MORAL IMPERIUM

Recent Titles in
Contributions in Comparative Colonial Studies

Constraint of Empire: The United States and Caribbean Interventions
Whitney T. Perkins

Toward a Programme of Imperial Life: The British Empire
at the Turn of the Century
H. John Field

European Colonial Rule, 1880-1940: The Impact of the
West on India, Southeast Asia, and Africa
Rudolf von Albertini, with Albert Wirz
John G. Williamson, translator

An Empire for the Masses: The French Popular Image
of Africa, 1870-1900
William H. Schneider

Western Women in Colonial Africa
Caroline Oliver

The Emergence of Modern South Africa: State, Capital,
and the Incorporation of Organized Labor on the South African
Gold Fields, 1902-1939
David Yudelman

The Second British Empire: Trade, Philanthropy, and
Good Government, 1820-1890
John P. Halstead

Completing a Stewardship: The Malayan Civil Service, 1942-1957
Robert Heussler

Double Impact: France and Africa in the Age of Imperialism
G. Wesley Johnson, editor

The Selling of the Empire: British and French Imperialist
Propaganda, 1890-1945
Thomas G. August

The Transition to Responsible Government: British
Policy in British North America, 1815-1850
Phillip A. Buckner

The India Office, 1880-1910
Arnold P. Kaminsky

MORAL IMPERIUM

Afro-Caribbeans and the Transformation of British Rule, 1776–1838

Ronald Kent Richardson

Contributions in Comparative Colonial Studies, Number 22

Greenwood Press
New York • Westport, Connecticut • London

Library of Congress Cataloging-in-Publication Data

Richardson, Ronald Kent.
  Moral imperium.

  (Contributions in comparative colonial studies,
  ISSN 0163-3813 ; no. 22)
  Bibliography: p.
  Includes index.
  1. Slavery—West Indies, British. 2. Anti-slavery
  movements—West Indies, British. I. Title. II. Series.
  HT1073.R53 1987   326'.09729   86-3154
  ISBN 0-313-24724-2 (lib. bdg. : alk. paper)

Library of Congress Catalog Card Number: 86-3154
ISBN: 0-313-24724-2
ISSN: 0163-3813

First published in 1987

Greenwood Press, Inc.
88 Post Road West, Westport, Connecticut 06881

Printed in the United States of America

10 9 8 7 6 5 4 3 2 1

Contents

	Preface	vii
1.	The Problem of Slavery	1
2.	The Foundation of the West Indian Empire and the Conditions for Colonial Dependency	19
3.	The Signs of Power	51
4.	Imperial Benevolence	97
5.	The Dangers of Slavery	133
	Conclusion	179
	Selected Bibliography	185
	Index	203

Preface

This essay is intended as a contribution to the social history of ideas. It in no way pretends to be either a definitive or a full treatment of the subject of the relationship between the development of anti-slavery thought and social movements in the British Caribbean. Instead, I have sought to outline a fruitful way of conceiving the relationship between the ideological formations of the imperial ruling classes, on the one hand, and the struggles and aspirations of the Afro-Caribbean people, on the other. My goal will have been achieved if this work succeeds in sparking debate over the impact of the outside, and particularly the Third World, on the development of what has generally come to be thought of as an autonomously developed tradition of Western humanism and liberalism.

Like all products of scholarship, the book builds considerably on the work of intellectual laborers who have paved the way. In particular, I have found the work of David Brion Davis, Roger Anstey, Charles Duncan-Rice, and Roger Buckley to be indispensable. From these pioneers I have drawn inspiration as well as edification. My teachers at the State University of New York at Binghamton were a constant source of encouragement and advice. Special thanks are due to Professors Malik Simba, Thadd Hall, and Norman Cantor, who each, in their own distinctive way, added significantly to my development as a scholar. If this offering has any merit, it is largely a result of their persistent advice and criticism. Whatever shortcomings that may be discovered in this work are entirely my own responsibility. The staff of Greenwood Press, especially Dr. James Sabin, Maureen Melino, and Lisa Reichbach, deserves special thanks for seeing me through the intricacies of the publication process.

Finally, I must thank Aloyah for her love and support, and my children, Khary, Ade, Kartina, and Endria, for their patience and understanding while this work was in preparation. This book is dedicated to them, to my mother, and to the memory of my father.

MORAL IMPERIUM

1

The Problem of Slavery

The problem of British slave emancipation continues to provide fruitful soil for historiographical debate. In the past decade or so, the debate has been immensely enriched by the outstanding work of historians such as David Brion Davis, Charles Duncan-Rice, Roger Anstey, and Howard Temperly. But strangely enough, the most important discussion in anti-slavery historiography continues to focus on the relative significance of ideals and material self-interest in British slave emancipation.

The British historian Roger Anstey illustrates the concern of historians of abolition and emancipation with weighing and measuring such factors. "For the present writer, the study of British abolition is of particular interest because it involves assessment of the relative importance of ideas, of religious 'enthusiasm,' of national interest and of political circumstances."[1] In a refinement of this type of conception, Duncan-Rice posits interaction among a range of categories. In his fine work *The Rise and Fall of Black Slavery* (1975), he wrote:

Slavery was overthrown when its profitability declined and when the classes who supported it themselves began to lose strength. This is not the same as saying that abolition was nothing but the product of changes in the economic needs of the class structure of western Europe. An abolitionist movement was produced by the interaction between such economic and social change, and a complex series of intellectual developments, philosophical, literary and religious.[2]

As profitable and learned as the work of these scholars has been, we have yet to develop an understanding of the impact of the Afro-Caribbean population on the development of anti-slavery thought and the anti-slavery movement as a whole. The present study attempts, in a modest way, to outline what I hope will be a profitable means of appreciating the relationship between English anti-slavery thought, as represented by the group known as the Clapham Sect, and its close associates, and the Afro-Caribbean population.

The problem that I wish to address can be approached by raising again the question asked by Wylie Sypher more than forty years ago. "It is peculiar, first of all that although popular feeling was stirred by tales of the Negro slave, no one in England seems to have taken seriously the countless plays and novels picturing slavery in the orient."[3] Sypher's indication of the selective concern of English benevolence for West Indian slaves and disregard for the plight of Indian bondsmen has not been followed up by an explanation.

Explanations have been given, however, for the emergence of the movement to free West Indian slaves. One of the most appealing and influential is the thesis that the British Caribbean was in a state of economic decline by the time a viable anti-slavery movement got underway. According to this argument, the economic decay of the sugar islands reduced their value as imperial possessions, thereby undermining the political strength of the West India lobby in Parliament.

This view has been supported by many historians.[4] Frank Klingberg wrote that "a serious economic decline of the West Indies actually and relatively reduced the influence of the planters."[5] Dale Porter argued that among the major factors accounting for the abolition of the British slave trade was "the brief conjunction of a set of economic conditions necessitating restrictions on the productive capacity of the British Caribbean colonies."[6] And even Reginald Coupland, whom Eric Williams claimed "represents the sentimental conception of history," gave passing nod to the role of economic forces in setting the stage for abolition.[7] Coupland's view was that by 1807, the West Indian interest still commanded the votes of those with interests in the islands, "but the value and therefore the weight of those interests had been undermined by insuperable economic forces."[8]

In the past, almost all historians of anti-slavery accepted the proposition of a West Indies in economic decline by the nineteenth century, or thereabouts. This consensus owed much to the "monumental labors" (the phrase is Eric Williams') of Lowell Ragatz. Ragatz' magnum opus, appropriately entitled *The Fall of the Planter Class in the British Caribbean 1763-1833*, is a massive analysis of West Indian economic history. In it, Ragatz attempts to answer a complex question. How did it come about, he asks, that one of the wealthiest possessions of the empire shrank to insignificance in three-fourths of a century?

In order for us to appreciate the originality and vigor of Ragatz' work, we should keep in mind that he was arguing against the notion that the destruction of slavery had ruined West Indian prosperity. "The decline of the British West Indies has been given but slight attention heretofore. Associated as it was with abolition and emancipation, those events have been seized upon as offering ready explanation. Yet they were mere contributing factors."[9] Quite apart from the anti-slavery effort were a set of economic conditions which can explain decline. Ragatz continued, "The American sugar producing areas within the empire had been overtaken by economic vicissitudes decades before the slightest obstruction to the free importation of new field hands was raised or the faintest popular demand for emancipation was voiced."[10] For Ragatz, then, anti-slavery falls within, not before, the process of decline.

Ragatz formulated the fundamental theme of the decline thesis when he wrote: "Had abolition never been instituted, had the regime of forced labor never come to an end, the properties there must still have suffered general ruin which engulfed them." A "wasteful" system of agriculture, competition from new sugar-producing areas, warfare, and trade restriction, not anti-slavery, were responsible for West Indian ruin.[11] The seeds of decline were sown in the establishment of the original West

Indian system itself, which Ragatz indicted for having "no national basis" and resting on monopoly of the home market for tropical commodities.[12]

Once the British Islands were faced with competition from foreign sugar producers and the newly won planting areas added to the empire after the 1760s and with the disruption of commerce because of war, the great profits of planters vanished and the underlying weakness of their system was revealed. Nevertheless, the West Indians still clung to their ruinous system.[13]

Ragatz did not claim, however, that the economic decline of the British Caribbean led to the abolition of the slave trade or the emancipation of the slaves. Rather, he indicated that the one was an economic process, the other a manifestation of the awakening moral consciousness of European man. Eric Williams' *Capitalism and Slavery* is the classic formulation of the thesis which links abolition and emancipation to the relative economic decline of the islands. Williams argued that abolition and emancipation must be seen in the context of the decline of mercantile capital before the onslaught of aggressive, free market, industrial capitalism. For Williams, slavery provided the foundation for the erection of a commercial system, which generated a significant part of the capital necessary for industrialization. Rapid industrial development in the late eighteenth century, however, gradually eroded the political, social, and ideological structures associated with the mercantile stage of capitalism. Monopoly now became a barrier to the further expansion of the market for British commodities. "The expansion of British exports depended on the capacity of Britain to absorb . . . raw materials as payment. The British West Indian monopoly, prohibiting the importation of non-British plantation sugar for home consumption, stood in the way."[14] In one of the great ironies of history, slavery, a progenitor of modern capitalism, became a brake on its further development. Socioeconomic progress demanded its destruction. "The commercial capitalism of the 18th century developed the wealth of Europe by means of slavery and monopoly. But in so doing it helped to create the industrial capitalism of the 19th century which turned round and destroyed the power of commercial capitalism, slavery, and all its works."[15] Slavery came to be identified with the archaic in economy. It was attacked and overthrown because it had become an essential support for an "unhealthy" economic system.

Williams was unable, however, to indicate a clear expression of an economic motivation by either policymakers or humanitarians. While admitting that "the humanitarians were the spearhead of the onslaught which destroyed the West Indian system and freed the Negro," he largely ignored both the content of their protest and the anti-slavery movement, despite its centrality to imperial abolition.[16] The problem with the Williams formulation is this inability to link economic change with a highly idealistic anti-slavery movement.

Despite the weight of consensus, however, is there reason to take a second look at the decline thesis? At least one scholar has done so. The American historian Seymour Drescher has leveled serious criticism at what he calls the "Ragatz-Williams" thesis. In particular, Drescher contends that the slave trade was more, not less, valuable to Britain during the period of intense debate on the imperial slave trade and the world slave trade than during the previous period from 1720 to 1775, when no organized abolition movement existed.

Drescher contends that Williams presents scattered material to show a decline in the value of the British West Indies in the period just before emancipation. But, he asks, what of the period between 1770 and 1820, the critical period for the campaigns against the slave trade? "To establish firmly the Ragatz-Williams thesis, it would also be necessary to demonstrate the relative decline of the slave economies in this interval."[17] But when Drescher examines the period which he has set up to test the Ragatz-Williams thesis, he finds that

neither imports from nor exports to the British West Indies declined at the end of the eighteenth century. On the contrary, both categories increased sharply in value toward 1800 and reached levels well above any putative "golden age" before the American Revolution. They therefore point to precisely the opposite conclusion from that indicated by Williams. Even more impressive are the figures of British West Indian trade as a percentage of total British overseas trade. . . . If we use Williams' terminal data year (1773) as our pivotal year between 1723 and 1822, the British West Indian trade accounted for a higher proportion of total British trade after 1773 than it did before. . . . Therefore, Williams' own principle measure of significance shows that the British West Indies were absolutely and relatively far more valuable to Britain during the period of intense debate on the imperial slave trade (1788-1807) and on the world slave trade (1814-1820) than during the period when there had been no organized British pressure against the trade (1720-1755).[18]

Drescher argues that decline followed the abolition of the slave trade, rather than caused it.

In a significant departure from mainstream anti-slavery scholarship, Drescher claims that the abolitionists feared that if the slave trade, fueled by a healthy West Indian economy, kept on growing at its present rate, it would soon become even more difficult to abolish than it was at the turn of the eighteenth century. Drescher asserts that the trade was abolished for cultural reasons. "Humanitarian historiography rightly treated the abolitionist movement not simply as an ideology, but as a national political movement with a humanitarian ideology." The cultural reasons appear to have had some relation to the development of Britain as a metropolis and the social changes concomitant on industrialization.[19]

Once abolished, for whatever reason, abolition set in motion forces which contributed mightily to the economic decline of the West Indies. The cutting off of the labor supply essentially "had rigidified British slavery," which for that reason "was losing its resiliency as a normal economic system by the early 19th century." After abolition, the British slave system could no longer expand. At last, the moral repugnance to slavery could be supported by the declining economic significance of the institution. Drescher writes that "there were accusations enough of moral decadence against slavery without the added one of economic decadence."[20]

In sum, Drescher's one telling point against Williams is the demonstration that the abolition of the slave trade was not part of a plan to dismantle the British West Indian sugar industry and its monopoly of the home market. The West Indies were not declining by 1807, nor did they block British capital accumulation.

On the other hand, Drescher provides support for the view expressed by Klingberg that "a serious economic decline of the West Indies actually and relatively reduced the influence of the planters." Thus it seems that we are on safe ground with the thesis that emancipation may have been facilitated by the relative decline of the British West Indies after 1807.

The major problem still remains, however. If Drescher has undermined Williams' argument on abolition, and if, as we argued, Williams was unable to demonstrate any significant connection between the motivation of the humanitarians and economic factors, we are back where we started. We must still account for British humanitarian focus on the "Negro."

I propose that we take a different approach. Instead of looking at things that the abolitionists did not speak and write about, we should turn our attention to the objects of their benevolence, the slaves. Was there anything about West Indian slaves and slavery which might help us to understand the humanitarian focus?

In this respect, one important difference between slavery in the West Indies and slavery in the Orient, or the United States, was demographic and racial. Whereas slaves formed minority islands in Indian and American society, slaves and freedmen formed the major part of the population of the Caribbean.

The most distinctive factor in Caribbean slavery was that the labor force was drawn from the continent of Africa. The demographic and racial factor is of demonstrated significance in the construction and development of Caribbean society. Ignored by economic historians and historians of anti-slavery, this theme has been pursued by historians of slavery. Moving in this direction, Elsa Goveia, Douglas Hall, and Franklin Knight have suggested that Caribbean society is most profitably seen as a "slave society." In this sense, the maintenance of slavery in the face of powerful resistance by the slaves necessitated the creation of a repressive regime. Because slavery was based on force, constant watchfulness came to condition all aspects of society.[21]

Despite a growing literature on slavery, the study of anti-slavery continues to ignore the impact of the slaves on the development of anti-slavery thought. The dichotomy between slavery and anti-slavery persists in the literature on abolition/emancipation. It is reflective of a deeper problem.

With the outstanding exception of Eric Williams, abolitionist historiography has been markedly anti-materialist and devoted to the celebration of the power of disinterested benevolence in effecting social change. Frank Klingberg, whose *The Anti-Slavery Movement in England* appeared in 1926, is representative of the best in this tradition. Klingberg pointed out the importance of the economic and social transformation of eighteenth-century English society to the rise of humanitarianism, but he was unable to explain what the relationship was. His formulation seemed to locate the origin of benevolence in the emergent sensitivity of bourgeois man.[22]

In this respect, Klingberg's treatment of humanitarianism is similar to that of Peter Gay. In *The Enlightenment: The Science of Freedom,* Gay exemplifies the idealist treatment of humanitarianism which we saw in Klingberg. "I have said," he wrote, in a discussion of the nature of the reform catalyst, "that the philosophes turned legal reformers because they were empiricists, because they found the need for reform appallingly apparent in their immediate experience—that is, once it was apparent. They had to be educated by spectacular cases before their latent, rhetorical humanity would become manifest and political."[23] Gay's formulation concerns the manner in which reformers become aware of social problems. To clarify his argument, Gay points to the Calais Affair, as providing the catalyst that activated Voltaire's latent reformism. But it is important to realize that for Gay, reformism was latent and its existence is explained by reference to cultural intellectual transformations. For Gay, it was the magnitude of the inhumanity involved in the Calais Affair which drew Voltaire's attention to it. It was symbolic of wider issues with which Voltaire was concerned.[24]

In a similar manner, Klingberg addressed the problem of the origins of humanitarian sentiment, of which anti-slavery formed a part:

Such rapid economic changes [as the industrial revolution], created a country of many new rich men and multitudes of poor. The Capitalist and laborer classes became more clearly marked in English society than they had been before. New social problems were created, which demanded settlement. In consequence, discussion raged upon such public questions as the distress and poverty caused by the new industrial system; the hardships created by the new agriculture with its extermination of many of the small farmers; and those phases of overseas expansion which seemed to pay too little attention to the rights of Asiatics and Africans. The trial of Warren Hastings and the investigation and destruction of the slave system were to be two of the dramatic expressions of this new spirit of inquiry and striving for justice.[25]

For Klingberg, then, the social transformation of the eighteenth century threw man's inhumanity to man into such sharp relief that it became clearly visible to men of sensitivity. Yet, like Gay's Voltaire, the British middle class had been prepared, by a process of enlightenment, to see problems in the world. Thus "the better instincts of the nineteenth century were opposed to the continuance of any cruel system."[26]

Reginald Coupland, the target of Williams' invective in *Capitalism and Slavery*, argued that economic conditions, the deepening field of British enterprise in India, and "the inevitable decline of the British sugar Islands" facilitated abolition. But he gave credit for abolition and emancipation to the disinterested efforts of the tireless band of humanitarian activists.[27] Earnest Howse celebrated *The Saints in Politics* as "a shining example of how society can be influenced by a few men of ability and devotion" and saw abolition and emancipation as "an illuminating reminder that spiritual factors in civilization may outweigh material factors, and men of prophetic minds are still the hope of history."[28]

Undoubtedly, the historiography of anti-slavery reached its most precise and sophisticated formulation in the work of David Brion Davis. In a sense, Davis' volumes on anti-slavery are a refinement of the Coupland-Klingberg tradition. His work on the problem of slavery can be seen as a brilliant refinement of the idealist conception of British slave emancipation.

Davis' contribution to the debate is his explanation of a process which previous writers left unexplained, the origins of "this new spirit of inquiry and striving for justice" and the precise nature of its relation to the industrial revolution. Davis elaborates his formulation of this relationship by way of a critique of Klingberg:

The theory that abolitionism was the natural outgrowth of a continuously swelling social consciousness fails to explain the long period when Negro slavery aroused virtually no protest and was accepted or regarded with indifference by the most benevolent of men. Britain's great expansion of the slave trade was not mitigated by centuries of developing domestic philanthropy.[29]

In attempting to adjust for Klingberg's failure, Davis argues that benevolence was tempered by a continuing respect for property and social order. He goes on to propound an alternative thesis to that of expanding benevolence, which, by placing emphasis on the symbolic value of anti-slavery, promises to explain the timing of anti-slavery. He writes:

British philanthropy, as one of the expressions of an emerging capitalist ethic, embodied the values of individual effort and responsibility. Yet if philanthropists went too far in their attempts to widen opportunities and promote self-reliance at home, they would undermine not only the old regime but the prevailing justifications for inequality and social rank. They might, however, experiment with liberal values by focusing their attention on a distant symbol of patriarchal society.[30]

In Davis' formulation, anti-slavery is seen as a mechanism for the working out of an industrial ethic, which helps to explain its absence during the rise of the slave economies.

As a tool for the formulation of a bourgeois ideology, anti-slavery offered a rich potential in symbolism. Thus slaveholders could symbolize anti-modern patriarchal society and "prescriptive authority." In this sense, "the slave system would stand for the insecurity and mobility of labor in a profit-oriented society; and yet the injustice of slavery could be identified with individuals rather than with impersonal forces. . . . His emancipation [the slave's] would not be like the elevation of a worker to an undeserved station; it would substitute the fear of hunger for the fear of the whip."[31]

Davis effected a re-orientation of the debate, clearly placing the emergence of anti-slavery in the context of changes in the Western class structure and class consciousness. It is used by the middle class as a means of working out an effective attitude toward the new industrial system in which there were capitalists and laborers. This is, however, as far as the analysis goes, as the "ideological needs" of the "various classes" of which Davis writes do not seem to emerge from the conflict of capital and labor in England, that is to say, from a palpable class struggle, or from the exigencies of their position within a world division of labor. Rather, they express the psychological imperative of the English middle class to confirm its self-image, not a response to the action and reaction of other classes. In Davis' formulation, the middle class seems to be a lone actor on the stage.

The furthest refinement of the Anglo-American tradition of anti-slavery scholarship is achieved in the following formulation by Davis: "The central question is: What led men to see the problem" of slavery? For the answer, Davis looks at the impact of industrialization on the Western cultural tradition. His effort is directed to an explanation of the manner in which slavery came to be conceived of as a problem, i.e., as a means by which the British middle class could resolve certain tensions arising from the impact of industrial capitalism on their liberal constitutional tradition, as well as a means of testing and elaborating a contractual conception of human relations.

We can recognize the same question of catalyst in the work of Thomas Clarkson, the historian of abolition who explained the rise of anti-slavery in terms of the expanding and deepening web of Europeans and Americans who realized the great wrong that slavery was. Comparing the progress of anti-slavery sentiment to the course of a great river, Clarkson wrote in his 1808 history of the abolition movement:

It would be considered by many who have stood at the mouth of a river, and witnessed its torrent there, to be both interesting and a pleasing journey to go to the fountainhead, and then to travel on its banks downward, and to mark the different streams in each side, which should run into it and feed it. So I presume the reader will not be a little interested and entertained in viewing with me the course of the abolition of the slave trade, in first finding its source, and then in tracing the different springs which have contributed to its increase.[32]

For Clarkson, this great movement, spanning 300 years, created the pre-conditions for the success of the abolition movement between 1787 and 1808, as it "brought the subject more or less into notice" and "more or less enlightened the public mind upon it."[33]

It would seem, then, that there is a fundamental agreement among Clarkson, Coupland, Klingberg, and Davis that the analysis of anti-slavery resolves itself into an explanation of how slavery became a problem for Western man. Their explanations indicate a movement from the extreme idealism of Clarkson to the interactionism of Davis, Temperly, Duncan-Rice, and Anstey.

This consensus indicates a significant link running through the historiography of anti-slavery, the persistence of what we have come to call Eurocentrism. The problem has not been addressed by historians of anti-slavery. Strangely enough, Davis, who is otherwise consistent in drawing out and clarifying the implications and problems in abolitionist scholarship, obscures the problem still further, in his eagerness to avoid the dangers of relativism. In *The Problem of Slavery in the Age of Revolution,* he has composed a revealing apologia.

The analysis of other peoples' ideologies has commonly been used as a weapon for discrediting their beliefs. By now, however, we should have moved beyond this rather naive level of self understanding. There is no reason that we should consider a moral judgment wrong simply because it was an artifact of history, and thus the product of a humanly fallible group or class. If one could demonstrate, for example, that the anti-slavery movements were the product of historical circumstances and that they served various ulterior purposes and functions, the demonstration in no way implies that their indictment of slavery was wrong.[34]

Implicit in his critique of the relativizers is the assumption that moral judgments bear universal significance. This assumption is central to abolitionist historiography.

Although it is clear that knowledge of the socioeconomic context of a judgment does not imply that the judgment is wrong, neither does it imply that the judgment is right. The judgments of two observers may sound the same, and yet the fact of verbal similarity does not necessarily mean identity of judgment. Two individuals may reach the same conclusions for divergent, and even contradictory, reasons. When this occurs, the context and the ulterior motives of the people making the judgments are certainly important. As I hope to show, both English humanitarians and Caribbean slaves came to the conclusion that slavery was morally wrong and should be abolished, but they did so for different reasons. Now as far as the obliteration of slavery is concerned, divergence of their rationales for calling for abolition may not have mattered, but it did matter if we extend our view to the type of society that abolition was expected to bring about. This is only to say that I do not know how one can separate a moral judgment from the actors' expectations of the consequences that will flow from that judgment.

The point here is that a judgment is neither right nor wrong until we establish criteria by which to judge its rightness or wrongness. The problem is that for judgments made within one culture, moral criteria are often implied, and the status of a judgment is therefore self-evident. But when we are dealing with two cultures and the judgments are made by actors in one about social conditions in the other, it becomes of the utmost importance to draw out the implied criteria by which judgments are evaluated. This also raises the question as to whose criteria we shall accept, or by what criteria we shall judge. The historiography indicates that we have accepted the perspective of the humanitarians. We can appreciate the limitations that acceptance of this humanitarian perspective can present if we keep in mind the fact that British humanitarians did not step in to implement a social program put forward by Afro-Caribbean slaves; nor did they consult black people when formulating their anti-slavery programs. What they did was to formulate under the rubric slavery a bundle of practices and conditions that conflicted with their own criteria of social justice. Those criteria were inserparable from the social situation and goals of the humanitarians.

The major point to keep in mind is that abolition and emancipation were carried out in the context of British rule and designed to create a social environment receptive to British needs. Those needs were conditioned by domestic and imperial problems that pressed on Britain's moral and political leadership.

The British West Indian aspects of that situation included a condition of social unrest. Thus, if abolitionists looked to their cultural intellectual heritage for arguments against slavery, and if the arguments which they developed were in some sense determined by the nature of that heritage, the problem which they addressed thrust itself on them. In this sense, Thomas Fowell Buxton was demonstrating more than astuteness as a politician appealing to the practical concerns of members of Parliament when, in the debate on imperial compensation to slave owners, he argued that, although

the amount [£20,000,000] was far surpassing what he thought the actual value of the slaves, and if the Government were only to wait till next year, they might buy emancipation at a quarter of the present price, but then in what state would the colonies be? He supported the grant for this reason; if emancipation was not given, more than £20,000,000 would be spent in military preparations; and what was worse, it would be against men who were merely asserting their natural rights. . . . If it [the emancipation bill] were not passed they would lose the colonies. Were they not cheap at the price of £20,000,000?[35]

Buxton leaves no doubt that anti-slavery forces were concerned with the issue of imperial security. Far from a mere symbolic value, we can see in anti-slavery a response to the dangers of slavery, a theme with which I shall be concerned throughout this work. Beside the English middle class, we have another actor on the stage, the Afro-Caribbean population.

Part of the dilemma in which abolition scholarship finds itself is rooted in a narrowness of vision. Such scholarship focuses, in the main, on the removal of labor conditions which appeared to be immoral and inhumane to enlightened Englishmen. Research has consequently been directed towards an archaeology of anti-slavery in an effort to unearth the earliest beginnings and the evolutionary course of a cultural intellectual tradition.

Although there are several studies of the period of transition from slavery to free labor in the British West Indies, they are, for the most part, analyses of the development and implementation of Colonial Office policy during the so-called apprenticeship period.[36] There has been little interest in studying the anti-slavery movement as an effort of social reconstruction, expressing the relationship of the British ruling elite to Afro-Caribbean people. Historians have persistently regarded abolitionist ideology as universal and progressive, resting on a community of interest between the British humanitarians and the West Indian slaves. Having begun with this assumption, Anglo-American historiography remains unable to achieve a social history of anti-slavery thought.

In this book, I analyze the Caribbean influence on the development of abolitionist thought. I pay particular attention to the impact of the late-eighteenth-century Anglo-French struggle for the hegemony of colonial empire on the British attitude towards imperial rule.

From this perspective, the problem with which we are confronted in anti-slavery is not a simple concern for the treatment of slaves, but the much wider issue of the perpetuation of the dependent and formal colonial status of a society integrated into the imperial system. This issue has been ignored because we have been slow to recognize the existence of a vibrant Afro-Caribbean community.

I hope to clarify the nature of the relationship between anti-slavery thought and the emergence of a viable Afro-Caribbean society in the West Indies. This book, then, is a study of the ideological aspects of the anti-slavery movement. Its core is an interpretation of the relationship between anti-slavery thought, as typified in the writings of Granville Sharp, William Wilberforce, Thomas Clarkson, James Stephen, Zachary Macaulay, and Thomas Fowell Buxton, an elite group of imperial humanitarians, and the sociopolitical aspirations of the Afro-Caribbean masses, as expressed through rebellion, day-to-day resistance, and, sometimes, in word.

NOTES

1. Roger Anstey, *The Atlantic Slave Trade and British Abolition, 1760-1810* (Atlantic Highlands, N.J.: Humanities Press, 1975), p. xx.

16   Moral Imperium

2. Charles Duncan-Rice, *The Rise and Fall of Black Slavery* (New York: Harper & Row, 1977), p. 153.

3. Wylie Sypher, *Guinea's Captive Kings* (Chapel Hill: University of North Carolina Press, 1942), p. 25.

4. See, for example, Reginald Coupland, *The British Anti-Slavery Movement* (London: Frank Cass & Co., 1964); Frank Klingberg, *The Anti-Slavery Movement in England* (London: Oxford University Press, 1926); and William Mathieson, *British Slavery and Its Abolition, 1823-1838* (New York: Octagon Books, 1967).

5. Klingberg, *Anti-Slavery Movement,* p. 278.

6. Dale H. Porter, *The Abolition of the Slave Trade in England 1784-1807* (Hamden, Conn.: Archon Books, 1970),p. 143.

7. Eric Williams, *Capitalism and Slavery* (New York: G. P. Putnam & Sons, 1966), p. 268.

8. Coupland, *British Anti-Slavery,* pp. 123-124.

9. Lowell Ragatz, *The Fall of the Planter Class in the British Caribbean, 1763-1833* (New York: Appleton-Century-Crofts, 1928), p. vii.

10. Ibid., p. viii.

11. Ibid., p. vii.

12. Ibid., p. viii.

13. Ibid.

14. Williams, *Capitalism and Slavery,* p. 154.

15. Ibid., p. 210.

16. Williams, *Capitalism and Slavery,* chapter 11.

17. Seymour Drescher, *Econocide: British Slavery in the Era of Abolition* (Pittsburgh: University of Pittsburgh Press, 1977), p. 16.

18. Ibid., pp. 16-17.

19. Ibid., pp. 185, 183.

20. Ibid., pp. 148, 149.

21. See, for example, Elsa Goveia, *Slave Society in the British Leeward Islands at the End of the Eighteenth Century* (New Haven, Conn.: Yale University Press, 1965), and Franklin Knight, *Slave Society in Cuba During the Nineteenth Century* (Madison: University Wisconsin Press, 1970).

22. Klingberg, *Anti-Slavery Movement.*

23. Peter Gay, *The Enlightenment:The Science of Freedom.* (New York: Alfred A. Knopf, 1969), p. 433.

24. Ibid., pp. 433-437.

25. Klingberg, *Anti-Slavery Movement,* pp. 24-25.

26. Ibid., p. 257.

27. Coupland, *British Anti-Slavery,* pp. 123-124.

28. Earnest Howse, *The Saints in Politics* (Toronto: University of Toronto Press, 1952), p. viii.

29. Davis, *Problem of Slavery in Western Culture,* p. 334.

30. Ibid., pp. 335-336.

31. Ibid., p. 336.

32. Thomas Clarkson, *The History of the Rise, Progress, and Accomplishment of the Abolition of the African Slave Trade by the British Parliament,* 2 vols. (London: Frank Cass & Co., 1968), 1:3.

33. Ibid., pp. 31, 33.

34. David Brion Davis, *The Problem of Slavery in the Age of Revolution* (Ithaca, N.Y.: Cornell University Press, 1975), pp. 14-15.

35. Hansard, *Parliamentary Debates,* 3d series, vol. xx, pp. 135-136.

36. See William Burn, *Emancipation and Apprenticeship in the British West Indies* (London: Jonathan Cape, 1937); William Green, *British Slave Emancipation* (London: Oxford University Press, 1975); Mathieson, *British Slavery.*

2

The Foundation of the West Indian Empire and the Conditions for Colonial Dependency

In the late seventeenth century, the political economist Charles D'Avenant considered how one might best determine the true extent of the wealth of a nation, especially whether it gained or lost by its foreign trade. He found that one of the first signs of wealth was an increase in the stock of shipping that a nation had at its disposal. "As handicraftsmen when they first thrive in the world furnish themselves with all instruments that are necessary for their respective callings; so whole nations, whom trade begins to enrich, increase their stock of shipping, which are the working tools of a trading people."[1] Associated with this is the nation's ability to set forth a strong navy to protect its merchant marine. When once the expense of a navy can be met without signs of weakness, "it is an evident mark that there are secret springs by which the expense is fed."[2]

Reflecting on the history of empires, D'Avenant asserted that the wealth of a nation is in the commercial, agricultural, and industrial skill of its people, rather "than even the possession of gold and silver mines." The case of Spain, the imperial giant of the past century, was ready to hand to make his point. Once rich in gold and silver, the Spanish had few natural resources and lacked the character of a free people, wisdom and justice in government, and the creative initiative essential to the creation of real wealth. With evident chauvinism, D'Avenant wrote:

The lazy temper came undoubtedly upon them, with that affluence of money which was brought into their country in the reign of Philip II presuming upon which, they neglected arts, labour and manufactures; and the common people being the stomach of the body politic and that stomach being thus weakened, and performing its due functions, the food that had been plentifully thrown in was not at all digested but passed through without giving any spirits, strength or nourishment to the members of the commonwealth.[3]

Spain's wealth was foolishly squandered in wars and luxury, fertilizing, through expenditures, the manufactures and commerce of foreign states.[4] To D'Avenant, the lesson was clear: "Trade and manufactures are the only mediums by which such a digestion and distribution of gold and silver can be made, as will be nutritive to the body politic."[5] If England would grow prosperous, then it would be on the basis of its human and natural resources. It should aim to become an entrepôt and avoid concentration on one or two trades alone, such as wool cloth. "It is in the interest of England," wrote D'Avenant, "to enlarge its traffic as much as possible."[6] By becoming merchants to the world, the English could ensure themselves a secure and continually expanding wealth.

The seventeenth-century merchant Dalby Thomas expressed similar views in a tract aimed at encouraging the development of the tropical American trade. A living link between Africa, the Caribbean, and Europe, Thomas was an active merchant and an agent of the Royal African Company. In many ways the epitome of the aggressive Englishman expanding his own and his nation's prospects overseas, Thomas developed a broad-based interest in the colonial trades. He was at the forefront of Caribbean exploitation, vigorously advocating a concerted national effort on behalf of colonial development.[7]

Writing in 1690, Thomas reflected on *The Rise and Growth of the West India Colonies*. Like D'Avenant, he argued that money was merely the medium of exchange, the oil that lubricated the engine of commerce, but was not, alone, sufficient to generate prosperity and security. Real wealth was to be found in the land and its products, together with the people who worked it.[8]

Thomas believed that one of the most productive employments of land and labor was in the sugar colonies, where, he thought, the fertility of the soil, the encouraging climate, and the political conditions favored the productivity of labor. These factors meant that workers employed in the islands were worth 130 times the value to the mother country of those engaged at home.[9] Thomas presented statistics to show that the approximately 600,000 white men and women now living in the colonies yielded the nation about 400 million pounds sterling each year.[10] In addition to this direct increment of wealth, each person living in the plantations caused the consumption of more English manufactures than did ten such persons at home. In the absence of colonial industries, the entire population of the English Caribbean was dependent on English manufactures. "Let it suffice in one word to say, that the produce and consumption with the shipping they give employment to, is of an infinite deal more benefit to the wealth, Honour, and Strength of the Nation, then four times the same number of hands the best employed at home can be."[11] Clearly support for plantation development would catalyze English economic growth.

For contemporaries like D'Avenant and Dalby Thomas, overseas trade and colonization offered the promise of prosperity in an increasingly competitive world. It could become an answer to the terrible competition with continental rivals in which English merchants found themselves. In this rivalry, particular importance must be given to the Dutch, who perhaps more than any other people were perceived to be a threat to England's commercial growth. The manufacture of cloth, especially the traditional woolens, had been England's major non-agricultural trade. Woolens traditionally went from England to markets in eastern Europe, Germany, and Holland, with small but growing markets in southern Europe and the Mediterranean.[12] After about 1614, however, England began to lose its monopoly of this extremely important commodity trade to continental, and especially Dutch, competitors.[13]

The Dutch were indeed a marvel. "The prodigious increase of the Netherlanders in their domestick and foreign trade, Riches, and multitude of shipping," wrote Sir Josiah Child, "is the envy of the present, and may be the wonder of all future generations."[14] Child felt that the Dutchmen owed their success partly to the influence of their merchants in their councils of state, but religious toleration, which attracted the industrious from other nations, and dedication to enterprise and craftsman-ship also played a large part.[15] Contemporaries agreed that the Dutch drove a better trade because they were better organized for commerce, breathed freer air, paid lower freight, and their merchants enjoyed state support.[16] The English, therefore, found themselves at a severe disadvantage in competition for what had lately been their accustomed trading grounds. Sir Walter Raleigh expressed an exasperation shared by many when he complained that

the wool, cloth, lead, tin, and divers other commodities are in England; but by means of our wool and cloth going out rough, undressed, and undyed, there is an exceeding manufactory and drapery in the low countries, wherewith they serve themselves and other nations, and advance greatly the employment of their people at home and traffick abroad, and put down ours in foreign parts.[17]

In this setting, the so-called old draperies began to decline. In 1598, the two major markets for English cloth were Germany and the United Provinces, which together took 71,000 short cloths from London. In 1614, the English sent 99,000 pieces to these markets, but the number subsequently declined from this peak. By 1632, it had dropped to below 60,000, and eight years later, in 1640, only 45,000 were sent.[18] Unable to meet the vigorous competition of Dutch, Silesians, and Venetians, the English were forced to accept a smaller share of the market for woolen cloth. They responded to this challenge by accelerated development of the new draperies, light cloth suitable for wear in warmer climates, but they also began to expand their geographic horizons and search for markets outside their traditional haunts.[19] "Few things stand out more clearly from the economic discussions under Elizabeth and the early Stuarts," wrote F. J. Fisher, "than the twin ideas that the old outlets for cloth were glutted and that new ones must be found."[20] Englishmen met the challenge of a new age by the exploitation of new markets and by diversification.[21] Londoners shipped few English products besides wool overseas. Instead, beginning to build a trading system based on the re-export of foreign products, by the 1640s, they were shipping East Indian wares to Russia,

Germany, the Netherlands, Italy, and the Levant, while they carried the products of the Mediterranean to the Netherlands, and European wares to Africa and the Americas. As early as 1640, re-exports equalled all English goods shipped besides textiles. But because most goods carried by English vessels were traded directly from one country to another without ever touching English soil, re-exports were only a minor part of the total trade carried by Englishmen.[22]

It seemed that the future of English industry lay in diversification and in the construction of an entrepôt trade. Barry Supple sums up the developments of the seventeenth century:

The previous hundred years had seen the establishment of a commercial network and industrial structure which, in spite of many dashing and enterprising exploits, was largely tied to the old drapries and to European markets north of the Mediterranean. When the Hanoverians came to the throne, and even for some years before, it was abundantly clear that businessmen were operating within a new framework, one whose important lines of communication extended westward to America and Southward into the Mediterranean, round Africa, and to the far East; whose trading products had been diversified to a revolutionary degree.[23]

Ralph Davis agrees with this assessment. As late as 1640, 80 to 90 percent of London exports were in woolen cloth, but by 1700, he points out, although woolens were still in the lead, they now accounted for only 47 percent of exports, while re-exports had reached a level of 30 percent of total exports. This development reflected the "enormous" growth of imports from America and the Indies. "English trade as a whole now depended to a great extent upon the extra-European world."[24] Thus, whereas in 1615 the English consumed 50,000 pounds of tobacco, by 1700 they were using 13 million pounds and re-exporting 25 million to Europe. A similar, if less spectacular, development occurred in the sugar trade.[25]

The growth of English commerce was gradual, however. In the late sixteenth century, England was not a significant maritime nation, lagging far behind Spain, which could boast of a huge merchant fleet. The most promising maritime people were the Netherlanders. In 1562, they had sent 1,192 ships into the Baltic for northern products, while the English sent a mere 51.[26] English maritime expansion began as a gradual movement, around the 1550s. Mariners of the southwestern ports took the lead in developing the fishing industry in Iceland, the North Sea, and especially New Foundland and the banks.[27] The revolt of the Netherlands from Spain provided the English with the opportunity to break into the Baltic and Mediterranean trades, taking advantage of the vacuum created by the temporary decline in Dutch activity.[28] By the beginning of the seventeenth century, however, the Dutch were able once again to turn full stride to their old commercial pursuits, and the two Western nations entered a period of intense competition. Disputes over the East Indian trade, whaling, and the fisheries were responsible for most of the Anglo-Dutch rivalry in the first half of the seventeenth century.[29] After 1648, their competition became more severe, and war broke out between the rivals three times in the century (1652-1654, 1665-1667, 1672-1674). Although England's commercial fortunes certainly improved after 1667, while those of Holland declined, there is no clear evidence that this was the exclusive result of the Anglo-Dutch wars. Dutch decline was due perhaps as much to internal problems as to English aggression, while England's success spoke in no small measure to the reorganization of domestic and commercial policy associated with the period of civil war and restoration. Undoubtedly, the great expense of war with England placed severe strains on the economy of the Netherlands and in this manner, perhaps more than in any other, contributed to the relative decline of the provinces.[30]

The seventeenth century was, therefore, an age of tremendous creativity for the English. Under the pressure of trade rivalry, forced to develop new ways of doing business and new markets for their wares, the English organized themselves more effectively for competition with the Dutch and, at the same time, began to cultivate what was to become a major area of later imperial activity. No Englishmen captured the sense of enterprise and adventure better than the two Hakluyts, chroniclers of Anglo-Saxon exploration. In his seminal tract on colonization, *Discourse of Western Planting,* Richard Hakluyt argued that American development could turn England's liabilities into assets. By providing land and work in abundance, colonization would put idle hands to productive purposes.[31] Because the western lands were situated far away from the internecine conflicts of the great powers, they had the added attraction of promising relatively peaceful settlement by smaller nations, like England. In addition, America offered the hope of economic self-sufficiency by providing a supply of raw materials such as pitch and tar, vital naval stores which England had to purchase from foreigners.[32] Hakluyt was careful to point to the success of Portugal in the exploitation of the Azores and Madeira to make his case that the future lay in western planting.[33]

Even as Hakluyt composed his message, Englishmen were scouring the Spanish Caribbean and making tentative essays into the African trade to America. But it was only with the decline of the age of the privateer and the apparent deterioration of England's commercial position in the early seventeenth century that active colonization of western lands was undertaken.[34] One of the first areas of English colonial activity was the Guiana coast. A Privy Council report describes the Guiana expedition that Captain Charles Leigh undertook in 1604, permitting us to catch the flavor of early Caribbean settlement.

Arrived in the country with fifty men, with whom he purposed to inhabit in some by place, away from the Indians; but accepted the offers of the natives to dwell amongst them in their best houses and gardens. Has resolved to remain with forty men, and return the rest for England with four Indian chiefs as pledges. The natives desire that he will send for men to teach them to pray. Doubts not but God hath a wonderful work in this simple-hearted people. Beseeches the council to send over well disposed preachers. Requests the King's protection and free passage to those who will come and settle there.[35]

This infant colony, established as a station for the promotion of trade with the Indians of the interior, was probably the first English settlement on American soil. The experiment was, however, short-lived. The adventurers were still active in 1605 when a Dutch slaver put in at the Wiapoco in hopes of selling slaves, but by 1606, the remaining settlers had embarked for home in a Dutch merchantman. During their brief residence, they had cultivated tobacco, flax, cotton, and sugarcane.[36]

The settlement that was to become the first real English colony in the Caribbean was made on the island of St. Christopher by Thomas Warner. An acquaintance of Jonathan Winthrop, Warner was from a comfortable Suffolk family and, like others of his generation, sought his fortune overseas. In 1620, Warner had gone to the Amazon with Captain Roger North and run a plantation there, before James I ended the enterprise. He then turned his attention to the Lesser Antilles in search of a safe and promising site for a new colony.[37] Eventually landing on the island of St. Christopher, he managed, through diplomacy, to win the friendship of the Carib chief, Tegreeman, thus ensuring initial freedom from Indian attack while the settlement gained a foothold. Once the colony was launched, Warner returned to England in order to raise money for plantation development, winning the support of backers who "did disburse their monies toward the setting forth a ship and men for the design of tobaccoes."[38] St. Christopher became a successful plantation colony, but the really spectacular developments took place further east, in Barbados, where one can glimpse in miniature the developing relationship between the Caribbean and the metropolitan center. In 1626, a company of Englishmen led by Captain Henry Powel and Simon Gordon settled Barbados on behalf of a syndicate whose moving spirit was the wealthy and influential merchant Sir William Courteen. With the backing of the Courteen syndicate, an initial colony was established, and cassava, corn, tobacco, and thirty-two Arawaks for labor were obtained in Guiana and transported to the colony. By 1629, the year of a devastating Spanish attack on St. Christopher, Barbados could boast of between 1,500 and 1,850 persons, and by then, the syndicate had already invested 10,000 pounds.[39]

Almost from the start, Barbados was embroiled in faction fights centering on conflicting claims to land ownership and governmental powers, conflicts that were an extension of the struggles over prerogative monarchy and the constitution at home. It was predictable that this conflict would center, at least in its initial stages, on the financial question because it was the area in which Parliament had most leverage. Unable to live within the resources of the crown, the king must either raise the additionally needed revenue outside of Parliament, by the use of patronage, through loans and the like, or go to the commons. The latter course necessarily involved concessions to the clamorings of Parliament, so kings like James I were eager to exploit other sources of revenue. In their search for income, the Stuarts naturally made use of the newly discovered lands over which it was their right to grant proprietorship. In this way the constitutional crisis was imported into the early colonial development of the islands, and as the eventual constitutional settlement came to strengthen responsible central government, even while limiting its arbitrary power, so too did the outcome in the islands mark an important stage in the growing power of the metropolis over colonial development.

A major controversy in the early history of Barbados was begun when James I granted the Lord Proprietorship of Barbados and several other islands in the Caribbean to James Hay, first Earl of Carlisle, one of his Scottish favorites. The grant conferred on Hay the property of the islands to hold by knight service from the king, broad governmental powers, and freedom from all duties on goods exported to England for a period of ten years.[40] The grant to Carlisle did not prevent James, who was not famous for consistency, from making a similar grant to Philip Herbert of Montgomery, and afterwards of Pembroke in the very next year.[41] Pembroke may have been acting on behalf of Sir William Courteen and a powerful group of London merchants.[42] Carlisle succeeded in the following year in obtaining a confirmation of his original grant, but that did not end the affair.[43] The Carlisle-Pembroke controversy became entangled in the larger struggles of civil war and interregnum when the divisions between court and country were reproduced in Barbados. On the outbreak of civil war in England, the estates of Carlisle, a Royalist, were sequestered and his proprietorship assumed by Parliament.[44] On November 24, 1643, Parliament created a commission to oversee plantation affairs. It was headed by Robert Rich Earl of Warwick and included, among others, Philip Earl of Pembroke, John Pym, and Oliver Cromwell. Pembroke and his merchant backers had been excluded from participation in Caribbean planting by the Carlisle monopoly and now intended to use governmental powers to their own economic advantage.[45]

But as the metropolitan government would find on many

occasions in the eighteenth and nineteenth centuries, the administration of empire at a distance depended heavily on political as well as military arts. Barbados tried hard to preserve its neutrality during the civil war, and no doubt to encourage its loyalty by pacifying the large number of Royalists living there, Parliament returned Carlisle's proprietorship to him in 1654.[46] Ironically, the success of the parliamentary armies led indirectly to the revolt of the colony by strengthening the Royalist party in it. A contemporary observed that

multitudes of the Royal Party being made prisoners, were sent thither to be sold as Servants, and many of the officers of that side to mend their fortunes, applyed themselves to that place, and in such considerable numbers, that by the Civility of the first settlers, they got into the principal offices of that Government, and by degree drew the people, if not absolutely to decline their former peaceable resolutions, yet in a great measure, to encline the lost Cavalier party, by making the current of all Preferements and Authority to stream to those that way affected.[47]

Parliament reacted to the growing disaffection of Barbados by dispatching an expedition to reduce the island. On February 1, 1651, instructions were given to Sir George Ayscue, Daniel Searle, and Captain Michael Pack, commissioners for the reduction of Barbados. The colonists were to submit to the government of the commonwealth, accept the acts against the kingship, the House of Lords, and the abolition of the Book of Common Prayer. They were to agree, in effect, to full parliamentary control over their affairs.[48] After a prolonged blockade, siege, and drawn-out negotiations, Barbados was brought to surrender on January 12, 1652.[49]

Factionalism continued to plague Barbados for some time. Colonists, no matter what their political inclinations, were not overly enthused by the prospect of tight metropolitan control, and the Royalist party still maintained a powerful hold on the local political situation. By September of 1653, Daniel Searle, now governor, was writing to inform the Council of State that all of the candidates whom he had recently recommended for assembly seats had been passed over in favor of those who were opposed to the commonwealth. Searle ended up by dismissing the Assembly, believing that its continued existence would have tended to make "this little limb of the commonwealth into a free state."[50] With the Restoration, Barbados entered on a brief period under a proprietary government, but finally, in 1663, a settlement was worked out that marked a milestone in the process of imperial consolidation. To satisfy the claims of all the disputants to proprietorship, and in order to induce the king to assume sovereignty over the island, Barbados' agents in England proposed laying a 4.5 percent duty on all commodities of native growth and on the export trade, which would provide sufficient revenue for the support of the colonial government and still leave a large surplus for the king. Anxious to develop any financial resource that might aid him in his bid to rule without Parliament, Charles readily agreed. The proprietary was dissolved and the crown assumed direct control of Barbados.[51]

The metropolis increased its influence over the islands in other ways as well. The civil war and interregnum were periods of growth for Barbados. During the 1640s and 1650s, the Leeward Islands and Barbados enjoyed virtual freedom of trade, the Dutch playing a critical role.[52] As late as 1652, the trade of Barbados was said to be mainly in Dutch hands, and so pronounced was the islands' dependence on the Dutch that Governor Searle complained to the Council of State that in consequence of the recent Act of Navigation, there had been a great scarcity of commodities in the island.[53] As early as 1633, the Privy Council had attempted to force all vessels coming from the English plantations to bring their ships and cargoes into British ports to unload before reshipment.[54] This attempt at creating a "staple" was designed to increase the customs revenue of the state and was pursued with vigor by the passage of the famous navigation acts of 1651 and 1660.[55] Although these acts did not bring immediate success, they laid the foundation for making England the staple of the colonial trade.[56] The navigation acts are evidence of the growing maturity in the administration of overseas enterprise. The motive is still a more or less immediate profit, not the construction of a durable imperial economy, but there is distinct progress in the move from total reliance on chartered companies as the agents of overseas development, through which the crown profited as patron, to parliamentary control of trade through legislation mandating that trade must center on England, where customs duties could be collected. Chartered companies still played an important role, especially when, as in the African trade, there was a large risk involved in the heavy outlay of capital on a highly perishable human cargo, but in the now relatively stable Caribbean, the economic and political role of the state was definitely growing. As W. Cunningham put it, "the plantation trade could be controlled without being confined to a privileged body of merchants, through the machinery of the Navigation acts."[57]

Probably a more powerful factor operating to tie the Caribbean colonies closer to the mother country was the manner in which they were financed. Here the pre-eminent place went to the big merchant operating alone or, like Courteen, in a syndicate. The seventeenth-century overseas trade, at least that to America and Africa, was one of the riskiest enterprises that one could engage in. If the returns could be high, losses could be catastrophic. For this reason it was the province of the merchant who engaged in it as one of many enterprises. As K. G. Davies wrote of the African trade, "it drew capital out of older established branches of England's commerce and applied it to a trade that was still undeveloped."[58] The big merchant was able to do this because he could stand the risk. Many times merchants were able to reap profits in the trade, despite the precarious nature of West Indian investment, because it was merely one facet of their commercial activity. As early as the 1562 voyage of John Hawkins, we can observe this phenomenon at work. Hawkins undertook the actual risk of life and limb, but behind him stood a joint stock company willing to experiment with a new avenue of commerce in order to promote a new market based on the linkage of Africa and the Caribbean.[59]

Because of his access to capital and credit, the merchant could step in and invest when the market was ripe and withdraw when danger threatened. He was even able to buy pieces of the future by experimenting in new trades, one of which was bound to pay and make up for others that had failed. One such enterprising fellow was the London merchant Thomas Hall. Hall had already made money in the Mediterranean, Indian, and African trades before he began to delve in another in the southern seas. It was with no sense of surprise, therefore, that a correspondent wrote to him: "As I heard lately, you changed quite your manner of business, and are now a great trader in Jamaica and Barbadoes goods."[60] This flexibility of the merchant with big capital should be borne in mind when we examine the performance of the African company. Although in the first twenty years of its existence, the company paid an average annual dividend of only 7 percent, the original shareholders who sold out before 1691 and moved on to other things did well and sometimes made a killing. James II, for example, made a profit of 6,000 pounds over a seventeen-year period.[61] Therefore, the companies must be seen as instruments by which men with venture capital could augment their private fortunes, not just as corporate entities whose success we judge by their overall performance. Because these companies fulfilled a quasi-public function, it is sometimes difficult to appreciate the fact that they were utilized, as was the state itself to some degree, by private interests.[62]

Perhaps nothing better symbolized the early power of the merchant vis-à-vis the colonial than these oft-despised chartered companies. The rationale for them had been the need to organize trades that the state was either unable or unwilling to promote, protect, and develop. As late as 1757, Malachy Poslethwayt was arguing the need for a monopolistic company to control trade on the African coast. The "late" African company had made American plantation agriculture possible by gaining the English entrance to the slave trade, and the continued prosperity of those plantations depended on the health of the African trade, best preserved by an African company.[63]

But the need for private or state monopolies did not appear as self-evident to debt-pressed planters in need of laborers to work their fields. Their continual complaints about the company crowd the colonial records. The company was unable to meet their labor needs at a reasonable cost. They preferred to patronize the independent traders, who, freed from the burdensome costs of upkeep on forts and factories, were able to sell cheaper than the company.

These early struggles between merchant and planter, with the
state as intermediary, represent the conflict of large and small
capital. They are illustrated in a seventeenth-century document.
In a 1667 petition from Barbados, we are able to hear the
colonial side of the argument. The petitioners complain

That whereas free trade is the best means of living to any colony, of
which these islands having for some years been debarred the planters
have been so impoverished and the enemy's trade so advanced that the
English to maintain a livelihood have been forced to fish with French
nets . . . that they may have free trade with the coast of Guinea for
negroes.

If free trade be refused, then the petitioners ask that the African
Company be compelled to sell slaves to them at a reasonable
price, or 17 pounds per head.[64] In addition, they pray for "free
trade with, and a supply of servants from Scotland and
permission for the present transport of 1,000 or 2,000 English
servants."[65] The reply was a clear formulation of mercantilist
policy and evidence of the centralizing tendencies in the
evolution of the Caribbean.

That open markets and free trade are Best for those that desire them is
certain, and so it is to Buy cheap and sell dear, and most of all to have
commodities for nothing, and if all his Majesty's Dominions and
plantations were made only for Barbados it might be expedient; But
since it is conceived that His Majesty will have regard to what may
preserve the trade of the nation and not only to what will gratify
Barbados, they think their desire of free trade will prove impractical and
pernicious to other public interests.[66]

With the restoration and the rising power of Parliament, the
days of proprietary rule and monopolistic companies drew to a
close, at least in the West. This did not signify simply an
ideological repugnance to such things; rather, the need for such
artificial devices declined with the maturation of the Caribbean
as an area of colonial enterprise and with the growing control
over the islands exercised by the metropolitan-based merchant.
Late in the seventeenth century, Barbados petitioned the king
for release from the operation of the Navigation Acts, as

all people are so generally indeted to the merchant that they have but a small portion in their own estates. Sugar is at so low a rate that the merchants send no goods to Barbadoes, but only empty ships to take away the sugar, which if they send away on their own account yields so contemptible a rate, for the merchants having them in their power can give what they list, for they have the market to themselves, and make us simple planters only the property of their gain.[67]

Although the total subjection of the colonies to the mother country was never achieved, in the struggle between merchant and planter, the whip was always in the hand of the former. The progress of imperial control over the affairs of the West India colonies was slow, and we can establish no definitive period by which an ideal form of rule had been created. In fact, the anti-slavery movement itself was a stage in the refinement of imperial rule, a process perhaps best described as an ongoing adjustment between the developing metro-state, the colonists, and the Afro-Caribbean population. But an important stage in the evolution of the British Caribbean was reached by the end of the seventeenth century.[68] By that time, direct island opposition to imperial authority was uncommon, and the West Indian colonies had entered a path that would prevent them from mounting the type of opposition to imperial control presented by the mainland colonies. The Assembly of Barbados might resolve in 1651 to "defend themselves against the slavery intended to be imposed upon them" by England, but by century's-end, they could pose little threat to the rule of the central government.[69]

In the historical development of the British West Indies, the conversion to sugarcane cultivation by slave labor is universally recognized as a major factor conditioning the type of society that emerged there and its momentous dependence on England. The cultivation of sugar was an expensive undertaking. It could be engaged in only by men with enough capital and credit to purchase the slaves and equipment needed, and with the ability to weather the loss of a crop owing to hurricanes, enemy raids, or sabotage. In view of the primitive agricultural techniques used by the colonists, sugar cultivation was best carried out on vast tracts of land with a large enough work force to give continual care to the young plants.[70] These conditions soon forced the small farmer out of the islands. They simply could not compete with the large merchant-backed planter. His land, which was under mortage, was held precariously, and any small disaster was likely to spell ruin for the small farmer. His loss worked to the advantage of the big planters, who were able to consolidate their holdings by buying up the land he had to forfeit. As he was forced off his land, even the labor of the small farmer was made superfluous by the employment of African slaves. Thus the poor white came increasingly to try his lot in migration to areas that seemed to offer a more promising life, like the North American colonies.[71]

By the eighteenth century, society in the British islands was everywhere dominated by a narrow aristocracy of sugar-rich planters and their agents.[72] This stratification of society was based on concentration of holdings that went on throughout the eighteenth century. While in some cases the number of proprietors increased, the average acreage per holding decreased. This happened in Jamaica between 1754 and 1774. In 1754, 1,620 planters held 1,671,569 acres. Their average estate size was more than 1,000 acres. In 1774, 2,178 proprietors held a decreased average acreage. There were 680 sugar estates with a total of 300,000 acres and 105,000 slaves. Additional settlements numbering 1,498 held 300,000 acres and 40,000 slaves. Of all estates, 31 percent were in sugar, with an average of 441 acres and 154 slaves per estate, and 69 percent cultivated crops other than sugar. Even some of these estates were involved in sugar-related cultivation, such as the growing of provisions for estate slaves. These estates contained an average of 200 acres each and supported 27 slaves per estate. F. W. Pitman, who compiled and refined these statistics, wrote that "while composing a little less than a third of the total number of proprietors, the sugar plantations had an investment in the island out of all proportion to their numbers and constituted a powerful aristocracy."[73]

In fact, only an aristocracy could build prosperous sugar plantations. In 1673, Richard Ligon calculated that in order to begin a plantation of 500 acres, the minimum he thought necessary for a chance of success, and stock it with slaves, servants, cattle, etc., a man would need about 1,400 pounds sterling.[74] In the late eighteenth century, Bryan Edwards found that a worthwhile plantation, one of at least 900 acres, required an initial capital of 30,000 pounds sterling.[75] Obviously, this type of money was not available to everyone, and when it could be borrowed, the conditions were often such as to facilitate the eventual transfer of the plantation into the hands of the lien holder.

The workings of the Navigation Acts, the rise in power and prominence of Parliament as a national institution, and the power of the merchant financier, all helped to account for the increasing dependence of the West India colonies on Great Britain, a dependence without which there could have been no anti-slavery movement like the one that agitated Britain in the late eighteenth and early nineteenth centuries. But these factors do not account completely for the leverage that the imperial government was to realize over the islands. They reflect and interact with a more significant problem—the absence of a local English community with a native loyalty and sense of the future. Early society in the West Indies was famous for its rough and unfinished quality. Contemporaries were fond of pointing to the boorishness and lack of cultivation of the islanders. Attempts at the establishment of learned societies, of education, and agricultural improvement projects came to nothing. Colonials seemed to enjoy spending their time in an orgy of eating and drinking. Tempers flared easily, cruelty was commonplace, and sexual license with slave women was a hallmark of society in the colonial Caribbean. Englishmen who remained for any length of time in the tropics appeared to degenerate, losing their sense of easy but restrained superiority over others and becoming petty tyrants.[76] James Stewart's views are typical of those expressed by contemporary observers from the seventeenth through the nineteenth centuries. "Arbitrary habits are acquired," wrote Stewart; "irritation and violent passions are engendered—partly indeed by the perverseness of the slaves—and the feelings are gradually blunted by the constant exercize of a too unrestrained power, and the scenes to which it is continually giving birth."[77]

The chance for a healthy white community in the Caribbean existed early on. It was destroyed not only by the rise of the sugar plantocracy, but also by the ending of the trade in white servants. Usually seen as a symptom of the triumph of capitalist monocrop agriculture and the conversion to slave labor, the demise of the white labor force can also be seen as a contributing factor in the success of the merchant-planter's bid to control the destiny of the Caribbean. If sufficiently large populations of white laborers had existed, they might have been able to fight off the monopolistic designs of the wealthy. The actual "failure" of the system of indenture, or contract labor, is difficult to explain. Certainly it was a popular form of labor in the seventeenth century, actively promoted by both planters and merchants. The emigration of Englishmen to the West Indies was seen as an avenue to economic advancement for them and their children. So Dalby Thomas thought that an English servant, if diligent, had a better chance of rising in the world in Barbados than at home.[78] Christopher Jeaffreson, writing from St. Christopher in the seventeenth century, was convinced that "it is seldome seene that the ingenious or industrious men fail of raising their fortunes," and it was certain that "they may live much better than thousands of the poor people in England."[79] Earlier, Richard Eburne had advocated that the authorities "take up all such vagrant persons as now contrary to the statute wander about the country loitoring, begging, etc., of which sort many are strong and able persons, such as could and would work and labor well if they were well ordered and employed."[80] If they were transported overseas to work, such persons might overcome their sordid pasts and "both richly increase their own estates and notably ease and disburden ours."[81] Such proposals had a rich history in English governmental experience with the poor. The hallmark of that experience over the past hundred years or so had been coercion justified by the assumption that the cause of poverty was idleness. Thus the act of 1531, which drew a distinction between those who were unable to work because of disability and the so-called sturdy beggars, directed that such people be "tied to the end of a cart naked and . . . beaten till [their bodies] be bloody." They were to be returned home and set to work.[82] In 1547, a statute directed that "vagabonds" be branded and enslaved for a term of two years.[83] The emphasis on coercion, which is seen as well in the Statute of Artificers of 1563, was carried over into legislation designed to address the seventeenth-century problem of the vagrant poor.

It was well known that many of the poor, despairing of survival through honest effort, turned instead to lives of crime, furnishing a rationale for the savageness of English law. The multiplication of offenses for which the death penalty was mandated had led to a situation in which juries would frequently fail to convict rather than send a fellow to the gallows for a relatively minor offense. Eager to demonstrate its mercy as well as its support for colonial ventures, the crown decided that a moderation in the severity of the law was warranted. In 1617, the Privy Council decided that it would henceforth be both humane and expedient to transport some of the condemned overseas to labor for the good of the nation.[84] Potential destinations for such labor are not indicated except for reference to parts "beyond the seas." By 1617, the English had already initiated activity in the Caribbean and were fishing off the Atlantic coast of North America. But aside from English activity in Virginia, there was as yet no significant English colony in the Americas, but the state had clearly grasped the potential importance of colonization and the critical need for labor with which to exploit it.

An early source of labor for Caribbean plantations was provided by the steady stream of political prisoners generated by the Civil War and the wars with Scotland and Ireland. Edward, the Earl of Clarendon, related that after the Royalist rising at Salisbury was crushed, many of those who were not hung were "sent as slaves to the Barbados."[85] After the total collapse of the king's cause, "the Parliament thought of nothing but transporting those families into Barbados and Jamaica, and other plantations, which might hereafter produce children of their father's affection, and by degrees to model their army that it might never give them more trouble."[86] The interest of public security was in this way made to coincide with the interest of private enterprise.

The return of peace with the Restoration did not disrupt the stream of servants pouring into the islands. As in France after the collapse of the Jacobin party, repression against the lower orders was pursued by the judiciary.[87] Instead of political prisoners, convict labor and voluntary and involuntary refugees from poverty provided a human cargo for the merchants of London and the outer ports. To this effort at labor recruitment the state once again lent a hand. In October of 1662, for example, the king "extended his grace and mercy to many prisoners in England and Wales conditionally on their being transported to the plantations and not returning again to this kingdom."[88] In December of the same year, license was given to Sir Thomas Bludworth and Sir William Turner, sheriffs of London, to have transportation of prisoners for twelve years.[89] In June of 1661, Jeremy Bonnell and Company of London, merchants with interests in the island of Jamaica, "having notice of many convicted persons, and others of loose and idle conversation who remain in the said prisons," ask that they may take and transport them overseas where they might be put to productive use.[90] In July of 1661, the king, in Council, ordered all who had been pardoned to be turned over to the petitioners.[91]

Other, less legal methods of labor recruitment included kidnapping, especially of young people.[92] By the 1650s, kidnapping had become a well-organized business, with its victims imprisoned in secret houses, at times for a month or more, before being shipped abroad.[93] Winked at by the law, little was done to discourage the activity of the "spirits" who conducted the business of stealing people. Moreover, it appears that efforts to control illegal recruitment were aimed more at the preservation of property rights than at the welfare of the poor. Although concern for the rights of the lower class is evinced, it is a tangential concern, one that is undergirded by the much more important need to protect private property. Thus kidnapping had provided an unexpected, and probably unwelcomed, means of escape for some who had been guilty of crimes or had escaped from prison. In addition, the very existence of "spirits" allowed dishonest people to accept pay for service overseas and then pretend that they had been kidnapped as a means of avoiding service.[94]

Towards the close of the seventeenth century, the English began to worry about a loss of manpower abroad. The islands became increasingly merely capitalist-run plantations dominated by slave labor, leading to the narrowing of opportunities for the social and economic advancement of small farmers. This resulted in an exodus to North America or home. In addition, with high rates of mortality for both Europeans and Africans and the harsh treatment meted out by cruel masters, the attraction of emigration to the tropical dependencies declined. The planter, faced with a renewed labor problem and having exhausted all other sources, turned at once to the African slave trade, thus initiating new world slavery on a grand scale.[95] The argument is plausible but not entirely convincing. It is tempting to speculate that there may have been other forces at work in the conversion to slave labor. The motive behind the servant trade, first of all, was neither planter demand for labor, imperial concern for overseas development, nor anxiety about the dangers presented by the rootless poor. Servants were carried into the Caribbean because of the merchant's desire for profit.

Over the course of the seventeenth century, thousands of English and Irish servants were transported into the Americas— 10,000 from the port of Bristol alone—and sold at a price well above shipping costs, delivering handsome profits to the merchants.[96] In the seventeenth century, Christopher Jeaffreson estimated the profit from the transportation of 300 servants to be about 3,000 pounds.[97] Still, as the century progressed, servants were becoming a precious commodity, and when, in 1655, General Venables stopped at Barbados to recruit servants for the conquest of Spanish lands, he met with discouragement, writing that "all the inhabitants were against our design as destructive to them."[98] It may not have been reluctance to ship whites overseas or the better availability of African slaves that accounts for the drying up of the servant trade. Perhaps it is worth considering the thesis that the English merchant played a larger role here than is usually recognized by pushing the slave trade over the servant trade as a better source of profit. Even as Caribbean colonization got underway with white labor, English merchants were in the initial stages of developing the African trading system. In 1664, black slaves were being sold in Barbados for 20 pounds a head, while English, Irish, and Scottish servants were bringing only 6 pounds apiece.[99] In 1662, a ship owned by John and Thomas Knight fell victim to Anglo-Dutch rivalry on the West African coast. Lost was a cargo of gold and elephants' teeth worth about 1,000 pounds and eighty-two blacks valued at 7,000 pounds sterling.[100] In 1665, John Style was still hoping that the labor problem could be solved with white labor. Perhaps in the knowledge that the crown had supported the search for white labor in the past, he wrote to Secretary Lord Arlington from Barbados: "Why should not his majesty as the Romans did send out a colony, one family from each parish, not your convict goal birds or riotous persons rotten before they are sent forth and at best idle and only fit for the mines."[101] But hopes for the growth of Anglo-Saxon, or even Anglo-Irish, communities were to be dashed forever.

While James Stewart used the existence of slavery as an excuse for the behavior of colonials, it is nevertheless true that slavery was the major problem, the critical factor tying the West Indies to Great Britain, as it was also the promoter of a violent and degenerate society. As abolitionists and other eighteenth-century critics pointed out, the habit of a more or less absolute power over multitudes of human beings bred harshness and cruelty in the slave master, a cruelty no doubt related to fear of the African slaves who outnumbered them. It was a fear coupled with a pragmatic need for security that led islanders to rely on imperial troops and ships as the ultimate guarantors of white supremacy.

Slave labor was not the necessary solution to the Caribbean labor problem caused by the destruction of the aboriginal population, but once sugarcane had been introduced, and the merchant realized the potential wealth to be made in the slave trade compared with the relatively moderate income from the transport of English indentured servants into the islands, it became the backbone of the Caribbean economy. By the late seventeenth century, the construction of an Atlantic commercial system linking America, Africa, and Europe was pursued with vigor. In 1672, the Royal African Company was chartered, organized specifically to exploit the slave trade. Its seal contained "the image of Our Royal Person in Parliament and on the other side an elephant bearing a Castle supported by two negroes."[102] Although ivory still maintained an importance, by 1672, its significance was surpassed by the importance of the slave trade, which was by then protected by the presence of English forts on the African coast. The rising demand for slaves in the Caribbean is captured by the comment of a seventeenth-century Surinam planter who wrote home to the government:

"Were the planters supplied with negroes, the strength and sinews of this Western World, they would Advance their fortunes and his majesty's customs."[103] The demand was met by a tremendous influx of African slaves, who fueled the growth of plantation capitalism and the famous triangular trade. At the same time, however, the demographic revolution, represented by the replacement of an Irish-English labor force by an African slave system, meant that the foundations were being laid for the rise of Afro-Caribbean communities. This could eventually come to present England with the type of colonial resistance that English planters were unable to mount. The potential for a colonial problem far more serious than that posed by Barbados in the seventeenth century was recognized early on, prompting one Barbados planter to complain that the replacement of white servants by black slaves was a revolution "by which the whole may be endangered; for now there are many thousands of slaves that speak English, and if there are many leading men slaves in a plantation, they may be easily wrought upon to betray it, especially on the promise of freedom."[104] Another writer put his finger squarely on the problem when he noted that "there are in Barbados not less than 60,000 souls, of which 40,000 are Blacks, whose different tongues and animosities have kept them from insurrection, but . . . the Creolian generation now growing up and increasing may hereafter emancipate their masters."[105]

The central problem in Caribbean history became not the lack of community, but the constant need to frustrate the emergence of any politically viable community with a consciousness of its own potential and the will to actualize it. Modern Caribbean history can thus be seen as a struggle between British planters and the imperial government on one side and Afro-Caribbean peoples on the other. The key to understanding that history is the effort of the British to prevent the emergence of a Caribbean society antithetical to imperial concerns.

At the end of the seventeenth century, Charles D'Avenant saw the promise of economic growth presented by Caribbean exploitation. He realized that the colonies represented a unique catalyst for commerce. The binding together of England and Africa through the American nexus allowed for the productive use of labor and resources which were unable to find employment at home. Dalby Thomas argued forcefully for the vigorous support of colonization. Englishmen overseas, because of their strategic position in a budding economic system, were able to be more productive than those at home. Well might Thomas argue in this manner. The colonist ruled over a host of unfree laborers. But neither D'Avenant nor Thomas grappled directly with the centrality of slavery to the British West Indies. Although their arguments revolved around the implicit recognition of opportunities and limitations inherent in a slave labor system, its importance was too axiomatic to be discussed at length. Slaves provided the indispensable foundations for Caribbean prosperity. The interrelationship of sugar and slaves made so well known by twentieth-century historians was just as well known to seventeenth-century Englishmen. Contemporaries were well aware of the importance of the so-called triangular trade to the future of the Western economy. They knew that this trade, by linking Europe, Africa, and America, provided a tremendous impetus to economic growth, and they therefore advocated its protection. The best of them knew that new world slavery was not, in its origin, a matter of race, but of economics. Africans, they believed, were used as slaves because they were abundantly available and were cheap compared with English servants, whose contracts were temporary. Like many modern historians, they focused on the European in the new world, having little or nothing to say about the African. This was not Eurocentrism on their part. It was not their purpose to illustrate the manifold ways in which Africans influenced the shape of colonial society and the form of imperial rule. However, if we are to understand the way in which British rule was transformed between the late eighteenth and the early nineteenth centuries, we must make up for this omission. We must probe the tenor of life in the Caribbean in order to understand what the relationship of master, slave, and empire was and, finally, to discern the ways in which slaves manifested what Frederick Douglass called the Signs of Power.

NOTES

1. *The Political and Commercial Works of Charles D'Avenant*, ed. Sir Charles Whitworth, 5 vols. (London: n.p., 1771), 1:356. D'Avenant,

born in 1656, was the son of the poet Sir William D'Avenant. From 1678 to 1689, Sir Charles was commissioner of the excise. In 1698 and 1700 he was a member of Parliament for Great Bedwin. In 1705, D'Avenant was made inspector general of exports and imports, a post that he held until his death in 1714. *Dictionary of National Biography*, 4:549-550. Hereafter referred to as *D.N.B.*

2. D'Avenant, *Political and Commercial Works*, pp. 1:356-357.

3. Ibid., pp. 382-383.

4. See also Thomas Mun, *England's Treasure by Foreign Trade* (Oxford: Basil Blackwell, 1949), pp. 22-24.

5. D'Avenant, *Political and Commercial Works*, p. 383.

6. Ibid., p. 393.

7. Dalby Thomas was English Agent General of the Royal African Company in 1703. During his tenure on the Gold Coast, he pursued an old Dutch idea of developing a plantation economy on the African side of the Atlantic. Importing seeds from the West Indies, he experimented with the cultivation of indigo. His attempt was a failure, and the company, preferring to cultivate the triangular trade, discouraged any future efforts of this nature. K. Y. Daaku, *Trade and Politics on the Gold Coast 1600-1720* (Oxford: Clarendon Press, 1970), pp. 45-46.

8. Dalby, Thomas, *An Historical Account of the Rise and Growth of the West India Colonies* (NY: Arno Press, 1972), pp. 2-3.

9. Ibid., p. 10.

10. Ibid., p. 9.

11. Ibid., pp. 10-11, 27.

12. Barry Supple, *Commercial Crisis and Change in England 1600-1642* (Cambridge: Cambridge University Press, 1959), p. 7.

13. On how the English tried to meet this competition, see Supple, *Commercial Crisis,* and A. Friis, *Alderman Cockayne's Project* (London, Oxford University Press 1927).

14. Sir Josiah Child, *Brief Observations Concerning Trade* (London, 1668), p. 5. See also Edward Misselden, *The Circle of Commerce, or the Ballance of Trade* (New York: Augustus M. Kelley, 1971).

15. Child, *Brief Observations,* pp. 3-5.

16. Roger Coke, *A Discourse of Trade* (London, 1670), pp. 41-42.

17. Sir Walter Raleigh, *Observations Touching Trade and Commerce, The Works of Walter Raleigh* (New York: Burt Franklin, 1829), 3:363.

18. Supple, *Commercial Crisis,* p. 50.

19. Ibid., p. 136. On the old and new draperies, see George Unwin, "The History of the Cloth Industry in Suffolk." in R. H. Tawney, ed., *Studies in Economic History: The Collected Papers of George Unwin* (New York: Augustus M. Kelley, 1966); J. de L. Mann, *The Cloth*

Industry in the West of England from 1640 to 1880 (Oxford: Clarendon Press, 1971), chap. 1; and the classic work of Alfred P. Wadsworth and Julia De Lacy Mann, *The Cotton Trade and Industrial Lancashire 1660-1780* (Manchester: Manchester University Press, 1931), pp. 19-20.

20. F. J. Fisher, "London's Export Trade in the Early Seventeenth Century," in W. E. Minchinton, ed., *The Growth of English Overseas Trade in the Seventeenth and Eighteenth Centuries* (London: Methuen, 1969), p. 71.

21. Ibid., p. 73.

22. Ibid., p. 76.

23. Supple, p. 135.

24. Ralph Davis, "English Foreign Trade, 1660-1700," in Minchinton, ed., *Growth of English Overseas Trade*, p. 78.

25. Ibid., pp. 80-82.

26. Ralph Davis, *The Rise of the English Shipping Industry in the Seventeenth and Eighteenth Centuries* (New York: Macmillan, 1962), p. 1. In 1582, the first comprehensive survey of shipping found that there were 66,714 tons of shipping of more than 10 tons weight, of which London accounted for 19 percent. W. G. Hoskins, *The Age of Plunder: King Henry's England 1500-1547* (London: Longmans, 1976), p. 177.

27. Davis, *English Shipping*, pp. 3-4; C. M. Macinnes, *Bristol: A Gateway of Empire* (New York: Augustus M. Kelley, 1968), p. 241.

28. Davis, *English Shipping*, p. 5. The decline of Dutch trade of which Davis writes here must have been that to the Baltic in the period from 1567 to 1572. An unusual factor in this long war was the continued growth in overall Dutch trade, especially to the new areas east and west. While Antwerp continued to decline, Amsterdam experienced a spectacular growth, replacing Antwerp as the leading commercial center. Violet Barbour, *Capitalism in Amsterdam in the 17th Century* (Ann Arbor: University of Michigan Press, 1966), pp. 13-21; C. R. Boxer, *The Dutch Seaborne Empire: 1600-1800* (New York: Alfred A. Knopf, 1979), pp. 16-30; B. Vlekke, *Evolution of the Dutch Nation* (New York: Roy Publishers, 1945), p. 110.

29. Davis, *English Shipping*, p. 9; Charles Wilson, *Profit and Power: A Study of England and the Dutch Wars* (New York: Longman, 1957), for a detailed discussion of the points of conflict which led to war between the two maritime nations.

30. Maurice Ashley, *Financial and Commercial Policy Under the Cromwellian Protectorate* (New York: Augustus M. Kelley, 1962), pp. 148-155. Boxer, *Dutch Seaborne Empire*, pp. 273-194; Charles Wilson, *The Dutch Republic* (New York: McGraw-Hill, 1977), pp. 230-236.

31. Richard Hakluyt, *Discourse of Western Planting, The Original Writings and Correspondence of the Two Richard Hakluyts.* (Hakluyt Society, 2d series, no. 76, 1935), p. 233.

32. *Calendar of State Papers. Colonial America and West Indies, 1574-1660,* p. 23. Hereafter referred to as *Cal. S.P. Colonial,* followed by dates and pages.

33. Hakluyt, *Discourse,* pp. 222-223, 270-273, 234-235; Richard Eburne, *A Plain Pathway to Plantations* (Ithaca, N.Y.: Cornell University Press, 1962), p. 34. On the motivation behind early colonization schemes, see the works of G. L. Beer, *British Colonial Policy, 1754-1765* (New York: The Macmillan Co., 1907); *The Old Colonial System 1660-1688,* 2 vols., (New York: The Macmillan Co., 1912) and *The Origins of the British Colonial System, 1578-1660* (New York: The Macmillan Co., 1908).

34. Arthur P. Newton, *The European Nations in the West Indies 1498-1688* (London: A. C. Black, 1933), pp. 131-132; Beer, *Origins of the British Colonial System,* pp. 5-60.

35. *Cal. S.P. Colonial,* 1574-1660, p. 5.

36. Newton, *European Nations,* pp. 132-134.

37. J. A. Williamson, *The Caribee Islands Under the Proprietary Patents* (London: Oxford University Press, 1926), pp. 21-22.

38. John Hilton, "The Relation of . . . John Hilton," in V. T. Harlow, ed., *Colonizing Expeditions to the West Indies and Guiana 1623-1667* (Hakluyt Society, 2d series, no. 56, 1925), pp.

39. Williamson, *Caribee Islands,* pp. 33-36; *Cal. S.P. Colonial,* 1574-1660, p. 485; John Oldmixon, *The British Empire in America* (New York: Augustus M. Kelley, 1969), 2:2-3; Richard Ligon, *A True and Exact History of the Island of Barbados* (London, 1673), p. 23. John Oldmixon was born in 1673 to an old Somerset family. He published a number of dramatic works before his *British Empire in America* (1708). Oldmixon died in 1742. *D.N.B.,* pp. 1010-1012.

40. *Cal. S.P. Colonial,* 1574-1660, pp. 85-86; Williamson, *Caribee Islands,* pp. 40-41.

41. Ibid., p. 43.

42. Ibid., pp. 44-45; D. C. Coleman and A. H. John, eds., *Trade Government and Economy in Pre-Industrial England* (London: Weidenfeld & Nicolson, 1976), p. 121. Courteen, born in 1572, was an Anglo-Dutch merchant who had built up a successful business in silk and linen. Courteen was involved in the trade to Guinea, Portugal, and Spain, in addition to the West Indies. At one time he had a fleet of twenty ships and employed some 5,000 sailors. *D.N.B.,* p. 1258. On the proprietary issue, see the work of V. T. Harlow, *History of Barbados 1625-1685* (New York: Oxford University Press, 1926); C.S.S. Higham,

The Development of the Leeward Islands Under the Restoration, 1660-1688 (Cambridge: Cambridge University Press, 1921); A. P. Thornton, *West India Policy Under the Restoration* (Oxford; Oxford University Press, 1956).

43. *Cal. S.P. Colonial,* 1574-1660, pp. 9, 83, 94, 96, 97, 98, 104, 291, 299-300, 305-306, 308, 313, 323-324, 327, 486.

44. Harlow, *Barbados,* p. 28.

45. Charles M. Andrews, *British Committees, Commissions, and Councils of Trade and Plantations, 1622-1675* (Baltimore: Johns Hopkins University Press, 1908), p. 21.

46. Harlow, *Barbados,* pp. 30-31.

47. British Museum Egerton mss. 2395, Papers Relating to the English Colonies in America and the West Indies, 1627-1699, "A Brief Relation . . .", f. 49.

48. *Cal. S.P. Colonial,* 1574-1660, p. 350.

49. Ibid., pp. 374-375.

50. Ibid., p. 408.

51. John Poyer, *The History of Barbados* (London, 1808), pp. 81-85; Beer, *Old Colonial System,* 1:179-188, 190, 202.

52. Cornelis Ch. Goslinga, *A Short History of the Netherlands Antilles and Surinam* (The Hague: Martinus Nijhoff, 1979), p. 36.

53. *Cal. S.P. Colonial,* 1574-1660, p. 390.

54. K. G. Davies, "The Origins of the Commission System in the West Indies Trade," *Transactions of the Royal Historical Society,* 5th series, vol. 3, 1952, pp. 89-90.

55. *Cal. S.P. Colonial,* 1574-1660, p. 165.

56. Beer, *Old Colonial System,* 1:63-67, 72-73, 75-78, 81-84; *Acts of the Privy Council,* 1613-1680, pp. 318-320, 334-335, 345-349; Charles Wilson, *Profit and Power: A Study of England and the Dutch Wars* (New York: Longmans, 1957), p. 87; Charles M. Andrews, *The Colonial Period of American History,* 4 vols. (New Haven, Conn.: Yale University Press, 1948), 4:44-49. These acts are discussed in detail in L. A. Harper, *The English Navigation Laws* (New York: Octagon Books, 1973).

57. W. Cunningham, *The Growth of English Industry and Commerce,* 3 vols. (Cambridge: Cambridge University Press, 1912), vol. 2, pt. 1, p. 472.

58. K. G. Davies, *The Royal African Company* (New York: Atheneum, 1970), pp. 66-74. For the early African trade, see George F. Zook, *The Company of Royal Adventurers Trading into Africa* (New York: Negro Universities Press, 1969).

59. William R. Scott, *The Constitution and Finance of English,*

Scottish and Irish Joint Stock Companies to 1720, 2 vols. (New York: Peter Smith, 1951), 1:8-9.

60. Conrad Gill, *Merchants and Mariners of the Seventeenth Century* (London: Edward Arnold, 1961), p. 74; Ashley, *Financial and Commercial Policy,* p. 14.

61. Wilson, *Profit and Power,* p. 154; Sir William Holdsworth, *A History of English Law,* 16 vols. (London: Methuen, 1966), 8:200-201, 209; V. T. Harlow, *The Founding of the Second British Empire 1763-1793,* 2 vols. (Cambridge: Cambridge University Press, 1964), 2:21; Ephraim Lipson, *The Economic History of England* (London: A & C Black, 1948-1949) 3 vols. vol. 3 (Claims that after 1660, London had 3,000 merchants, two-thirds of whom were in foreign trade (p. 191).

62. See Wilson, *Profit and Power.*

63. Malachy Postlethwayt, *Britain's Commercial Interest Explained and Improved,* 2 vols. (New York: Augustus M. Kelley, 1968), 3:203.

64. *Cal. S. P. Colonial,* 1661-1668, p. 495.

65. Idem.

66. *Cal. S.P. Colonial,* 1661-1668, p. 542.

67. Ibid., p. 45.

68. K. G. Davies, *The North Atlantic World in the Seventeenth Century* (Minneapolis: University of Minnesota Press, 1974), p. 244 and chap. 5.

69. *Cal. S.P. Colonial,* 1574-1660, p. 357.

70. Frank W. Pitman, *The Development of the British West Indies, 1700-1763* (New Haven, Conn.: Yale University Press, 1917), p. 91; "Extract from Henry Whistler's Account of the British Expedition Which Conquered Jamaica," in C. H. Firth, ed., *The Narrative of General Venables* (New York: Longmans Green, 1900), p. 145; John Cardy Jeaffreson, ed., *A Young Squire of the Seventeenth Century. From the papers (AD. 1676-1685) of Christopher Jeaffreson* (London: C. Hurst & Blackett, 1878). 2 vols. 1:211.

71. Richard S. Dunn, *Sugar and Slaves* (New York: W. W. Norton, 1972), p. 24.

72. Ibid., p. 132.

73. Frank W. Pitman, "The Settlement and Financing of British West India Plantations in the 18th Century," in *Essays in Colonial History Presented to Charles McLean Andrews by His Students* (New Haven, Conn.: Yale University Press, 1931), p. 266.

74. Ligon, *History,* p. 108.

75. Bryan Edwards, *The History, Civil and Commercial of the British West Indies,* 3 vols. (London, 1819), 3:87-296.

76. See Chapter Three.

77. J. Stewart, *A View of Jamaica* (London, 1823).
78. Thomas, *Historical Account*, p. 27.
79. Jeaffreson, *Young Squire*, 1:256.
80. Eburne, *Plain Pathway*, p. 10.
81. Ibid., p. 32.
82. Roger Lockyer, *Tudor and Stuart Britain, 1471-1714* (London: Longmans, 1969), p. 138.
83. Ibid., p. 139; J. R. Poyer, *Society and Pauperism. English Ideas on Poor Relief 1795-1834* (London: Routledge & Kegan Paul, 1969), p. 2; Samuel McKee, *Labor in Colonial New York 1664-1776* (New York: Columbia University Press, 1935), p. 89; C. A. Herrick, *White Servitude in Pennsylvania* (Philadelphia: John Joseph McVery, 1929), p. 6; P. A. Bruce, *Economic History of Virginia in the Seventeenth Century*, 2 vols. (New York: Peter Smith, 1935), 1:576-582, 592-594; Marcus Wilson Jernegan, *Laboring and Dependent Classes in Colonial America 1607-1783* (Chicago: University of Chicago Press, 1931), pp. 46-47.
84. *Acts of the Privy Council*, 1613-1680, pp. 10-11.
85. Edward, Earl of Clarendon, *The History of the Rebellion and Civil Wars in England*, 6 vols. (Oxford: Oxford University Press, 1958), 4:256-259.
86. Ibid., 6:43. Maurice Ashley notes that Cromwell had at one time approved a plan to transport the entire population of New England to Jamaica. *Financial and Commercial Policy*, p. 134.
87. See especially Richard Cobb, *The Police and the People* (Oxford: Oxford University Press, 1970).
88. *Cal. S.P. Colonial*, 1661-1668, p. 117.
89. Idem.
90. *Acts of the Privy Council*, 1613-1680, p. 310.
91. Ibid., pp. 314-315.
92. *Cal. S.P. Colonial*, 1661-1668, p. 117.
93. Abbot Emerson Smith, *Colonists in Bondage. White Servitude and Convict Labor in America, 1607-1776* (Chapel Hill: North Carolina University Press, 1947), p. 69; Jernegan, *Laboring and Dependent Classes*, p. 49.
94. *Cal. S.P. Colonial*, 1661-1668, pp. 23, 98.
95. See Eric Williams, *Capitalism and Slavery* (New York: G. P. Putnam's Sons, 1966); Dunn, *Sugar and Slaves;* Carl Bridenbaugh and Roberta Bridenbaugh, *No Peace Beyond the Line. The English in the Caribbean, 1624-1690* (London: Oxford University Press, 1972).
96. Smith, *Colonists in Bondage*, pp. 4-5, 35-36; William Bowman, *Bristol and America. A Record of the First Settlers in the Colonies of North America, 1654-1685* (Baltimore: Genealogical Publishing Co.,

1967), pp. 3-5; John Camden Hotten, *The Original Lists of Persons of Quality . . . Who Went from Great Britain to the American Plantations 1600-1700* (Baltimore: Genealogical Publishing Co., 1968).

97. Smith, *Colonists in Bondage,* p. 66; Warren B. Smith, *White Servitude in Colonial South Carolina* (Columbia: University of South Carolina Press, 1961), pp. 22, 52-53; K. F. Geiser, *Redemptioners and Indentured Servants in the Colony and Commonwealth of Pennsylvania* (New Haven, Conn.: Tuttle, Morehouse & Taylor, 1901), p. 45; Edward Morgan, *American Slavery American Freedom* (New York: W. W. Norton, 1975), p. 176.

98. Firth, ed., *Narrative of General Venables,* p. 8.

99. *Cal. S.P. Colonial,* 1661-1668, p. 229.

100. *Acts of the Privy Council,* 1613-1680, pp. 328-329.

101. *Cal. S.P. Colonial,* 1661-1668, p. 313.

102. Cecil T. Carr, ed., *Select Charters of Trading Companies, 1520-1707,* Selden Society, vol. 28 (1913), p. 189.

103. *Cal. S.P. Colonial,* 1661-1668, pp. 119-169.

104. Ibid., p. 530.

105. Ibid., p. 586.

3

The Signs of Power

If the existence of slavery in the British Caribbean was founded on the support of the imperial government, the anti-slavery movement called for a reassessment of the terms on which support should be given. It was part of a movement to create an instrument of governance suitable to the needs of a far-flung empire. By the 1830s, as a result of the dynamic, well-organized, and popular anti-slavery campaign, the imperial government had come to share the humanitarians' contention that slave society would have to be transformed by the imperial government if the colonies were to form a productive and peaceful part of the empire. But far from being exclusively the product of cultural changes in England and Europe, this conclusion was reached through reflection on the evidence of the unstable nature of slave society. In this sense, it was the slaves themselves who, through their day-to-day struggle against the oppressive conditions of their lives, waged an unlabeled but highly visible anti-slavery movement. The history of that movement is the story of the relationship of master and slave.

The establishment of sugar cultivation in the British Caribbean led to the growth of slave communities. Cultivation of sugar began in Barbados about 1640. Three years later, there were 6,400 slaves in that island. By 1683, the slave population had exploded to 46,602, as the sugar boom there neared its peak. In 1773, the servile population of Barbados stood at 68,485, and at emancipation in 1834, compensation was paid for 66,683 bondsmen.[1]

Conversion to slave labor came a bit later in the Leeward Islands. The sugar revolution occurred there between 1678 and 1713. In the earlier year, there were 8,449 blacks in that group, but in 1708, after the introduction of sugar, their numbers stood at 23,500.[2] Elsa Goveia estimates that, at the end of the eighteenth century, the combined slave population of Antigua, St. Kitts, Nevis, Monserrat, and the Virgin Islands was about 81,000.[3]

Jamaica, which was settled later than Barbados or the Leewards, developed more slowly than the older islands. In 1661, there were only 514 blacks. By 1673, the black population had grown to more than 9,504 for this largest British island.[4] Jamaica eventually outran all other British Caribbean colonies, coming to possess the largest slave population. In 1768, there were 167,000 slaves in Jamaica, and by 1820, the servile population stood at 339,000, which was just about its highest point.[5]

By 1807, when the slave trade was abolished, there were more than 700,000 slaves in the British Caribbean.[6] The large number of blacks meant threatening ratios between master and slave. In Barbados, there were about four slaves to every white throughout slavery times. In the Leewards, it peaked at eight blacks to one white in the eighteenth century. But the ratio was at its worst in Jamaica, where most British slaves lived. During the seventeenth century, there were more than ten slaves to every white, and the ratio climbed to thirteen to one in the nineteenth century.[7]

The Afro-Caribbean population presented a problem in management for their approximately 51,000 British rulers.[8] What was the problem? How did planters meet it? Why did it become overwhelming by the 1830s?

The maintenance of slavery necessitated positive action and a high degree of internal discipline within the "dominant" group. Central to the process of social control was the institution of positive law. "In Fact," wrote Elsa Goveia, "the experience of the British colonies makes it particularly clear that police regulations lay at the very heart of the slave system and that without them the system itself became impossible to maintain."[9]

The earliest known slave code for the British West Indies, the Barbados code of 1661, addressed the need for continual vigilance on the part of whites if they were to maintain dominance over the blacks, whom it characterized as "an heathenish, brutish and uncertaine, dangerous kinde of people."[10] It directed plantation overseers to keep the cabins of blacks under tight surveillance. These should be searched twice a month for stolen goods as well as for clubs and wooden swords.[11]

Contemporary observers attest to this vigilance. Writing in the late seventeenth century, Richard Blome noted that planters were careful to keep all weapons away from the slaves, whose diversity of languages was also a hedge against rebellion. Christopher Jeaffreson wrote to his steward in St. Christopher, urging him to "keep a strict hand over" his slaves, as they must be kept in "awe" of their rulers. W. W. Bridges thought Africans a "strange and barbarous people" to be governed harshly. Even the reform-minded Clement Caines warned of "the restless and sharp sighted dishonesty of the slaves always on the watch to avail itself of the negligence of the masters." In the words of the ex-slave Esteban Montejo, "everything was based on watchfulness and the whip."[12]

This constant need for supervision led the planters to develop an elaborate set of slave codes outlining the treatment that was expected to keep slaves in check. A high priority of West Indian laws was the maintenance of the proper relationship between master and slave. The supremacy of all whites was an important ideological prop of the regime and was supported by strict laws. A challenge to the authority of any white was thought to be a challenge to the stability of white society.

The attempt to legislate white supremacy is reflected in the savageness of the legal reprisals for crimes against whites, ranging from insubordination to striking a white person, for which the slave could be subject to whipping, mutilation, or death.[13] While, on the other hand, the murder of a slave was seldom punished with anything severer than a heavy fine.[14] In this way, the law sought to protect property, but, at the same time, avoided the suggestion that the lives of blacks and whites could be equated. The savageness of the law may also be an indication of the insecurity of white colonials who saw themselves surrounded by hostile "savages" ready to resist their every demand.

A host of regulatory laws were enacted to guard against escape, the most obvious avenue of resistance to slavery. Slaves were forbidden to go off estates without written passes, blow horns, or beat drums because these activities facilitated movement within the slave's world.[15] The St. Kitts acts of 1711 and 1722 directed that the houses of blacks be regularly searched for the detection of runaways.[16] In order to limit support for runaway slaves, a Jamaican act of the seventeenth century ordered the destruction of plantations deserted for six months to prevent them from becoming places of refuge for such slaves.[17]

The Antigua codes of 1702 and 1723, which were concerned with capture and punishment of runaways, specified the penalty for concealment of such slaves to be whipping "upon the bare back, with any number of stripes, at the Discretion of the Justice."[18] For free persons, fines were substituted, with varying terms of imprisonment for delinquency.[19]

As an aid in their effort to apprehend runaways and to discourage this response to slavery, planters attempted to gain allies among the black population. "A slave, taking up a runaway, and bringing to the owner or to the next gaol," ran a Jamaican law of 1696, "shall receive a shilling per mile for the first five miles, and eight-pence per mile for every other, so that the whole does not exceed forty shillings. Any person, depriving or defrauding the slave of such rewards, shall forfeit treble the value."[20] A Barbados act of 1661 provided that slaves who apprehended runaways should be decorated "with a Badge of Red Crose on his right Arme, whereby he may be knowne and cherished by all good people."[21]

These efforts at control dealt out violent reprisals for violators, but they clearly extended incentives to those who were willing to cooperate with the regime. This was a tactic that planters used throughout the history of Caribbean slavery, and one that was crucial to the security of the regime. Regulations and control had the overriding objective of facilitating the production of sugar. But this, too, involved management and drew on skill and experience.

Dr. Collins, a twenty-year resident in the sugar islands, advised planters that slaves could be "seasoned" through a process of manipulation that used careful supervision by an African from the slave's own country, who would be with him constantly day and night. The role of this trusted companion was nothing short of assisting in the enculturation of the recent arrival.[22] Collins indicated strong preference for psychological coercion rather than physical coercion, which experience had shown him was not effective, recommending that "if any of them should refuse to go to the field when they are required, you will turn them into ridicule, laugh at their indolence, and excite your other negroes to do the same."[23] The emphasis on psychological manipulation is much more apparent when Collins explained that when physical punishment is to be meted out, the guilty party and the slave community must both be made to see that the punishment is deserved.[24] The interesting thing about Collins' advice is the degree to which it depends on the cooperation of the slave community to engage each member in a common enterprise and assume common standards of behavior. Although one of the few planters to express so openly the importance of the attitude of the slave community for plantation discipline, Collins was scarcely the only one to offer instructions for good management that placed heavy emphasis on non-violent manipulation.

A well-educated planter, Edward Long, nevertheless was content to compare blacks with orangutans, to whom, he believed, they might be related. But he thought them sufficiently elevated above their simian relations to agree with the abolitionist Thomas Clarkson in the view that the Negro's character could be molded by his master. Long especially recommended that planters try to cajole Creole slaves, who could be motivated by rewards, as well as by punishments. A keen student of the psychology of slavery, he reflected that "on every well-organized plantation they eye and respect their master as a father, and are extremely vain in reflecting on the connection between them. Their master's character and repute casts, they believe, a kind of secondary light upon themselves, . . . and the importance he aquires, in his station of life, adds, they imagine, to their own estimation among their neighbour's Negroes on adjacent estates." Creoles were thus capable of being integrated into a British cultural complex. But Long was careful to warn that overseers must be careful of the artfulness of Creoles, whose "principal address is shown in finding out their master's temper, and playing upon it so artfully as to bend it with most convenience to their own purposes." If he is not careful, the Negroes' subtlety will "very soon bring his government to disgrace."[25] Even the most cooperative slaves had agendas of their own.

The Jamaican planter Thomas Roughley devoted a great deal of thought to the business of slave management. His *Jamaican Planters Guide* (1823) was intended to facilitate the scientific management of slave populations on estates. Significantly, Roughley paid close attention to the business of the overseer, the representative of the planter and, ultimately, of imperial power. The effective overseer must ensure that the slaves were kept to their work, without overburdening them by excessive demands. He should inflict punishment when necessary but avoid abusing his power. He must respond to their needs promptly, always taking care not to be deceived by their artfulness.[26] Above all else, he should be careful not to "encourage the spirit of obea" among them, lie with their wives, prevent the care of their provision grounds, or neglect upkeep of their houses. By any such negligence, good slaves can be turned into runaways and estates ruined.

In essence, Roughley advised planters that the transgression of what the slaves had come to regard as their customary rights would alienate them. Despite their lack of effective legal protection, or of institutionalized power, Jamaican slaves had succeeded in demonstrating their willingness to defend what they regarded as their minimum rights. Roughley's recommendations are a significant indication of the existence of a powerful slave culture.

The strength of this culture was expressed in numerous ways. For example, Roughley related the story of an overseer who was murdered by slaves in retaliation for cruel treatment. He included it in his Guide in order to "warn others not to tread in such fearful paths, when human nature, however depressed or subjugated, but stung by anguish of a poison directed to its very existence, will form some desperate design to rid itself of its torment.''[27] Roughley's warning is clear—push them too far and even the most loyal bondsmen will fight back.

In the context of a vigilant slave population, the art of plantership entailed the knowledge of how to define the bounds of legitimate authority. Roughley provided some clues. He felt that a particularly outrageous act in the eyes of a slave was the destruction of his provision grounds or the pulling down of his house. "It may easily be conjectured what will be the consequence, when the slave views his beggared starving family, his comforts fled, his happiness annihilated and expiring." Roughley's warning that the violation of the rights of family and home would be likely to provoke hostility provides support for the argument of humanitarians, like Clarkson, who urged that slaves be granted homes and copyhold tenure as means of attaching them to the community.[28]

As a result of the abolition of the slave trade, the percentage of African-born slaves in the population would continually decline. Roughley saw that the planter would have to give great care to the condition of the Creole, or island-born, slaves, who would now form the backbone of the labor force. Their health must be attended to, their provision grounds and houses well ordered, the sanctity of their family lives respected, and especially important, the enlightened planter should strive to "lessen their propensity to vice, cabalistic or obea arts, induce them to receive Christianity."[29] In its attention to the moral, as well as the physical, improvement of the slaves, Roughley's program sounded quite like the classic abolitionist prescription for social health. The obvious similarity was that both abolitionist and enlightened planters like Roughley were interested in how to achieve a society in which order and economic prosperity could be based on cooperation rather than coercion.

The similarity in approach went even further. Despite his willingness to use force, Roughley understood that social stability could only be protected as long as the slave population remained susceptible to the proper psychological coercion, or incentives. This was, it will become clear, a key anti-slavery

position. But at this point, there was great disagreement
between colonials and metropolitan humanitarians as to how far
society could rely on such natural incentives alone. The planters
were sure that force must remain the final arbiter, and they
rested their claim on their experience with slaves. That
experience had taught them that there were two types of
slaves—those "good Negroes" who could be cajoled and the
mass of "bad Negroes" who invited the use of force.

What did planters have in mind when they spoke of
"cooperative" slaves? The position of "head Negro driver" was
one of the most important that a slave could attain. Because
drivers were responsible for the orderly and productive work of
the hands in the field, the position was central to the accomplishment of estate goals. The selection of a head driver was, therefore, an important one. Roughley believed that an intelligent
head driver "is the life and soul of an estate." Such a slave
should be athletic, healthy, possessed of a fine character and
reputation. "He should be respectful to white people; suffering
no freedoms from those under him, by conversation or trifling
puerile conduct."[30] The picture, in short, is that of a "Negro"
copy of the ideal British overseer.

As a man who moved between two worlds, charged to carry
out the bidding of one, the driver had to be a dependable
character. A slave would appear dependable if the planter
recognized in him a tendency to identify with the master class.
The position of head driver brought power and responsibility to
those who enjoyed it but only in return for cooperation with the
regime. Cooperativeness in the Jamaican slave society meant an
ability to juggle conflicting demands—those of the planter and
those of loyalty to one's fellows. The strain of such a position
could be endured only by unique individuals, and it is no wonder
that many of them were to be found in the leadership of
nineteenth-century slave revolts. For their part, planters
recognized the difficulty of meeting these criteria. "It is rare
indeed," mused Roughley of the qualifications he had outlined,
"to find this mass of perfection in a negro."[31]

Roughley meant to disparage the character of the slave by
what he saw as the absence of the moral development necessary
to fit a person for the position of driver, but if we recognize that

what he called perfection was more in the manner of an aberration, in the context of slave society, his interpretation can provide us with insight into the degree of cooperation that the slaves were prepared to provide to the regime.

James Stewart, like many whites familiar with slave behavior, observed that the slave accounted it no crime to steal from the master, while theft from a fellow slave was severely censured.[32] This was a code by which a driver or a head man might not always be able to abide. Roughley, for example, explained that the head cattle and mule men who had supervision over a good part of their master's property, must be vigilant in guarding against slave theft.[33] He emphasized this point because readiness to betray a fellow bondsman was uncommon, and one would imagine that it became increasingly so as society became more Creolized. What planters called honest bondsmen did exist, but their scarcity drew praise from planters, who regarded them as striking exceptions to the general rule.

Mrs. Carmichael, who had lived in the eastern Caribbean, complained with bitterness how her husband's "kindly" treatment of his slaves was repaid with treachery. On one occasion, she was warned by two slaves of a plot to kill him. Several weeks later, another attempt was made on her husband's life, when again she was alerted by "good negroes." Thankful for the existence of these rare types, Carmichael defined the behavior which marked good negroes who were the backbone of any estate. "When I use the term good negro, I wish my readers to understand it as we do in the West Indies—industrious, civil, with some sense of his own dignity, and a wish to retain a place in the good opinion of his master and all around him." She knew such slaves to be vigilant in seeking runaways, whose capture brought financial reward.[34] But she lamented that they were rare indeed and were not themselves free from imperfections. "Such a man is seldom altogether proof against occasional deceit and theft, to an extent that would ruin the character of a servant at home; but compared with the majority, 'he is a good negro.'"[35] From the planter's perspective, "good negroes" were the best of the lot, but their scarcity frustrated attempts to rule without force. Carmichael saw herself surrounded by "bad and idle characters, who form too often the majority upon an estate." Quick to break any promise on their part, they were "strict enough in exacting the performance of one in their favour."[36] She saw such people as faithless enemies.

When she anguished over the "deceit," "theft," and "treachery" of her slaves, who seemed incapable of being touched by kindness, Mrs. Carmichael simply gave expression to a phenomenon frequently noted by observers of slave society, that slaves saw no basis for adhering to a contract with their masters that was not backed by force.

Colonials realized that slaves behaved as if they were under no moral obligation to their masters, but like Mrs. Carmichael, they attributed slave reluctance to act "honestly" to defects in their characters. John Poyer, the historian of Barbados, argued against the admission of slave testimony against whites in court with the warning that "were the testimony of slaves once allowed, Barbados would be no place of abode for any honest man who had a regard for his reputation, his interest, or his personal safety." By defining colonials as "honest" and slaves as "deceitful," Poyer avoided confronting the conflict inherent in the relationship of master and slave.[37] If the slave's rebelliousness could be made to spring from character defects, rather than from his drive for as much freedom as possible in any given situation, the planter could more easily justify the reality of terror tactics needed to maintain control. John Oldmixon, an eighteenth-century historian of the British Empire, reflected the planter attitude that "negroes are generally false and treacherous. Some instances of great fidelity have been found among them . . . but for the most part they are faithless, and dissemblers." Oldmixon excused the planters for the savage treatment that they dealt out to their slaves as a virtural necessity if social order was to be maintained.[38]

Living in the midst of African slaves, colonials looked with outrage on the anti-slavery doctrines of imperial humanitarians. They believed that although abolitionists might be men of good intentions, they were in general ignorant of Negro character. John Davy, who directed the army's medical department in Barbados in the 1840s, was quick to come to the defense of the much-abused planter and delighted to tell his readers that post-emancipation social conditions were proof that the abolitionists had misjudged the Negro. Claiming that the changed social environments after 1838 had made little impact on the slaves' character, Davy wrote: "The great majority of these people, since emancipation have improved less in moral than in physical condition, to the disappointment of many of their well wishers of sanguine dispositions who did not make sufficient allowance for inbred vices."[39]

Other planter sympathizers came to this conclusion long before emancipation. R. C. Dallas, historian of the Maroons and a resident of Jamaica, repented of his early liberal sympathies as a result of the St. Domingue rising, confessing that the French revolution in the Caribbean had led him to "substitute the words happiness and order, for liberty and right."[40] Men like Dallas used the St. Domingue revolution as a standing indictment of humanitarians, wondering how men who were aware of the fragility of slave society could be naive enough to believe that social stability could be guaranteed without reliance on force.

Planters were not averse to the use of incentives, but they believed that the only people who were capable of safely using psychological manipulation were the slave masters themselves, who, they claimed, had come to know the African character through close and open association with slaves. Robert Renny explained that Jamaican slave masters took great interest in the affairs of their slaves, thereby getting to know them on a basis of intimacy not known between European masters and servants.[41] The solicitude which Renny observed was motivated not by humanitarian sentiments, but by the necessity of looking into the hearts of the bondsmen, in order to know what lurked there, and so to be prepared with contingencies for all manner of behavior.

If colonials stereotyped slaves as "thievish, lazy, and dissimulating," they also knew that control depended heavily on detailed knowledge of the slave.[42] Slave owners, therefore, paid close attention to the gathering of data which could aid them in this effort at control. Edward Long advised that "the choice of Negroes for different purposes requires experience and particular attention." Another planter agreed and recom-

mended that care also be taken to select slaves from parts of
Africa where they had become accustomed to hard physical
labor before reaching adulthood.[43]

None put his gift for understanding human nature to better
effect than the popular writer M. G. Lewis, who created a bad
reputation for himself among Jamaican planters by implemen-
ting reforms on his Jamaican estates that his neighbors feared
might raise the expectations of their own blacks. His aim was
not to make his slaves happy, but to create a more cohesive and
productive plantation unit, a goal that entailed a modified
approach to control, not its abandonment. The significant point,
however, was that his project was based on sharp observation
and acute analysis of slave psychology.

As a writer of imaginative power, Lewis was aware of the
strength of human emotions and their ability to produce
dynamic effects when properly channeled. Although advised
that an estate could not be managed without resort to the whip,
Lewis applied his own principles of management and wrote
proudly that "I have positively forbidden the use of it on
Cornwall."[44] But enlightened as he was, Lewis did not disdain
the use of violence. He had simply learned that violence was not
always the most effective motivator. Discovering that the blacks
had a most morbid hatred of imprisonment, Lewis sought to use
that fear to influence their behavior. "They cannot bear it, and
the memory of it seems to make a lasting impression upon their
minds, while the lash makes none but upon their skins, and lasts
no longer than the mark."[45] By playing on their fears, Lewis
tried to substitute a psychological motivation for a physical one,
an internal imperative for an external one. The objective was to
obtain the cooperation of the slave by allowing him to decide to
avoid the deprivation of something he valued, rather than by
making him submit to a pain he could decide to bear.

Other slave owners tried to appeal to the bondsmen's nobler
sentiments and to rule through kindness or the influence of
religious ideas. Lady Maria Nugent ruled her domestics with the
enlightened treatment appropriate for a governor's wife. "Re-
flect(ed) all night upon slavery," she wrote in her diary, "and
make up my mind, that the want of exertion in the blackes must
proceed from that cause. Assemble them together after

breakfast and talk to them a great deal, promising every kindness and indulgence. We parted excellent friends, and I think they have been rather more active in cleaning ever since."[46] J. B. Moreton believed that blacks "are human flesh and blood, and have souls and intellects as well as whites; and if their geniuses were properly cultivated, would make a great improvement in all the polite arts and sciences as whites." He was convinced that slaves whose masters fed and treated them well would show love in return.[47]

Masters who understood that slaves were people, similar if not equal to themselves, recognized that manipulation was more politic than coercion. The Reverend Hope Waddell, wary of planter opposition to missionary endeavor, was obviously encouraged when the owner of Barrett Hall estate, a large Jamaican plantation, agreed to allow him to preach to his people. But Waddell found this planter's motivation to be less than spiritual. "He said that he found his people had a desire for religious instruction, and it was better for them he should provide it of an approved character than leave them to seek it themselves," adding perceptively, "and perhaps err in the search." Mr. Barrett attempted in this artful manner to forestall the growth of potentially disruptive Negro sects as well as to supply his folk with a more encouraging set of principles. "But I must in candour own," he told Waddell, "that I am not influenced by religious principles myself in this matter, but simply by self-interest. I have a bad set of people. . . . If you can bring them under fear of a God or a judgement to come, or something of that sort, you may be doing them and me a service."[48]

Barrett was engaging in a little psychological warfare. Waddell could become an ally in the effort to subdue what the planters saw as the recalcitrant and rebellious attitude of the blacks. Left to themselves, they might very well turn their psychic energies into dangerous paths. An instance of such danger is recorded by a contemporary observer of the 1831 rebellion in Jamaica. "The Woodstock slaves were almost all Baptists, and acknowledged they had punctually attended the Montego Bay Chapel, for the purpose of hearing about their freedom."[49] By interpreting Christianity in terms of their own cultural orientation and needs, the rebels had found in that doctrine support for a radical social movement. Africa-derived cults threatened evils as well. Thomas Atwood, reflecting on his experience in Dominica, attested to the ascendancy that obeah people maintained over the other blacks. He warned that they were dangerous and had caused the death of white people.[50] Thomas Southey estimated that in 1788, the Moravians, the largest missionary establishment in the Caribbean, maintained a converted congregation of only 16,000 in all.[51] But on the other hand, Afro-Caribbean sects and religions seemed to thrive.

James Phillippo, a Jamaican missionary, thought that in slavery times, every estate had a myalist priest or priestess.[52] R. R. Madden, who knew of Muslim slaves as late as the 1830s, wrote: "I had a visit one Sunday morning very lately, from three Mandingo negroes, natives of Africa. They could all read and write Arabic; and one of them showed me a Koran written from memory by himself—but written he assured me, before he became a Christian." One of these slaves, Edward Dolan, wrote Arabic well and had been a man of rank at home before he was enslaved about the year 1804. Madden was convinced that Christianity was often only a veneer covering the stubborn persistence of what he called superstition. "Few, very few, indeed, of the native Africans who have been instructed in their creed or their superstition, which you please, have given up their early rites and observances for those of the religion of the country they were brought to. But this they do not acknowledge, because they are afraid to do so."[53]

As cultural historians like Lawrence Levine and Albert Rabateau have skillfully shown, slaves adapted old cultural forms to new circumstances, striving in this way to maintain a distinct cultural identity. The problem was that the development of a really autonomous culture could be a powerful threat to the continued existence of the slave system by providing the bondsmen with the vision of a world in which their needs and values could be met and expressed. Once this occurred, it would only be a matter of time before the vision was translated into action. In this context, enlightened planters like Barrett knew what they were doing by encouraging "safe" Christian missionaries. Like the abolitionists, they knew that as dangerous as Christianity could be, it could, if properly presented, help to bind the slaves in a value system with the planter and so act to constrain their freedom of action. But at the same time, the force of law was called in to control the activity of obeah men and slave preachers.[54]

Near the end of the slave period, obeah appeared to be coming under control. W. J. Gardiner, a Jamaican historian, wrote that the abolition of the slave trade had led to a gradual diminishing of the prevalence of obeah. This was due, he felt, to the declining numbers of Africans in the population, over whom the cult had its greatest influence. What he believed to be the slow but real growth of Christian sentiment among the slaves was responsible for a decrease in the popularity of obeah among the Creole population. Part of the explanation for this was itself to be found in the slaves' superstitious conviction that baptism rendered the newly Christianized safe from the power of obeah. Gardiner philosophized that "superstition is among the last of all evils corrected by Gospel teaching."[55]

Attempts to control belief, to limit the emergence of a coherent Afro-Caribbean culture was a form of psychological warfare. The combination of physical and psychological persuasion seemed to make an impression on many. But there were slaves who could not be persuaded, who had decided that they would pursue their own course, even at the cost of life and limb, and for this reason, planters insisted on the need for flexibility in determining the use of violence. Because slavery was fundamentally a war, the rulers of a slave society had to have force at their disposal to use as they saw fit; they could not be hampered in the exercise of their judgment by the program of metropolitan idealists. Even "humane" planters, like the knowledgeable Dr. Collins, recognized that slavery was fundamentally a matter of violence. Collins wrote of the slave that there was always "the necessity of terror to coerce his obedience."[56]

At times, planters seemed to be more aware that slaves were capable of genuinely unusual behavior than were the humanitarians, whose preachings assumed that blacks would, if given the chance, act just like Englishmen. The slave owner, on the other hand, for all his racism, knew that blacks were not simply Englishmen of a different color. He realized that they had their own values or, in his terms, aberrations which could frustrate the success of any policy that assumed the existence of a uniform human nature. In a strange way, planter insistence on force as the final arbiter was a tribute to the existence of a vital Afro-Caribbean culture embodying a vision of society that conflicted with that of both the planters and the humanitarians.

An example of such difference was the case of the slave Plato, a runaway, who, by 1780, had set himself up in the Moreland Mountains of Jamaica, gathered a following, and preyed on the countryside. A large reward was placed on his head, but it was said that his practice of obeah allowed him to avoid capture. When, at last, he was taken and executed, "he died heroically," telling his black jailer that he should die soon afterwards. The unfortunate jailer died before the end of the year.[57] Such defiance, especially when coupled with a leadership position in the African cults or the Christian church, could threaten to undermine the entire regime if the example should spread. It was with good reason that such slaves were horribly executed as an example to others.

Once again in their resort to terror, the colonial authorities demonstrated just how bankrupt they were when confronted with manifestations of idealism which were so obviously informed by the slaves own cultural values, and which could not help but to inspire other bondsmen. Such examples could be quite remarkable indeed. While on duty in the Caribbean, Dr. George Pinckard observed the barbaric execution of a Bush Negro captured during a campaign in the interior. He was burnt alive after the skin was first flayed from his limbs with hot pinchers. The sentence was carried out, but the slave endured it all with the greatest composure, leading Pinckard to comment that "the conduct of this negro furnishes a striking example of the powers of the human mind in subduing our bodily suffering."[58] Such episodes highlighted the substratum of terror which supported the system.

Quite clearly in defense of their own position and the justice of slavery, planters took such things as proof of the ignorance and animal-like nature of the slave, preferring to think that the blacks' silent endurance of pain sprang not from the highest sentiments, but from a disregard for the value of human life. To the master, the slaves' capacity for sensibility was so diminished that cruel treatment was demanded in order to make any impression on them.

The perceptive overseer or resident owner realized that resistance was the slave's attempt to do as little as possible for the master in order to preserve as much freedom as possible for himself. But it was this assertiveness on the part of the slave that made force necessary. Alexander Barclay might wax romantic about slavery being a contract between a master and his people, with rights and obligations on both sides, but that did not prevent him from seeing the crux of the matter. Barclay observed that where the English master held over his servants' heads the continued threat of dismissal, with the difficulty of survival in a hostile world, the slave master had only the threat of punishment, so that without the ultimate freedom to use physical force, there could be no control over the slave.[59]

Barclay realized that far from being servile, "Negroes" possessed a well-developed spirit of independence and maintained a sharp sense of justice where their interests were concerned. Inventive, and vindictive, they had many means of offering opposition. "The canes are destroyed by the cattle, the cattle themselves are neglected, the sugar is spoiled in the manufactory, the mill is broken, thefts are committed, in short, everything goes wrong."[60] Planters needed flexibility to deal effectively with such a creative and resilient people. It was this flexibility, this freedom to decide on and apply methods of management suitable to each occasion and to each slave, that the humanitarians wanted to take away from them. In fact, planters agreed with Clarkson's insight that the essence of slavery was the master's power over the slave. The abolition or radical modification of that power would mean the destruction of the system. But in the place of the master's discretion, the humanitarians wanted to put rigid laws binding not only the slave, but the master as well. The planters argued against it, that the Negroes were not like Europeans and would not, therefore, respond to the removal of the master's overriding power in the ways that the abolitionists wanted them to. It was much more likely that they would pursue their own goals.

Mrs. Carmichael described the situation on her husband's Jamaican estate on the eve of emancipation. She related with bitterness that the planters were put on the defensive with their slaves by the agitation of the slavery question in Parliament. Echoing a common planter complaint, she wrote that news of such parliamentary proceedings was quickly conveyed among the bondsmen, making them far less manageable. Aware that their future was being debated, and that a great party in England supported eventual emancipation, "there was a total change of conduct."[61] In this politicized environment, the slaves on the Carmichael estate stubbornly resisted any directive from their masters.

Puzzled by their obstinancy, Mrs. Carmichael was surprised that even her determined efforts to be kind were ignored by slaves "who were now determined to be influenced by no treatment however kind." Strangely enough, she appeared to be unaware that her kindness was obviously self-serving and was hurt that the slaves now "showed in their every action that they looked upon me, being their proprietor, as necessarily their enemy." This was certainly an equation that most masters wished to avoid.

Like many colonials, Mrs. Carmichael blamed the English anti-slavery forces for her troubles. In her mind, their ignorance of Negro character led them to make mistakes that only made the colonial situation worse. In the first place, the abolitionists were operating with a definition of freedom to which, she claimed, the Negro could not relate. English intellectual opponents of slavery thought that freedom for the slave would mean a state in which "the negro is no longer to be the property of his master," but is to work as do laborers in England. But, Carmichael explained, the Negro had his own definition of liberty, which was quite different, "for they tell me," she wrote, "that it means no massa at all, and Massa King George is to buy all the estates and let them live upon."[62] Ironically, neither colonials nor humanitarians envisioned a post-emancipation Caribbean composed of small farmers who were totally removed from the plantation economy.

But if Carmichael realized that there was a connection between the anti-slavery movement in England and slave unrest in the Caribbean, she was wrong in making the influence all in one direction, for the condition for the rise of an anti-slavery movement was that very unrest that she preferred to think had been bred by the anti-slavery controversy. Carmichael's problem was in her failure to see that the interests of master and slave had always been in contradiction and that the slaves needed no outside agitators to reveal this to them. This was one of the major contentions of the abolitionists, who were not creating, but identifying the problem. They were constantly reminding slave owners that one day the slave would be in a position to refuse to accept this contradiction and act on a definition of freedom that required an end to slavery. What abolitionists advocated was that the contradictions in slave society be removed by a program of amelioration leading towards the restructuring of society. This was preemptive reform, a device that the English would find quite useful throughout their modern empire.

But despite abolitionist preachings, colonials were sure of the superiority of their vision and were ruffled by what they saw as the agitation of irresponsible men in England. James M'Queen commented with biting sarcasm that slavery had existed and been accepted for more than 3,000 years under every form of government "till Mr. Clarkson came to open their eyes to truth and justice." Attacking the "unconstitutional" committee of the London Society for the Mitigation and Abolition of Slavery, he emphasized the selective nature of its vision. "They set out with stating their object to be the abolition 'of slavery in the British Dominions' and yet at a leap they pass over the millions of slaves in India."[63]

In this way, M'Queen raised the question which we considered at the outset: Why did the anti-slavery movement focus on the Negro slave in the Caribbean? For M'Queen, the answer was simple. Slavery was attacked when and where it was convenient to attack it, and it was not convenient to disturb slavery in India, a developing part of the empire. If this selective humanity was disturbing, it was also downright dangerous. Thus, when M'Queen reminded Clarkson that the slaves, not the French, had destroyed slavery in St. Domingue, he had in mind that their victory was prepared by divisions within the ruling class, divisions which abolitionist activity could produce in England, and by the late eighteenth century, that class in England was in fact divided on the question of slavery.[64] Increasingly, sensitive men were coming to question the slave owner's vision and the wisdom of continued metropolitan support for the Caribbean labor system. Slavery was becoming a problem.

"The Problem of Slavery," then, was not simply the expression of cultural shifts and strains, but a formulation of the significance of the manifestations of violence and unrest in slave society. It was a reassessment of Caribbean history from the perspective of the age of revolution. Behind that reassessment, lending it coherence, was not simply, or even primarily, a cultural heritage, but a social danger. To be a slave owner, or even to live in the sugar colonies, meant to be surrounded by multitudes who could have no real interest in the welfare of Englishmen. James Stephen was neither the first nor the last to recognize that the delicate thread which bound up the social fabric was not only physical, but psychological as well, the disposition of the slave and his awe of the master. An American planter's wife put it graphically when she recognized that it was vital to "make them stand in fear."[65] That fear was communicated through physical punishment. But punishment could provoke fear only as long as the slave remained a psychological captive, an object that was not free to choose not to be afraid. For this reason, awe of the master was essential and its perpetuation demanded that the slave be kept ignorant and prevented from developing a self-conscious cultural identity of his own. Once that bond of fear was loosened and the Negro saw the white as a man who wished to do him harm, slavery could not long survive.

Frederick Douglass came to that conclusion after an encounter with the slave breaker Covey. Pushed by cruel treatment to resist the attacks of the man who had beaten him on many occasions, Douglass found his "fingers firmly attached to the throat of my cowardly tormenter." He successfully defended himself and was never again touched by Covey. Having overcome his oppressor, Douglass wrote that the expression of violence, the release of pent up psychic energies, "recalled to life my crushed self-respect and my self-confidence and inspired me with a renewed determination to be a FREEMAN." In words which parallel the ideas of Frantz Fanon, Douglass contended that "a man, without force, is without the essential dignity of humanity. Human nature is so constituted, that it cannot honor a helpless man, although it can pity him; and even this it cannot do for long, if the signs of power do not arise."[66] The "Signs of Power" arose over and over again in the colonial Caribbean, making indelible marks on planter psychology. But the significance of such signs depended on perspective. They convinced planters of the need for slavery and abolitionists of the need for freedom.

The greatest signs of the power and hostility of slaves to European rule were the actual and threatened acts of violence committed by slaves who struck for freedom. And of these, the most impressive were the groups of runaway slaves who had formed themselves into communities in secluded and inaccessible regions. Such Maroon communities existed all over the Americas. In the southern United States, groups of escaped slaves united with Seminole Indians to form areas of sanctuary in the Florida swamps, providing one of the rationales for the annexation of Florida in 1819.[67] The French islands and Brazil experienced the Maroon phenomenon. The great Quilombo of Palmares in the seventeenth century and rebellions in nineteenth-century Bahia were examples of the slaves' ability and inclination to gain and defend freedom.[68]

Richard Price and Orlando Patterson have argued that maroonage was a phenomenon of the frontier days of slavery, before the accelerated development of sugar with its absorption of land and the consolidation of planter regimes made this response to slavery much more difficult. But in the seventeenth and early eighteenth centuries, the option of withdrawing from slave society and attempting to reconstruct an African way of life had strong appeal, especially to African-born bondsmen.[69]

The most spectacular, as well as the most threatening, communities of rebel slaves existed in colonies where the geography presented opportunities for the development of subsistence economies in relative isolation from the colonial establishment. John Stedman, who participated in the campaign to put down the Bush Negro revolt in eighteenth-century Surinam, felt that the shelter provided to fugitives by the immensity of the wilderness may have been a factor in the origins of the revolt.

He pointed out that the rapid extinction of the 1761 slave uprising in Berbice was due to the limited and negotiable nature of the woodland area, which could not provide the rebels with safe refuge.[70]

Like the Bush Negroes of Surinam, the Maroons of Jamaica were blessed with a terrain suitable to their enterprise. Maroons had existed in Jamaica since the Spanish occupation of the island. But the Spaniards did not develop a large slave population, and the number of Maroons consequently remained small. Under British occupation from 1655, the slave population grew rapidly. By 1730, there were said to be 100,000 Negroes in Jamaica. With this demographic base to draw from, the rebel communities grew in size and strength, eventually becoming a threat to colonial security. John Atkins, who visited Jamaica in the 1730s, thought that there were at least 80,000 slaves, compared with 8,000 whites. To this disparity in numbers and to the "severity of their patrons," he assigned the causes of Maroonage, observing that "many hundreds of them have at different times run to the Mountains, where they associate and commit little Robberies upon the defenceless and nearest plantations." Hunted with dogs, a price of 5 pounds was put on their heads. Atkins felt that their situation must have been desperate in the extreme to have driven them to adopt such a lonesome and insecure existence.[71]

The Maroons were not the only ones who were insecure. Their "little Robberies" on isolated properties soon came to pose a serious threat to the early economic development of the colony. The planters represented to the Board of Trade that the rebels had made entire country districts unsafe for white occupation. Trade to the coast from the interior had been stopped, and many settlers had left for the northern colonies, abandoning the area to the Africans. So severe had the decrease of small tradesmen, seafaring folk, and farmers become that there was said to be a shortage of small coin and that large contracts were now paid in foods. Fed by a stream of runaways from the plantations, the blacks had "made themselves several large plantations, towns and settlements, in the most fertile valleys among the midland and eastern mountains, which are by natural passes and precipices almost inaccessible." The danger was increased by the unreliability of the white indented servants, who, of course, had no reason to defend their masters' property at risk of life and limb. Perhaps even more threatening because it suggested the possibility of a growing and fatal unity in the black population, free blacks were said to be sympathetic to the rebels and to provide them with arms and ammunition.[72]

Maroons were in constant communication with plantation slaves with whom they traded. The danger that the example of their independence, reinforced by their boldness, might prove infectious and eventually lead to a general slave uprising was ever present. The government moved to limit the danger deriving from the greater mobility which free men enjoyed over their enslaved brethren by passing laws to restrain their movement and compelling them to go on expeditions against the rebels.[73] Acts were passed for the amending of highways, for compelling estate owners to keep sufficient numbers of white servants, and for the better regulation of the slaves, as well as for the reduction of the rebels.[74] These measures were not entirely effective, and stronger measures were made more urgent by the fear of Spanish aid for the rebels, who had apparently been in contact with the Spaniards in neighboring colonies, offering up the island in return for their freedom. The imperial government, sensitive to the danger that internal rebellion in wartime could offer an opening to foreign invaders, was ready to listen to colonial cries for aid.[75] In October of 1730, the imperial government sent two regiments of troops to the island, urging that the assembly provide support.[76] The troops, unused to the island terrain, were easily outclassed by the resourceful Maroons.

By 1731, the plantation population was reported to have grown insolent. The example of the Maroons was affecting the slaves.[77] The imperial government advised a change in tactics. Resort was had to "Blackshot" and Indians from the "Mosquito" shore. The Indians and blacks were used to great effect against the rebels. Where the colonials had failed, the mercenaries were able to locate and destroy the rebels' provision grounds and to keep up a constant harassment of them, leading the Maroons to remove to the secure "cockpit" area in the Northwest.[78]

Although the Maroons were never decisively defeated, fatigue and the desire for peace in which to pursue their semi-independent existence predisposed them to accept the government's offer to negotiate. The government, for its part, concerned with the unrest on the plantations, was fearful of a general conflagration should their war efforts fail.[79] By the terms of the Treaty of 1739, the government not only brought an end to the immediate danger, but also derived a new support for the regime. The Maroons were limited to their areas but, more important, agreed to wage war on the remaining rebel groups and, henceforth, to return all runaways to the British.[80] The independence of the Maroons, therefore, became a prop for planter hegemony. Former enemies were now guarantors of plantation integrity.

The terms of the treaty were not rigidly adhered to, and the failure to return all runaways was one of the causes of the second Maroon war of 1795. This episode, which was once again concluded by treaty, was instigated by the government, which was fearful of the independent blacks in its midst during the period of the St. Domingue revolution (1791-1804). Dallas thought that had the Maroons demonstrated to the slaves that their rebellion was not a passing thing, but a permanent "and successful opposition to the Government," a general revolution would have occurred.[81] As it was, the 1795 war occurred in the midst of the Anglo-French struggle in Europe and the Caribbean. French agents were known to be at work in the Caribbean fomenting unrest among the slaves. The potential danger of a foreign invasion during the Maroon war increased the government's willingness to come to terms.[82] On this occasion, treachery was used by the English, and a large body of Maroons was transported out of the colony after surrendering its arms.

In this way, the planter elite rid their society of some of their most dangerous enemies. But in so doing, they also removed potential allies and helped to make the slave population more homogenous, while the closure of the frontier made slavery potentially more explosive.

Planter fears of an invasion linking up with an internal rebellion were dramatized and given heightened reality by the activity of the notorious French agent of revolution Victor Hughues. The mulatto Hughues was a disciple of Robespierre. In the late 1790s, Hughues was active in the Caribbean, where he proclaimed the emancipation of all slaves. With an army of ex-slaves, Hughues had reconquered St. Lucia from the British.[83] With men like Hughues lurking in the area, isolated rebels and restive colored freedmen could become the agents of mass revolt similar to the one raging in St. Domingue.

In the closing years of the eighteenth century, revolt broke out all over the Caribbean as if in fulfillment of such fears. In March of 1795, the slaves rose in Grenada. The revolt led by the colored planter Julien Fedon involved more then 7,000 slaves and lasted for more than a year, during which time the rebels virtually controlled the island. In the same year, the black Caribs of St. Vincent and the Jamaican Maroons, pressed by fear-ridden planters, were at war with the empire. J. B. Fortesque, a historian of the British Army, observed that "the greater part of the Negroes in the West Indies were now in open revolt."[84]

A result of these events was the establishment of the 2nd West India Regiment of black troops for the defense of the colonies. In December of 1794, General Vaughan, commander of the British expeditionary force in the Caribbean, wrote home to Henry Dundas, secretary of war, informing him that in the present circumstances, the "whole army of Great Britain would not suffice to defend the Windward Islands." He urged the raising of a black regiment as the most effective means of providing for defense. If the local governments continued their opposition to the plan of arming slaves, then the government should import such people directly from Africa and use them as soldiers.[85] His requests were denied, and Vaughan wrote again in April of 1795, this time in stronger terms: "I do not hesitate to say that unless my advice be taken, these colonies will very soon be wrested from us. The French blacks will invade us and gain ours by the promise of freedom."[86] The danger of revolution was real.

Concern for the security of the empire eventually won out over the objections of the planters, who were reluctant to part with valuable slave labor and disturbed by the idea of blacks possessing weapons and military training. A compromise solution was reached whereby local slaves were to be used but only on condition that they not be removed from the island and that they were returned to their owners at the termination of service. When the requisition of plantation slaves proved inadequate, the imperial government finally resorted to the purchase of slaves in Africa to use as soldiers in the Caribbean. In order to make them more amenable to military service, Dundas ordered that such slaves be emancipated.[87] Here was clear recognition of the abolitionist's position that slavery could never provide the foundation for a healthy society. Soldiers should be highly motivated if they were to be depended on to risk life and limb for the crown. For this reason, they were to be given something worth fighting for, the possession of their own persons.

The unrest at the close of the eighteenth century was different from such earlier manifestations as Maroonage and the 1760 revolt of Coromantee slaves in Jamaica. Unlike the earlier risings, the slave revolts of the "Age of Revolution" began to display heavy involvement by Creole, or island-born, slaves. The leadership of rebel slave groups such as the Maroons was heavily African. Orlando Patterson points out that all of the major revolts in Jamaica were initiated and/or carried out by Africans or their sons.[88] Edward Brathwaite relates that Jamaicans saw the African as the center of rebellion and the Creole as a much more reliable laborer.[89] This was certainly true of Edward Long, who believed that Creoles were easier to manipulate and not as assertive as Africans.[90] If these claims have general validity, then, for Jamaica at least, revolt was undertaken by those who were in possession of a relatively autonomous culture. It was those groups that had some sort of ideology and were able to effect group discipline that engaged in revolt. When planters moved to rid themselves of the more distinct and assertive groups, they were in fact promoting the Creolization of society, a process of homogenization that was facilitated by the economic and demographic forces set in motion by the abolition of the slave trade.

Michael Craton and Barry Higman have demonstrated the negative demographic impact of the abolition of the slave trade on slave society. By cutting off the source of Africans, abolition accelerated the process of Creolization. But the same process created problems of its own and generated tensions which would ultimately lead to emancipation. The ending of the slave trade into the British West Indies was not followed by improvement in the conditions of the slaves and the natural increase of the population that the abolitionists had hoped for. Instead, as Barry Higman has shown, 1807 was followed by a demographic decline. With the birthrate failing to supply a natural increase, the "non-effective" labor force, those such as the colored population who were not normally assigned to field work, came to represent a larger proportion of the population.[91] Significantly, although the number of field hands decreased, productivity per unit actually increased. Concentration and consolidation of agricultural units, which had been proceeding since the eighteenth century, were now accelerated as planters attempted to take advantage of temporarily favorable conditions by marketing the largest possible crops. Increased and even stable levels of productivity in the context of the demographic revolution were purchased by heightened exploitation, which, in turn, reinforced the inability of the population to sustain itself.[92]

After about 1820, as the demographic forces set in motion by abolition worked themselves out, average productivity per hand began to decline as the population structure became top- and bottom-heavy. At the same time, the increasing size of the colored population continued to reduce the flexibility of the work force.[93] Under these circumstances, slavery began to weigh heavily on those Creole slaves who had come to expect opportunities to rise to relatively better positions within slave society.

Reflecting on slavery in the Caribbean, Alexander von Humbolt wrote: "There are degrees in the sufferings of the human species. The slave who has a hut and a family, is less miserable than he who is purchased, as if he formed part of a flock."[94] Slave society owed much of its tenuous stability to its stratification, a fact early recognized by planters. The free sector, whether colored tradesmen or Maroons, could serve as allies of the regime, trading support in return for limited freedom. William Robertson, one of Wilberforce's favorite writers, noticed the importance of such divisions when he wrote in his *History of the Discovery and Settlement of America* of the creation of a Negro elite group in Spanish America that it served as an important buffer between the Spaniards and the indigenous population, while skillful use of a divide-and-rule policy prevented any potential anti-Spanish alliances from coalescing.[95] While such an elite group did not exist in the English Caribbean, there were narrow opportunities to rise in the social structure. Opportunities for moving into the skilled or managerial sector of the labor force helped to alleviate some of the tensions of slave society while recruiting numbers of the more astute slaves into positions of alliance with the master class. It was better to be a driver than to be driven, and some believed it better and more secure to win a measure of freedom in return for oppressing slaves than to risk running away or actually fighting whites. But with demographic and economic decline, such safety valves began to close.

As noted earlier, Lowell Ragatz believed that the Caribbean economy was basically unsound because it rested on the artificial supports of temporarily high prices and restrictive monopolies. The abolition of the slave trade added to these basic problems by causing a labor shortage just as competition from foreign rivals cut into continental sugar markets. Ragatz argued that by the early 1820s, the planter class was in crisis. As the returns from plantations fell, so did the value of West Indian property, making it increasingly difficult for owners to raise loans against mortgages. By 1822, the planter class was hopelessly in debt to British agents, who "held the whip hand."[96] This situation led to greater pressure on the work force to produce more with less.

Barry Higman maintains that after about 1820, the system entered a period of rapid decline. Demographic forces set in motion by abolition reduced the size of the most productive portion of the work force, those men between the ages of twenty and forty-five. The growth of the colored slave population, which traditionally worked in skilled and domestic pursuits, further limited the flexibility of the labor force, and those slaves with expectations of enhanced status in the system, or even total freedom, were frustrated by the increasing rationalization of the labor system. Higman argues that these tensions were among the major causes of the 1831 Jamaican rebellion.[97]

As we have seen, slave rebellions occurred regularly throughout British Caribbean history. Orlando Patterson wrote that "rebellion, or the threat of it, was an almost permanent feature of Jamaican slave society."[98] Servile war was immortalized in such literary classics as Stedman's *Narrative of a Five Years' Expedition Against the Revolted Negroes of Surinam,* Dallas' *History of the Maroons,* Bryan Edwards' *History of the West Indies,* and Edward Long's *History of Jamaica.* Almost all memoirs and travel accounts from the period of slavery mention rebellions and plots either witnessed by or reported to the author. Far from being a strange or an unfamiliar phenomenon to educated Englishmen, slave resistance was part of the popular picture of the sugar colonies. The abolitionists, who were some of the best educated Englishmen of their day and who read parliamentary reports and papers, were thoroughly conversant with the slave's propensity to rebel. In fact, their pronouncements as to the danger of slavery and the threat of rebellion, whatever conclusions one wishes to draw about them, drew on their knowledge of the violent relationship of master and slave, which ran the gamut from day-to-day resistance and discipline to rebellion and reaction.

In his 1827 *Chronological History of the West Indies,* Thomas Southey listed slave revolts and conspiracies for the eighteenth century. He found incidents in Antigua in 1736; in Berbice in 1763, where slaves quickly took over the colony and were only put down with the assistance of Caribs and Indians; in Jamaica in 1760, when Coromantee slaves rose in an extensive rebellion, after which the Jamaica Assembly tried to limit the importation of Africans; a 1768 conspiracy in Montserrat; a 1769 conspiracy in Kingston; and the 1772 Surinam rebellion.[99]

Southey's list did not exhaust the record of rebellion. Orlando Patterson lists more or less continual Maroon-type rebellion from 1655 to 1722. From 1725 to 1740, other forms of slave resistance were overshadowed by the first Maroon war, which led to the British recognition of the independence of that group. Patterson has determined revolts or conspiracies for 1766, 1769, 1777, 1784, and 1798.[100]

Serious conspiracies also were discovered in 1806 and 1815, and three between 1823 and 1824. In 1808, revolts broke out in Jamaica among Coromantee slaves in the West India regiment and in Guyana, where skilled and elite slaves were in the lead.[101] In 1816, a rebellion broke out prematurely in Barbados. The British commander there related that the rebels proclaimed "that the island belonged to them, and not to white men, whom they proposed to destroy, reserving the females."[102]

In 1823, revolt erupted in British Guyana involving fifty plantations. These slaves were not after limited objectives or withdrawal from society, but demanded total emancipation.[103] Ground down by overwork and maltreatment, they had learned of the agitation in England over slavery and taken the opportunity presented by divisions among their rulers to strike for freedom. The sons of Wilberforce asserted in their biography of their father that it was the crown's prohibition of the whip which set in motion the process which led to revolt. The passage is pertinent:

The arrival of this order caused such alarm among the whites, that the local governors would not venture on its publication. Yet the domestic slaves soon gathered from the violent language of the planters that some great measures which concerned their race had been urged upon their masters. Fame magnified the rumor, and it was whispered that they alone stood between the black and liberty.[104]

Significantly, these slaves acted to secure what they believed had already been granted to them. This belief, erroneous though it was, provides a window through which to look critically at slave culture and resistance strategy, a point we will come back to in connection with the 1831 rising in Jamaica.

The revolts of the nineteenth century can be said to have had holistic objectives, while those of the seventeenth and eighteenth centuries were limited. From this perspective, planter complaints that the agitation of the slavery question in England made the slaves restive makes a good deal of sense. The revolution in St. Domingue took place amid divisions in the ruling class in the island and in France. The "Black Jacobins" seized the opportunity presented by this internal struggle to strike for their own freedom.

In the British Caribbean, revolts such as those in 1808, 1823, and 1831 coincided with high points in the anti-slavery struggle, indicating a sort of dialectical relationship in which slaves drew conclusions from the anti-slavery movement and acted on their own to secure freedom, while the imperial humanitarians and statesmen were spurred by slave unrest to renewed efforts to ameliorate and, finally, end slavery. This was far from the experience of the French in St. Domingue, but in acting on a belief that a party in the imperial metropole was working on their behalf against their masters, Caribbean slaves were certainly making use of philosophic and strategic divisions in the ruling class. Such phenomena do not take place until a culture and a society have achieved a well-developed self-consciousness, a shared set of values, a vision of the future capable of transcending group, ethnic, and caste rivalries, and a communications infrastructure allowing for the rapid spread, assimilation, and critique of information. The synchronization of slave risings with the rise and decline of the anti-slavery movement is, therefore, an expression of the emergence of an Afro-Caribbean culture, the very thrust of which was towards ultimate freedom and independence.

The proclamations of black rebels, who claimed to be fighting to secure the freedom they believed their masters were withholding from them, are frequently dismissed as confused notions of ignorant slaves, or simply wishful thinking. But this is to miss the significance of such sentiments. Although the slaves of Demerara, for example, were mistaken in believing that freedom had been granted, they were correct in their general analysis of the relationship between colony and metropole. They were aware that the imperial government was generally for some type of rights for blacks, while planters stood opposed. Objectively, the planters were the enemy and the imperial government should be the ally. If we define ideology as a tool that allows for the effective exploitation of contingency in pursuit of political goals, then we can have no doubt as to the existence of an ideology among Caribbean slaves, even if we cannot yet describe it. Because few slaves were able to write, we have almost no direct evidence of their thoughts. Lacking the usual material for intellectual history, we can perhaps do little more than extrapolate belief from behavior, something which historians of medieval and early modern Europe have pioneered.

A major indication of the slaves' ability to put contingency to good use is the Jamaican rebellion of 1831. Perhaps more than any other, the so-called Baptist War demonstrates the significance of Afro-Caribbean culture and of the slaves' own vision of post-slave society in accounting for the social instability that finally signaled the approaching end of slavery. By looking sympathetically at the testimony of both participants, and white colonials, we can learn much about the motivation of the rebels and clarify who they were actually rebelling against.

A particularly striking circumstance of the 1831 rebellion was not only the way that it took the establishment by surprise, a reflection of the deep-seated and almost stylized arrogance of the planter class, but also the secrecy in which the rebel leaders were able to plan the rising. The rebellion really got underway on December 27, 1831, but the governor, the Earl of Belmore, related that it was not until Thursday, December 22, that he had any account to lead him to suspect that anything at all was in the offing, and he did not finally convene a council of war until December 29, or about two days after the rebellion was already under way.[105] Even as late as the afternoon of the twenty-seventh, Henry Bleby, who composed an important account of the revolt, traveled on horseback through the country which was soon to form the seat of the rebellion. He was struck by the deserted state of the usually well-traveled roads and the uncommon quiet but otherwise found no hint of the storm which would soon break.[106] The suddenness of the rising bespeaks much about the communication and organizational infrastructure of Jamaican slave society.[107] The slave Linton, in prison under sentence of death for his part in the events of December and January, claimed that the revolt had been in planning or contemplated for at least three years and included a great many blacks.[108]

One of the most important means by which the conspiracy was promoted among the slaves was through skillful use of one of the few freedoms that the combination of slave resistance and English anti-slavery agitation had won for the slaves. The program of amelioration which the imperial government had pursued since 1823 had pushed the importance of religious education for blacks and especially, since the persecution of the Reverend John Smith in Demerara, had discouraged colonial interference with the work of missionaries to the slaves. Once again seizing on an opportunity presented by the metropolis, the slaves turned the church organization and philosophy to their own uses.[109] Although the white missionaries probably did not, as planters accused them, directly provoke the slaves to revolt, they did provide the bondsmen with religious teaching and literacy which were used for revolutionary ends. Mary Reckord, who studied this rising, wrote that it was "characterized by the fact that the missions were the source of the slaves' philosophy and the missionaries themselves were cast in the role of the slaves' allies."[110] She points to the existence of a network of independent churches which had grown up around the missions and which facilitated concerted action.[111]

Planters were right in trying to keep Christianity away from their slaves. That religion, which could be made to support slavery and the status quo, had often provided inspiration for revolt and millenarian movements.[112] If abolitionists like Granville Sharp and Thomas Clarkson could find anti-slavery doctrines in their creed, there was no reason why slaves could not do the same. At least two ex-slaves published works which based a condemnation of slavery on Christian doctrine. Gustavus Vassa had been captured as a boy in Benin and taken as a slave to the Caribbean. He eventually purchased his freedom and became a leader of the black community in England.[113] Vassa was atypical of British slaves. Literate, well-traveled, educated and a Christian in the eighteenth century when so few slaves were, he is most distinguished from his fellows by the fact that he published his autobiography. In its pages, Vassa clearly indicated the importance that Christianity held for him and told of his cathartic conversion, which marked a turning point in his life. Convinced of the reality of sin and the overriding need for salvation, Vassa's condemnation of slavery was couched in Christian terms. The slave trade and human bondage violated the golden rule and cast thousands of God's creatures into an abyssmal darkness.[114]

Less well known than Gustavus Vassa was Ottobah Cugoano. Born around 1757 in Ghana, he was captured in 1770 and taken to Grenada as a slave. Like Vassa, Cugoano won his freedom and became a leader of the black community in England. He was a friend of Gustavus Vassa and in close contact with Granville

Sharp.[115] As a leader of London's black community, Cugoano wrote to the Prince of Wales in 1786, urging him to consider the abolition of the slave trade. In 1787, he published his book *Thoughts and Sentiments on the Evils of Slavery* and sent copies to the Prince of Wales, Edmund Burke, and King George III.[116] Cugoano argued on the grounds of humanity and Christianity that slavery should be ameliorated and the slave trade abolished. By continuation in an immoral and sinful trade, European nations would bring the wrath of God upon them.[117]

Slaves, like abolitionists, could interpret Christianity in ways favorable to the attainment of their goals. But as Michael Craton has pointed out, there was more than religion involved in the 1831 rising. Church membership also provided the chance for slaves to get out on their own, achieve status, and organize for their own purposes.[118] Its utility as a cover for organization and planning was perhaps the greatest attraction the church held for the Jamaican rebels. Testimony before the committee of inquiry that the Jamaican House of Assembly instituted to investigate the rebellion, as well as contemporary accounts, confirms the importance of the Baptist and other non-conformist churches to the spread of the conspiracy. A typical method of recruitment was for the slave ministers or leaders who were involved in the plot to use the Sunday meeting as an opportunity to arrange for secret meetings, or simply to exchange information.[119] Thus it was that Gardiner, one of the ringleaders, confessed that the "business" was settled at the Montego Bay chapel after morning prayers on Christmas Day in a meeting attended by Samuel Sharp, who was by all accounts the prime mover, and Taylor, Johnstone, Guthrie, Dove, Tharp, and Gardiner himself.[120]

Although colonial accusations of missionary implication in the conspiracy were never demonstrated, it is clear that slave members of the Baptist church were prominent in the rebellion and figured heavily in leadership positions. They had apparently found that the Baptist variety of Protestantism could be interpreted in ways that were supportive of their world view. The Reverend John M'Intyre, relating the confession he had received from a condemned slave named Adam, revealed how after church, the "leaders" would interpret the ministers' teaching to their fellows.[121] These "leaders" were frequently those who occupied the highest stratas of the slave hierarchy and whether associated with the church, or not, were influential people in slave society. The Reverend Thomas Stewart, rector of the parish at Westmoreland, thought that "it is a very remarkable fact, that the head and confidential slaves, and consequently the most intelligent, have been the most active rebels."[122]

We can speculate that the ability to read and write and the occupation of prized positions in the slave hierarchy would facilitate elevation to positions of authority in the church, but it would probably be wrong to attribute the influence of such slaves in the community to religious authority alone. These were, in all likelihood, men who commanded respect in the community by merit of the ideals and attitudes that they reflected in their conduct. In other words, what the church provided was another vehicle which could be used by the community to attain its own ends. The authority of slaves like Samuel Sharp would not have derived from position in the church, but on the contrary, the usefulness of the church as a mode of organization to those members of the slave community who were dedicated to social change would have derived from the ability of men like Sharp to gain position within it. By all reports, it was Sharp's great persuasive skills which accounted for the adherence of many slaves to him and the program of rebellion.[123] But this is little more than to say that Sharp was able to formulate and vividly express the grievances and hopes of the masses of bondsmen.

Examination of the origins of the revolt throws additional light on the effectiveness of the emergent Afro-Caribbean culture in generating a set of assumptions and expectations about slavery and freedom that were, in all likelihood, more or less uniformly held. There were basically two sets of explanations offered for the revolt. Almost all contemporary accounts, as well as testimony before the committee of inquiry, blamed the revolt on the agitation of the slavery question in England and on the carelessness of colonials who openly displayed their opposition to emancipation. Bernard Senior, a contemporary of the revolt, insisted that anti-slavery activity had generated acute discontent among the slaves. He explained that through education, the slaves "had become capable of subsequently discussing the merits or demerits of the subject expatiated on by the different members of Parliament. On almost every property there was a Wilberforce, a Stephen, a M'Cauley."[124] It is clear from Henry Bleby's account that Samuel Sharp and his colleagues expressed a condemnation of slavery based on both natural rights and the teachings of Christianity, two pillars of the anti-slavery arguments. According to Bleby, Sharp "asserted the natural equality of men with regard to freedom" and claimed that whites had no right to enslave blacks.[125]

The use of such arguments implied more than a simple copying of a fashionable European style; it implied that the rebels were employing arguments that expressed their feelings and goals in a form that they found appealing and useful. They were using the language of those in England whom they had come to think of as allies and with whom they shared a similar philosophic outlook on slavery. Through their knowledge of the anti-slavery movement in England and its opponents in Jamaica, the slaves had formed the notion that the imperial government had granted them freedom, and the colonials were refusing to comply with the order.[126] Regarding the anti-slavery forces both in and out of government as their allies and defenders, it was but a simple step to the conclusion that the imperial army and navy would not intervene if they were simply to refuse to work any longer as slaves. This was the plan that Sam Sharp and his associates attempted to put into effect. There would be a work stoppage after Christmas 1831, a non-violent strike for freedom which would throw the moral onus on the imperial government. As envisioned by Sharp, the rising would involve no violence towards either whites or their property and would remain peaceful as long as the strikers were not attacked. The conspirators were determined, however, to gain their freedom and were prepared to fight in self-defense.[127] Given the resolution of the planter regime, the primitive nature of the slaves' military-political organization, and their flawed analysis of the likely attitude of the imperial power, there was little chance that violence could have been avoided. There is also the fact that Samuel Sharp, for all his influence in the slave

community, was nothing like a paramount chief on the scale of
Tussaint L'Ouverture.

Unquestionably, the rising was doomed to failure, but it
illustrates the degree to which Caribbean slave society had
become homogeneous and points up the strains that were
threatening to tear it apart. An important element was the
pressure to rebellion by the Creole elite that was being
threatened by the worsening economic conditions of the 1820s
and 1830s, and who were finding their opportunities to rise in
the world increasingly limited by economic change. The
Reverend Hope Waddell was in Jamaica before, during, and
after the rebellion. He described the attitude of this young and
aggressive class:

The Creoles—young, strong, and giddy with the newborn hope of
liberty, which they said the King had given them and their masters
withheld—resolved to stand out for the wages of free labour, and if
needful, to fight for their rights. The old people discouraged the
attempt. They had seen worse times, and were sensible of a growing
amelioration of their condition. The experience also of former
insurrections taught them to dread the consequence of failure.[128]

This giddiness, this active hope for liberty, was a new
phenomenon. It reflected a growing sense of community and
awareness of the strengths and weaknesses of the system. What
Waddell and Senior observed were the effects of Creolization.

By 1823, the planters could look back at the early days and feel
a bit more encouraged at the increasing civilization of the slaves,
meaning, of course, the diminishing manifestation of African
cultures and languages. They would have been wrong, however,
if they had mistaken their efforts for the causes of this
phenomenon. The abolition of the slave trade in 1807 had
accomplished in one stroke what the planters might not have
been able to do in fifty years. By cutting off the source of "raw"
Africans, it served to catalyze the growth of a native-born, or
Creole, population, sharing a common language, common
values, similar aspirations and expectations. But that process,
far from creating a secure and stable society, generated its own
tensions, which confirmed the humanitarians in their basic
perception that slavery could never really be ameliorated.

The process of the homogenization of society can be illustrated by the changing proportions of Africans and Creoles in the Jamaican slave population. Around 1807, when the trade was abolished, Africans represented about 45 percent of the slave population, but by 1838 their percentage had fallen to only 10 percent.[129] While the African population declined, the mulatto segment grew. By 1832, 10 percent of all Jamaican slaves were colored. Thus a radical shift in the composition of the slave population had been accomplished by abolition.[130]

Although Elsa Goveia dates the beginning of Creolization to the end of the eighteenth century, she sees its influence in terms supportive of our view. For Goveia, it brought about "a certain homogeneity of culture, common to the majority of the slaves."[131] This Creole culture provided the medium in which the ideology of freedom could grow. In this sense, Creolization represented the emergence of the homogeneous community that planters had all along been trying to frustrate and which the abolitionists had indirectly brought about by the removal of the slave trade.

The abolition of the slave trade, the first success of the anti-slavery forces, did not push planters to improve the lot of their slaves, but the economic and social changes that it set in motion undermined the safety valve of limited upward mobility. It would have been bad enough if those strains had fallen on a society torn by African ethnic and national rivalries, but the fact that it occurred in the context of a slave population with a greater awareness of a more homogeneous society meant that there was a greater chance for a united and programmatic response by the Creole population. This situation presented a different but potentially a much more ominous danger than the "savage" danger of the African rebel. A black coxswain summed up the meaning of those changes when he advised M. G. Lewis to suspend the use of the whip, "for blacks must not be treated as they used to be; they can think, and hear, and see, as well as white people; blacks are wiser, massa, then they were," adding prophetically, "and [they] will soon be still wiser."[132]

The "Signs of Power" of which Frederick Douglass wrote were always visible in the colonial Caribbean. They appeared in 1823 when the slaves of Demerara rose to force their masters to proclaim the emancipation they believed the king had granted. They were revealed in the mysterious and sudden death of a hated overseer, or in the stolid silence of field hands refusing to work and gone up to the hills to tend their grounds. The question was how to read them correctly. This was not such a difficult task if one understood the basic tenor of slave life, which was set by the irreconcilable conflict of master and slave. The slave desired freedom and understood by that term not an abstract principle, but life without "massa." That might mean a moment of rest in the field, a lifetime in the mountains, or the destruction of the colonial regime. The master wanted the cultivation of the cane and the production of sugar, which meant the continual effort to limit the slave's freedom. This was indeed an irrepressible conflict.

The slave master responded with a combination of force and incentive. Those who were vulnerable were enticed to join the regime as allies, trading cooperation for small comforts. Such slaves, captured runaways, informed on rebels, served as "Black Shot," Negro drivers, and the like. They were "good Negroes." The mass of the slaves, who were characterized by planters as "bad Negroes," had to be forced to work, to remain on the plantation, and to abandon their more alien ways. These slaves resisted. The most spectacular type of resistance was rebellion. The evidence indicates that slave rebellions changed over time from attempts to escape slave society and reconstruct an African life-style in the back country to attempts to overthrow slavery altogether.[133] Maroonage, the flight from slavery, occurred during the early days of colonization, when the regime was still weak and the frontier expansive enough to allow for the existence of separate communities in the interior. This was the great age of the African slave trade, which peopled the Caribbean with the members of African ethnic and national groups that supplied the leadership of the early rebellions and formed the first Maroon groups.

Ironically, although the Maroons were a threat to social security, their limited aims allowed for cooperation with the regime in return for a circumscribed independence, as in 1739, when the Jamaican Maroons won a margin of freedom in exchange for their agreement to capture runaway slaves. Thus the limited goals of Maroonage, made possible by the still relatively open nature of early slave society, helped to frustrate the emergence of a united independence movement, just as the prevalence of African national and ethnic rivalries discouraged the emergence of a common vision of justice and freedom. Instead of supporting rebellion, Maroons, in effect, helped to support the status quo when, in the pursuit of their own goals, they helped planters to protect the integrity of the regime.

By the close of the eighteenth century, soil exhaustion in the old islands and exploitation of the newer islands pushed the expansion of sugar cultivation to the edge of the wilderness, thereby limiting the opportunity for Maroonage. The removal of a large segment of Maroons from Jamaica in 1795 and the closing off of the slave trade in 1807 led to a further homogenization of society. At the same time, the economic decline of the islands meant that more slaves with higher expectations were finding that their efforts to rise in the existing society were blocked by the constricted economic environment.[134] Some of these slaves eventually found elements of a radical ideology in the versions of Christianity taught by black preachers.

The slave risings of the nineteenth century took place in this context of closing frontier, rising expectations, and limited opportunities to advance in slave society. When these slaves rose, they aimed at total freedom.[135] The situation appeared particularly explosive because Creoles now possessed an emergent ideology combining elements of Christianity with what can be called a natural rights philosophy, and were believed even by abolitionists to be susceptible to "Age of Revolution" principles. By the early nineteenth century, slaves had become too aware and slave society too explosive to control through force alone, and this is what abolitionists were saying. This is how they read the signs of power.

NOTES

1. Noel Deer, *The History of Sugar,* 2 vols. (London: Chapman & Hall, 1949-50), 1:165-166.

2. Richard Dunn, *Sugar and Slaves* (New York: W. W. Norton, 1972), table 14, p. 141.

3. Elsa Goveia, *Slave Society in the British Leeward Islands at the End of the Eighteenth Century* (New Haven, Conn.: Yale University Press, 1965), p. 203.

4. Dunn, *Sugar and Slaves*, table 16, p. 155.

5. Edward Brathwaite, *The Development of Creole Society in Jamaica 1777-1820* (London: Oxford University Press, 1971), p. 151.

6. Barry W. Higman, *Slave Populations of the British Caribbean 1807-1834* (Baltimore: Johns Hopkins University Press, 1984), p. 72.

7. Orlando Patterson, *The Sociology of Slavery* (Rutherford, N.J.: Fairleigh Dickinson University Press, 1969), p. 274.

8. Richard B. Sheridan, *Sugar and Slavery, An Economic History of the British West Indies, 1623-1775* (Baltimore: Johns Hopkins University Press, 1973), p. 13.

9. Elsa Goveia, "The West Indian Slave Laws of the Eighteenth Century," *Revista de ciencias sociales,* vol. 4, no. 1 (March 1960), pp. 75-105, 20.

10. Dunn, *Sugar and Slaves,* p. 239.

11. Ibid., p. 240.

12. Richard Blome, *The Present State of His Magesties Isles and Territories in America* (London: H. Clark, 1967), p. 44; John Cardy Jeaffreson, ed., *A Young Squire of the Seventeenth Century,* 2 vols. (London: C. Hurst & Blackett, 1878), 2:232; G. W. Bridges, *The Annales of Jamaica* (London: Frank Cass & Co., 1968), 2:430, 403; Clement Caines, *Letters on the Cultivation of Otaheite Cane . . .* (London: Robinson & Co., 1801); Miguel Barnet, ed., *Esteban Montejo, The Autobiography of a Runaway Slave* (New York: Vintage Books, 1972), p. 23.

13. George Metcalf, *Royal Government and Political Conflict in Jamaica 1729-1783* (London: Longmans, 1965), p. 5.

14. Goveia, "West Indian Slave Laws," p. 25.

15. Ibid., p. 23.

16. Goveia, *Slave Society,* pp. 156-157.

17. Robert Smith, "The Legal Status of Jamaican Slaves Before the Anti-Slavery Movement," *Journal of Negro History*, vol. 30, no. 3, pp. 293-303.

18. Goveia, *Slave Society,* p. 158.

19. Ibid., p. 158.

20. Edward Long, *The History of Jamaica,* 3 vols. (London: Frank Cass & Co., 1970), 2:490.

21. Dunn, *Sugar and Slaves,* p. 241.

22. [Dr. Collins], *Practical Rules for the Management and Medical Treatment of Negro Slaves in the Sugar Colonies, by a Professional Planter* (Freeport, N.Y.: Books for Libraries Press, 1971), p. 57.

23. Ibid., p. 64.

24. Ibid., p. 69.

25. Long, *History of Jamaica*, 2:405, 410, 411.

26. Thomas Roughley, *Jamaica Planters Guide* (London: n.p., 1823), pp. 41-42.

27. Ibid., p. 45.

28. Ibid., pp. 43-44.

29. Ibid., pp. 77-78.

30. Ibid., pp. 80-81.

31. Ibid., pp. 81-82.

32. James Stewart, *A View of the Past and Present State of the Island of Jamaica . . .* (New York: Negro Universities Press, 1969), p. 249.

33. Roughley, *Jamaica Planters Guide*, pp. 83-84.

34. Mrs. Carmichael, *Domestic Manners and Social Conditions of the White, Colored, and Negro Population of the West Indies*, 2 vols. (New York: Negro Universities Press, 1969), 2:217-219, 31, 25.

35. Ibid., p. 31.

36. Ibid., pp. 193, 108.

37. John Poyer, *The History of Barbados* (London: Frank Cass & Co., 1970), p. 143.

38. John Oldmixon, *The British Empire in America*, 2 vols. (New York: Augustus M. Kelley, 1969), 2:130-131.

39. John Davy, *The West Indies Before and Since Slave Emancipation* (London: Frank Cass & Co., 1971), p. 99.

40. R. C. Dallas, *History of the Maroons*, 2 vols. (London: Frank Cass & Co., 1968), l:xii.

41. Robert Renney, *History of Jamaica* (London: n.p., 1807), pp. 213-214.

42. Ibid., pp. 165-166.

43. Long, *History of Jamaica*, 3:403; Collins, *Practical Rules*, pp. 33-39.

44. M. G. Lewis, *Journal of a West India Proprietor 1815-1817*, ed. Mona Wilson (New York: Houghton Mifflin, 1929), p. 104.

45. Ibid., p. 316.

46. Frank Cundall, ed., *Lady Nugent's Journal* (New York: Adan & Charles Black, 1907), p. 21.

47. J. B. Moreton, *Manners and Customs in the West India Islands* (London: W. Richardson, 1970), pp. 140-162.

48. Rev. Hope Masterton Waddell, *Twenty-nine Years in the West*

Indies and Central Africa 1829-1858 (London: Frank Cass & Co., 1970), p. 37.

49. Bernard Senior, *Jamaica, as It Was, as It Is, and as It May Be* (New York: Negro Universities Press, 1969), p. 196.

50. Thomas Atwood, *History of the Island of Dominica* (London: Frank Cass & Co., 1971), pp. 269-271.

51. Captain Thomas Southey, *Chronological History of the West Indies,* 3 vols. (London: Frank Cass & Co., 1968), 3:14.

52. James M. Phillippo, *Jamaica, Its Past and Present State* (London: Davidson of Pall Mall, 1969), p. 249.

53. R. R. Madden, *A Twelve Months' Residence in the West Indies,* 2 vols. (New York: Negro University Press, 1970), 1:99, 108, 101-102.

54. Long, *History of Jamaica,* p. 489.

55. W. T. Gardner, *A History of Jamaica* (London: Frank Cass & Co., 1971), p. 391.

56. Collins, *Practical Rules,* p. 170.

57. Lewis, *Journal,* pp. 82, 83, 85.

58. George Pinckard, M.D., *Notes on the West Indies,* 3 vols. (New York: Negro Universities Press, 1970), 3:249.

59. Alexander Barclay, *A Practical View of the Present State of Slavery in the West India Colonies* (Miami: Mnemoyne Publishing Co., 1969), p. 35.

60. Ibid., p. 80.

61. Carmichael, *Domestic Manners,* 2:244.

62. Ibid., pp. 245, 246-247.

63. J. M'Queen, *The West India Colonies* (New York: Negro Universities Press, 1969), pp. 127, 247.

64. Ibid., pp. 197, 2-9.

65. Kenneth M. Stampp, *The Peculiar Institution* (New York: Vintage Books, 1956), p. 146.

66. Frederick Douglass, *My Bondage and My Freedom* (New York: Dover Publications, 1969), pp. 242, 246-247.

67. Herbert Aptheker, *American Negro Slave Revolts* (New York: International Publishers, 1974), p. 30.

68. Robert Brent Toplin, *The Abolition of Slavery in Brazil* (New York: Atheneum, 1971), p. 203.

69. Richard Price, *Maroon Societies* (New York: Doubleday, 1973), pp. 2-4; Orlando Patterson, *The Sociology of Slavery* (Rutherford, N.J.: Fairleigh Dickinson University Press, 1969), pp. 267-271.

70. Captain J. G. Stedman, *Narrative of a Five Years' Expedition Against the Revolted Negroes of Surinam* (Amherst: University of Massachusetts Press, 1971), pp. 4, 42.

71. John Atkins, *A Voyage to Guinea, Brazil and the West Indies* (London: Frank Cass & Co., 1970), p. 245.

72. *Calendar of State Papers, Colonial,* 1730, pp. 222-223; hereafter as *Cal. S.P. Colonial,* followed by year and page number.

73. Ibid., p. 106.

74. Ibid., p. 69.

75. Ibid., pp. 24, 160, 164, 293.

76. Ibid., p. 328.

77. Ibid., p. 333.

78. Dallas, *History of the Maroons,* 1:37-38.

79. Ibid., p. 47.

80. Ibid., pp. 58-65.

81. Ibid., 2:2-3.; *The Proceedings of the Governor and Assembly of Jamaica, in Regard to the Maroon Negroes* (Westport, Conn.: Negro Universities Press, 1970), pp. 14-15.

82. Ibid., p. 3.

83. Lowell Ragatz, *The Fall of the Planter Class in the British Caribbean 1763-1833* (New York: Appleton-Century-Crofts, 1928), pp. 219-220; Roger Norman Buckley, *Slaves in Red Coats. The British West India Regiments, 1795-1815* (New Haven, Conn.: Yale University Press, 1979), p. 83.

84. Michael Craton, *Testing the Chains. Resistance to Slavery in the British West Indies* (Ithaca, N.Y.: Cornell University Press, 1982), pp. 180-210, 190-206; John Fortescue, *A History of the British Army,* 13 vols. (London: Macmillan, 1899-1930), 4:pt. 1:427.

85. Ibid., p. 425.

86. Ibid., pp. 431-432.

87. Ibid., pp. 453, 543.

88. Patterson, *Sociology of Slavery,* p. 275.

89. Brathwaite, *Development of Creole Society in Jamaica,* pp. 164-166.

90. Long, *History of Jamaica,* 2:405, 410, 411.

91. Barry W. Higman, *Slave Population and Economy in Jamaica, 1807-1834* (Cambridge: Cambridge University Press, 1976), p. 224.

92. Ibid.

93. Ibid., p. 231.

94. Alexander von Humbolt, *Personal Narrative of Travels to the Equinoctial Regions of America,* 3 vols. (London: Henry G. Bohn, 1853), 3:244.

95. William Robertson, *The History of the Discovery and Settlement of America* (New York: Harper & Bros., 1842), pp. 357-358.

96. Ragatz, *Fall of the Planter Class,* pp. 346-356.

97. Higman, *Slave Population in Jamaica,* p. 232.

98. Patterson, *Sociology of Slavery,* p. 266.

99. Captain Thomas Southey, *Chronological History of the West Indies,* 3 vols. (London: Frank Cass & Co., 1968), 2:258, 261, 366, 384, 396, 400, 409.

100. Patterson, Sociology of Slavery, pp. 267-272.

101. Ibid., p. 272; Michael Craton, *Sinews of Empire* (New York: Doubleday, 1974), p. 231.

102. Eric Williams, *Capitalism and Slavery* (New York: G. P. Putnam's Sons, 1966), p. 204; Craton, *Testing the Chains,* pp. 257-264.

103. Williams, *Capitalism and Slavery,* p. 205; Craton, *Testing the Chains,* pp. 269-289; Joshua Bryant, *Account of an Insurrection of the Negro Slaves in the Colony of Demerara* (Georgetown, Demerara: A. Stevenson, 1824), pp. 71-80.

104. Robert Isaac Wilberforce and Samuel Wilberforce, *The Life of William Wilberforce,* 5 vols. (London: John Murray, 1839), 5:201.

105. "Belmore to Goderich," *Parliamentary Papers, 1831-1832,* vol. XLVII; hereafter referred to as P.P.

106. Henry Bleby, *Death Struggles of Slavery* (London: n.p., 1868), p. 7.

107. Michael Craton, "Slave Culture, Resistance and the Achievement of Emancipation in the British West Indies, 1783-1838," in James Walvin, ed., *Slavery and British Society, 1776-1846* (London: Macmillan, 1982), p. 105.

108. "Confession of Linton a Prisoner in Savannah La Mar Gaol," *P.P. 1831-1832,* vol. XLVII.

109. Ibid., p. 196.

110. Mary Reckford, "The Jamaican Slave Rebellion of 1831," *Past and Present,* no. 40, July 1968, pp. 108-125.

111. Ibid., pp. 108-109.

112. See especially Norman Cohen, *The Pursuit of the Millennium* (New York: Oxford University Press, 1970).

113. "The Life of Olaudah Equiano, or Gustavus Vassa, the African," in *Great Slave Narratives,* ed. Arna Bontemps (Boston: Beacon Press, 1969).

114. Ibid., chaps. 10 and 12.

115. Paul Edwards, "Introduction to Ottobah Cugoano," *Thoughts and Sentiments on the Evil of Slavery* (London: Dawsons, 1969), pp. v-vii.

116. Ibid., pp. xx-xxi.

117. Ibid., pp. 3, 4, 90, 103.

118. Michael Craton, "The Passion to Exist: Slave Rebellion in the

British West Indies 1650-1832," *Journal of Caribbean History*, vol. 13 (December 1981), pp. 1-20.

119. "Examination of Reverend John M'Intyre," *P.P. 1831-1832*, vol. XLVII.

120. "Confession of Robert Gardiner," *P.P. 1831-1832*, vol. XLVII, Bleby, *Death Struggles of Slavery*, p. 131.

121. "Examination of Reverend John M'Intyre" *P.P. 1831-1832*, Vol. XLVII.

122. "The Examination of Reverend Thomas Stewart," *P.P. 1831-1832*, vol. XLVII.

123. Bleby, *Death Struggles of Slavery*, pp. 127-128, 132.

124. Senior, *Jamaica*, p. 160; "Return to an Address . . . ," *P.P. 1831-1832*, vol. XLVII.

125. Bleby, *Death Struggles of Slavery*, p. 123.

126. Ibid., p. 123.

127. "Examination of Reverend John M'Intyre," *P.P. 1831-1832*, vol. XLVII; Craton, *Testing the Chains*, pp. 300-302; Bleby, *Death Struggles of Slavery*, p. 125.

128. Waddell, *Twenty-nine Years in the West Indies*, p. 51.

129. Higman, *Slave Population in Jamaica*, p. 76; Michael Craton, *Searching for the Invisible Man* (Cambridge, Mass.: Harvard University Press, 1978), p. 74.

130. Higman, *Slave Population in Jamaica*, p. 142.

131. Goveia, *Slave Society*, pp. 244-245.

132. Lewis, *Journal*, p. 139.

133. Eugene Genovese, *From Rebellion to Revolution* (New York: Vintage Books, 1981), p. 3.

134. Higman, *Slave Populations of the British Caribbean*, p. 67.

135. Ibid., pp. 387-394.

4

Imperial Benevolence

To a slave living in the British Caribbean at the end of the eighteenth century, the most visible and impressive manifestation of the imperial presence would have been the ships of war that called from time to time at the tiny island ports, bringing with them the red-coated soldiers of the crown. They were tangible symbols of the link that bound the sugar colonies in a political, economic, and military network with Britain. They were proof of the vulnerability of the white ruling class, whose ultimate security, as Samuel Sharp realized, depended on the willingness and the ability of the imperial government to support them.

The critical military and economic dependence of the West Indies on Great Britain was an essential precondition for the rise of the anti-slavery movement in England. Had the island colonies been able to live on their own without recourse to British guns and finance, there would have been little pretext for imperial intervention in the relationship of master and slave. As it was, West Indian vulnerability implied imperial responsibility. From this perspective, the problem with which we are confronted in anti-slavery is not the simple concern for the treatment of slaves, impelled by a newfound belief in the value of the individual, or an evangelical conviction of the sin of slaveholding. To be sure, these forces were real and at work in

English society, but they emerged within the parameters of a much broader structural problem: the need to provide an effective social and political foundation for a portion of the old empire that would serve to ensure its stability and productivity.

This problem arose because by the close of the eighteenth century, Afro-Caribbean society was rapidly coming of age as an autonomous and fairly homogeneous society, unlike the frontier outposts of Africans and Europeans of earlier times. The confrontation with another culture was not a problem in and of itself. Indeed, the British had been successful in India, which was certainly an alien environment, but in India, the English confronted an ancient society replete with a well-established class structure and indigenous forms of authority and discipline. British rule could be imposed on top of a pre-existing structure. If there was misery and injustice in India, at least it was not the creation of the British, whose rule could, if pursued properly, lead towards the enlightenment of the population.

If British India represented the indirect rule of an ancient state, the Caribbean was almost called into being by the English. Unlike the case of India, Englishmen could not dismiss the cruelty and misery created by British rule as the unavoidable result of centuries of the superstition and ignorance of the local culture. In the West Indies, the British themselves had created the conditions in which inhumanity was bound to flourish by allowing the existence of slavery in law and guaranteeing its existence in fact. The use of imperial troops, guns, ships, and money to support slavery in the Caribbean meant that it was now a form of imperial rule, and it was only in the Caribbean that the British imperium took such a form.

As weighty as these considerations were, however, they were not enough by themselves to create a reaction as profound as the anti-slavery movement. As in most cases of humanitarian behavior, injustice had first to be brought to the attention of the altruistic and then kept before them. In the words of Frederick Douglass, the "Signs of Power" had first to arise. It was the slaves themselves who, by their behavior, created the problem of slavery with which the abolitionists grappled. Had they been merely passive victims of exploitation instead of active freedom fighters, anti-slavery would certainly have existed as a sentiment, but it is likely that there would have been no vigorous movement to abolish slavery.

It was only in the 1820s that a popular and full-scale anti-slavery campaign got under way. It was also during the same period that some of the greatest and most extensive slave risings took place, in 1816, 1823, and 1831. But it was not slave revolts alone that attracted humanitarian attention to the problem of slavery; it was also the clear and persistent evidence that slaves hated and resisted slavery continually, on a day-to-day basis, and in the more spectacular rebellions. So that if abolitionists felt that slavery was repugnant to the human spirit, that perception was certainly reinforced by the behavior of black slaves, who made it clear that it was repugnant to them.

We can think of the movement of anti-slavery as a dialectical relationship of forces, reflecting the action and reaction of black slaves and imperial humanitarians in England. Thus, if, on the one hand, there was evidence of slave resistance, now expressed in Maroonage, now in rebellion, and, more typically, in the daily struggle of master and slave, there was, on the other side, a party in England sophisticated and sensitive enough to perceive in these disjointed phenomena a growing problem for the benevolent empire that they envisioned. There was, therefore, a meeting and adjustment of two social visions: that of the abolitionists, expressed in print, through speech, and in political behavior, and that of the slaves, stated in their deeds. It was the genius of the abolitionist party that it achieved a vision of the British imperium as a multi-ethnic empire in which loyalty would find a basis in the common values of a supernational culture, transcending race and class. It was a vision that excluded slavery because it undermined the basis for any legitimate claim to moral leadership. Yet it must be remembered that this was not a vision drawn from a cultural heritage alone, but a reading of experience with Caribbean slaves through the prism of culture. These two factors are inseparable: the Caribbean slaves, who had all along refused to accept bondage as a way of life, and the English humanitarians, whose vision of what Britain should be inclined them to read the signs of power in a progressive manner. Had they not done so, had there not been an anti-slavery movement, the signs would still have existed, but the outcome for Afro-Caribbean social development would have been different, for surely slaves would not have abandoned the struggle for freedom for lack of allies in Britain.

The future of Afro-Caribbean society and of the empire of which it formed a part was profoundly affected by the intervention of moral reformers in imperial affairs. The advent of humanitarian activism in imperial politics over the question of slavery signaled the beginnings of a revolution in the way in which the British elite conceived of the subject races of the empire and envisioned Britain's relationship with them. If we conceive of culture as patterned behavior that operates to secure the well-being of the individual and the group by providing a set of ready assumptions with which to approach typical situations, and as ways of looking at the world that serve the general interest of the participants, then we can characterize this change in imperial perception as a cultural revolution.[1]

Cultural revolutions take place in response to challenges to the effectiveness of given cultural formations. Thus, if traditional modes of behavior and thought no longer seem to facilitate the attainment of desired ends, then culture modification can be a response to the new situation. If the culture is successfully modified, the group should be more effective in its efforts to deal with the problem that provoked change. If it is not, a breakdown in culture may occur which can threaten the integrity of the group. If we see culture in this manner, then change must be considered as one of its essential characteristics, and the study of culture change can be a significant means of understanding the relation of a people to its political, social, and economic environment, by helping us to understand the types of pressures exerted on them by external forces.[2]

Although culture change is unceasing, there are periods when it assumes dynamic and revolutionary forms. In such periods, it is common for a particular group to take the lead in restructuring aspects of cultural life. It is characteristic for such movements to be quite self-conscious and understandably self-righteous.[3] The movement of enlightenment in eighteenth-century France, the psychoanalytic movement in early twentieth-century Europe, and the civil rights movement in mid-twentieth-century United States are all examples of campaigns for cultural change in the sense in which I have presented that concept. By this I do not mean that they set out to do something as abstract as to elicit a change in culture, but that the innovations at which they all aimed amounted to significant changes in cultural orientation. Such movements may advocate the need to see some aspect of physical, social, or economic life in a new and novel way in order to facilitate the achievement of their objectives, but this frequently cannot occur without change in patterned behavior.

Both the enlightenment and the psychoanalytic movement were highly self-conscious attempts at cultural change, in the sense that changes in the conceptualization of mental and social processes at a fundamental level and in what was to be considered desirable or acceptable behavior were primary goals.[4] In the case of the civil rights movement, the ultimate goal was the civil liberties of Afro-Americans. This politico-legal goal involved a legal and political campaign, but from the beginning, the close connection between these social domains and the general American culture was appreciated. Civil rights advocates understood that full civil rights for America's black population could not be achieved without the simultaneous creation of a cultural environment that induced white Americans to pay attention to, understand, and accept the case that they were making for federal and local action to remedy the damages of the historical legacy of anti-black discrimination and racism. The campaign to bring about this cultural revolution went far beyond the bounds of the legal-political movement and involved academia, the church, and the media. It attacked the cultural premises of racism across the board, as well as the specific incidents of racism in American life.[5]

The challenge to the integrity of American culture presented by the civil rights movement was met and surmounted by the forging of a new cultural consensus on race and constitutional rights which supported the civil rights leigislation and the economic reforms of the Kennedy, Johnson, and Nixon administrations and the local initiatives in business, industry, and education. The successful readjustment of American cultural attitudes towards black Americans had ramifications in related cultural attitudes towards other minorities, the third world, and women.

Having gone through the process, Americans ended up feeling that they had attained a new moral level, so that the very process of cultural change served to validate the self-image of American whites as a good and progressive people. This phenomenon can be observed as well in the English anti-slavery movement, which has been celebrated in the historiography as the triumph of English benevolence over material self-interest.

It is helpful to regard English anti-slavery as a movement for change in English cultural attitudes and behavior towards Afro-Caribbean people. As such, it can be conceived of as one facet of a general movement that sought to construct new and more productive relationships between Britain and the subject races of the empire. Formulated in this way, the anti-slavery movement, like the response of the American government to the civil rights movement, came into existence because of the perception of a persistent sociopolitical problem, which seemed to pose a relatively clear choice to the highly cultured Englishmen who supplied the intellect and political leadership of the movement.[6]

The anti-slavery leadership engaged the conscience of the nation essentially by asking where the imperial power should be exercised in the Caribbean. Should it protect the planter in the enjoyment of the right of property in human beings, or should it confirm the black in the enjoyment of those rights which the English believed to be the birthright of every man? The planter represented a virtually unrestrained power, or despotism. Support for the plantocracy involved the empire in a type of rule that pitted the interests of the Afro-Caribbean population against their imperial masters. Modern thinking emphasized that government should be founded on the welfare, if not necessarily the consent, of the governed. This cultural heritage conspired with currents of unrest in the Caribbean to reinforce the case for imperial intervention on behalf of freedom and against tyranny.[7]

The wider imperial environment had an important influence as well. A striking characteristic of the late eighteenth and early nineteenth centuries was the simultaneous upsurges of revolutionary activity throughout the Atlantic system, which must be appreciated in their cumulative impact on contemporaries. So that while the imperial humanitarians contemplated the injustice of slavery from the perspective of the cultural revolutions of enlightenment and evangelical Christianity and were impacted by the organized slave risings in the Caribbean, they also witnessed the mobilization of the French people in the name of liberty and against tyranny, at home, throughout Europe, and in the wars of revolution in the West Indies.[8] At the same time, from their vantage point near the pinnacle of imperial society, the anti-slavery humanitarians could contemplate the lessons of the American revolution, fought for self-determination and against British "tyranny."

The loss of the Thirteen Colonies and the revolutions in France and the continent underlined the intoxication of the age with the conviction that legitimate power must be bound by the consent and interest of those whom it touched. Expressed powerfully in America, this faith provided the ideology of the revolution. In France, the call for representative government through a national assembly had originally been part of the program of the aristocracy in its struggle with the king, but it was taken to its logical and radical extension by the popular movement. Finally, the writings of Tom Paine captured the spirit of the age in a form that was readily accessible to the common person. Events in France had demonstrated how dangerous it could be to underestimate, as the French monarchy and aristocracy had done, the power of the new ideology or the capacity of the people for independent and revolutionary action. Ideas that seemed like harmless philosophical speculation on the surface could become deadly under the pressure of events.

The British elite absorbed the lessons of popular revolution and national independence movements. The loss of the American colonies provoked momentary bewilderment, but it was quite rapidly replaced by a renewed determination to preserve the remaining empire and set it on a sure footing.[9] Of this, the most important area was the Caribbean, and then there were the remaining North American settlements in Canada and Nova Scotia; Ireland, the closest and oldest imperial possession; and India, a newly rising star. Much was done to secure the loyalty of the remaining American colonies and Ireland by constitutional settlements.[10] Already sharing a common culture and much history with Great Britain, the North American colonies did not draw significant humanitarian attention; neither, strangely enough, did Ireland. The great areas of humanitarian endeavor were all in what we now call the Third World, in particular the Caribbean, India, and Africa. British benevolence towards the outside world was geared to the darker races of the empire, not towards the Anglo-Saxon or even Celtic colonies.

As the first major modern imperial nation, late-eighteenth-century Britain was groping towards an ethic of empire which would generate constructive and secure relations between the metropolis and the subject races overseas.[11] At the forefront of this movement were the evangelicals of the so-called Clapham Sect. Celebrated for their opposition to slavery in the British West Indies, they were also involved in propounding an imperial attitude towards Africa and India, where British merchants had been active for more than 200 years.

At the beginning of the nineteenth century, Africa was not a big field for British commerce, with the notorious exception of the slave trade.[12] Opposition to the slave trade and slavery in England led humanitarians to the African continent itself, where their efforts centered on stopping the illegal slave trade from the West African coast and establishing the colony of Sierra Leone. It was pressure from English blacks on their patron, Granville Sharp, that galvanized the humanitarian network to establish an African home for the black poor of London. Founded in 1787, when Granville Sharp arranged for the settlement of several hundred blacks on the West African coast, the colony was administered by the Sierra Leone Company. The company's board of directors included Henry Thornton, Thomas Babington, and Zachary Macaulay, who served as colonial administrator between 1793 and 1799. After 1807, Sierra Leone developed into a refuge for slaves freed from illegal slavers by the British West African Squadron, but it never fulfilled its original promise of becoming a model colony that its founders hoped would spread civilization throughout the "dark" continent.[13]

The Clapham group, who founded the Sierra Leone Company, saw Africa as a continent sunk in ignorance and immorality. To them, the answer to Africa's dilemma was the introduction of

Christianity and the development of legitimate commerce and industry.[14] The establishment of the Church Missionary Society with evangelical support around 1799 was a step towards bringing this social vision to birth.[15] Unfortunately, while the slave trade remained, there seemed little hope for the growth of a legitimate commerce. At any rate, Britain's trade with Africa remained modest until well into the nineteenth century. Africa did not have the internal economic base from which to sustain a vital foreign trade, and European penetration, when it came, may have done far more to weaken the continent further than to catalyze the development of its natural resources.[16]

In the late eighteenth century, it was India, after the Caribbean, that seemed to offer most from Britain's overseas adventure and that presented a problem of imperial governance second only to that of slavery. In both India and the Caribbean, British enterprise had begun as a private affair with little government interference. But in the Caribbean, the age of private control through chartered companies rapidly gave way to a relatively tight supervision by the metropolitan government. Through the precedent of countless orders, dispatches, and memoranda, the government in London gradually built up a recognized supervision over Caribbean affairs, even before the influence of the anti-slavery movement began to be felt. At its most complete in the crown colonies, it is arguable that the practice of central supervision made it easier for the metropolitan government to juxtapose itself between master and slave than would otherwise have been the case.[17]

The advent of imperial rule in India represented more of a radical break with the past than the intensification of central direction in the Caribbean. Like colonial development in the Atlantic world, trade in the East Indies began as the province of a chartered company, but in India, the company remained the governing power, actually growing in importance until, by the close of the eighteenth century, it had become the paramount power in India. By the 1780s, when debate opened over the company's affairs, the issue had become the degree to which imperial control was necessary in order to ensure that unrestrained individual enterprise would not endanger the overall interests of the empire in the East.[18]

For the present study, the most salient issue in that debate was the question of the nature and responsibility of British rule over people believed to be at a lower stage of cultural development. This seemed to represent both a danger and a trust. The wrong attitude towards the Indian population could foment active opposition to imperial rule. At the same time, as a superior Christian civilization, the British had a divinely ordained mission to bring the blessings of Protestantism and Western morality to the subcontinent. As so often in the history of empires, important segments of the politically active class believed that the path of humanity and light should happily coincide with the true interest of empire. The problem was that this coincidence depended on human initiative, and historical progress would not necessarily take place unless the central government exerted the appropriate control over its agents abroad. This was the thinking of the humanitarians at Clapham.

Wilberforce presented the evangelical case for an active Indian policy to the Parliament. Like Edmund Burke, the evangelicals were hostile to the system of dual control of Indian affairs symbolized by the names of Clive and Hastings because it was founded on what they believed was the erroneous notion that Hindu culture was suitable, and even advantageous, for the Indians. Wilberforce and Charles Grant, the evangelical chairman of the board of the East India Company, argued that Hindu culture and the civilization which it supported were fundamentally depraved.[19] Wilberforce saw the problem in simple terms, as the moral obligation of a superior civilization to rescue millions of Indian souls enslaved by the "double yoke of political and religious despotism" which was the legacy of Hindu culture. He saw Indian civilization as "one grand abomination" and believed that the British were obliged to bring about moral reformation.[20]

Moral renovation through Christianization was a cardinal theme of the evangelical corpus. Because Charles Grant and John Shore, both evangelicals, were members of the governing body of the company, and the "Saints" an influential group in Parliament, the policy of Anglicization by way of religion and education in the English language was able to exert an influence on Indian affairs far out of proportion to the numerical strength of the reform party. Grant, who had established his career in Indian affairs, was as certain of the need to bring Chritianity to the heathen Hindu as was Wilberforce. Grant believed that Protestantism was largely responsible for the great growth in Western civilization since the sixteenth century. By liberating the European mind from medieval superstition and barbarism, Protestantism had made the achievements of the Western world possible. It could perform a similar civilizing and liberating service for the Indians as well and in so doing secure the relationship between metropolis and colony by the bond of a common value system.[21]

Both Grant and Wilberforce believed that the dictates of self-interest were aligned on the side of Indian reform. If the Indian empire was to be made secure, it would have to be founded on something more than the force of conquest; neither could it continue to rest on the abomination that was Hindu culture. The Indian population should be drawn into a cultural community with Britain so that it would be able to appreciate the advantages of British rule and come to recognize a community of interests between ruler and ruled. As Wilberforce put it, "our oriental empire indeed is now a vast edifice; but this lofty and spacious fabric rests on the surface of the earth without foundations." The introduction of Christianity and education in the English language would succeed in time in introducing the whole range of Western values and turn ignorant Indians, not indeed into little Englishmen, but into proper-thinking people, fit for life in the modern world.[22]

This was plain cultural imperialism, designed to produce a stable foundation for British rule through what was, in effect, cultural engineering. The intent and dynamic of this program were succinctly put by the Bishop of Calcutta writing to Wilberforce on the value of English language training for Indians. "Between the English and the native languages there is not more difference than between our modes of thinking and theirs upon the common questions of life."[23] The point was not that English education would remove the Indians' sense of self-interest, leaving them prey to European exploitation, but that the evangelicals were convinced that Hindu civilization had to be drastically modified in order that the Indians might be able to receive the blessings of English culture that would come with English rule.

At the heart of the imperial culture of the Clapham Sect was the powerful conviction that a British imperium guided by Christian principles was inherently progressive. To be precise, one must say that for the evangelical reformers, there was an all but indistinguishable identity between Christian and British. British civilization was Protestant civilization. The faith gave it its freedom and value. Religion was the inner dynamo that accounted for Britain's spectacular success. The Clapham Sect was practically incapable of distinguishing between Protestant values and what they considered to be the highest British values, and in truth, there was little to distinguish between them. When they critiqued the latter, it was only in terms of its departure from the former, so that the language of religion became a means of evaluating and adjusting aspects of their culture.

I have called Clapham culture imperial not because its finest representatives consciously engaged in the exploitation of subject peoples, but because the culture in which they lived and worked and the cultural revolution which they led were oriented towards the preservation of patterns of behavior at home and abroad that tended to protect and preserve the position of dominance overseas, on which much of Britain's material prosperity depended. This dymanic culture emerged in its first clear expression and became aware of its inherent responsibilities, and possibilities in the movement to reform Caribbean society. It remains now to look more closely at the moral elite who were responsible for this strident reform movement and at the faith that gave them the courage and persistence for which they are well known.

The core of evangelical Christianity lies in the conviction that human nature is fundamentally corrupt.[24] Salvation is possible only through the grace of a loving God and is absolutely the most important thing in the world. The duty of every Christian is to prepare for the judgment to come by doing everything possible to become worthy of salvation. This personal mission means that the "serious" Christian must be constantly vigilant against the forces of evil that act to seduce him from the true path. In the evangelical creed, the devil is not a metaphorical figure, but a

real and personal presence whose sole ambition is the perversion
of souls. The pilgrim must guard against the manifold snares of
this devil, while striving to carry out the injunctions of God as
revealed in the Bible.

The evangelical is deeply impressed and, at conversion, often
virtually crushed by the staggering burden of human guilt and
the terrible odds against successfully navigating the reefs and
shoals of a dangerous world on the way to salvation. The trauma
of rebirth, the center of the evangelical experience, shakes the
pilgrim's entire being and should be moderated by the wisdom of
a spiritual guide, someone who has already passed through the
door to new life and who is living the "serious" life. As a
powerful support in the spiritual quest, evangelicals sought the
company of like-minded people, who could reinforce their own
convictions, watch over one another, and help to surmount the
bouts of self-doubt.

The nuclear family provided a natural institution in which the
values and convictions essential for salvation could be fostered
and preserved. From the beginning, Christianity had recognized
the family as the appropriate vehicle for a Christian life. Within
its protective shell, sexual drives could be channeled into their
only legitimate function in reproduction, children could be
inculcated with the articles of the faith, and respect for earthly
laws and institutions could grow up naturally. As children were
impressed with the hierarchic structure of the family itself, the
lessons of respect for authority and station and the expectation
of reward for obedience and hard work, or punishment for lax-
ness and disobediance, would be carried over to their behavior in
society.

Evangelicalism made the family even more central to
Christian life. The evangelical family consisted of an ever-
widening circle of relatives and friends who maintained close
communication with one another, discussing moral problems,
rigorously evaluating one another's behavior, and reinforcing
common beliefs.

Evangelicalism enjoined on its adherents a far more positive
reason for association than its value as a prophylactic. The
brotherhood of man in God obliged its soldiers to bring the light
of revealed religion into every corner and rescue those who were

asleep to the word of God from their oppressive ignorance. The evangelist was, therefore, inherently a missionary, both at home and abroad, so much so that the word has come to symbolize the fervent religious teacher ardent for the conversion of new souls. There is no greater distinguishing mark of evangelicalism than the disturbing immediacy with which its adherents approach the spiritual problem. It is a life lived at fever pitch, in the often terrifying belief that humankind is rushing headlong over the precipice. Evangelicals, individuals and group, are a people living in a state of siege.

A group faith, a missionary force, an intensely individual experience, evangelicalism would have been a potent force in any social class, but with its emergence in late-eighteenth-century Britain among successful first- and second-generation upper-middle-class Englishmen, just when the British elite was redefining and reassessing the nature of imperial rule, it was able to achieve a profound influence on the development of imperial culture.

The classic anti-slavery argument was expressed by a close-knit and highly self-conscious group of Englishmen drawn from the upper middle class. This group, which was imbued with the evangelical spirit, was so homogeneous and easily identifiable and so strident in its moralistic approach to social and political problems, that they were called "Saints" by contemporaries who were as disturbed by their single-mindedness as they were impressed by their dedication to principle. The Saints, or the Clapham Sect, as they were called from the London suburb of Clapham, where many of them resided, found its center in the home of John Thornton. Fitting the Protestant ideal of the righteous patriarch, Thornton had amassed a fortune in business and saw his sons, Henry, Samuel, and Robert, win seats in Parliament.[25] One biographer of Wilberforce claims that Henry Thornton deliberately instigated a colony at Clapham.[26] But whether planned or not, a community of like-minded spirits did develop around the Thorntons.

About 1756, the evangelical preacher Henry Venn set up his ministry at Clapham, and his son John became rector there in 1793.[27] Wilberforce, who was a nephew of John Thornton, purchased a home at Clapham when he married in 1797. Zachary

Macaulay moved there in 1803, after having served the Sierra Leone Company in Africa. James Stephen, the most prolific abolitionist author, and Charles Grant, of the East India Company, also lived at Clapham.[28]

The intellectual and spiritual associates of the Clapham Sect were a diverse group, including the abolitionists Thomas Clarkson and Granville Sharp, the ex-slave trader, and now Reverend John Newton, Isaac Milner, Charles Simeon from Cambridge, Thomas Gisborne, Josiah Pratt, and Hannah More. The Saints were connected by sentiment and cooperative effort with almost every conservative reformer of their time. Through Simeon and Milner they were brought into contact with the intellectual hub of evangelicalism, and their service in Parliament closely connected them with the powerful.

The Clapham Sect was also bound together by family ties, which were extremely important in a faith that stressed the primacy of family. James Stephen married Wilberforce's sister, and their son James became an outstanding colonial servant, virtually guiding British colonial office policy on the West Indies during the transition from slave to free labor. Charles Elliot married John Venn's sister, and the son of James Stephen married John Venn's daughter.[29]

The Saints were united by their devotion to what Wilberforce had dubbed "serious" Christianity, as the key to personal salvation and a remedy for the immorality of an age distinguished for its moral laxity. The problem was that often what they condemned as immorality was simply the expression of legitimate discontent with the prevailing sociopolitical system. Because they regarded lower-class radicalism as evidence of cultural weaknesses, they responded with an ideological offensive designed to preserve the integrity of English culture and society as they saw it.

It is difficult to appreciate the significance of this ideological offensive unless we keep in mind the vastly different scale of eighteenth-century English government from the modern edifice that we are accustomed to think of. Elie Halevy's classic picture of the informal governmental apparatus of England at the turn of the century conveys the flavor of a nation governed by and large by amateurs.[30] Without the benefit of a large and professional repressive agency, the English upper classes had to rely for the maintenance of order on local judicial authorities and, most important, the good disposition of the population. The English state was never strong enough to withstand a well-organized and broad-based popular movement, but then again, it never had to.

For all the stresses and strains accompanying the transition to agrarian and industrial capitalism in the first industrial nation, England never experienced anything close to revolution or its threat on the continental model.[31] On the contrary, English radical movements aimed more at modifying the new economic system in ways that would preserve an older artisan-based way of life. But neither the abandonment of capitalism nor its control in the interests of the working class had much appeal for the middle class. By and large, the relatively slight middle-class support for lower-class radicalism is perhaps the major reason why England did not experience the type of radical movement that one sees in France, this and the fact that radicalism did not have wide support in the lower class. Nowhere in Europe could one point to a successful revolution that had been mounted by the lower orders on their own. So that as weak as the repressive agencies available to the English state were compared with some continental states, they were fully adequate for dealing with the situation in England, given the lack of middle-class and broad-based working-class support for radical movements.

In the classic formulation of George Lefebvre, the French revolution involved three stages. It began with an aristocratic challenge to the crown, was radicalized by the revolt of the Third Estate, and was popularized and the middle-class revolution saved by the intervention of the people in town and country.[32] In England, there was no critical clash between aristocracy and middle class, and one is tempted to conclude that this contributed powerfully to the continuity of English society. In light of upper-class unity, one would not expect radicalism to have had much opportunity for gaining wide support or of developing into a sophisticated critique of society with a viable reform program of its own.

The English aristocracy was not a backward-looking caste clinging to feudal privileges in reaction to a challenge from the crown. It was heavily involved in the new economic system, participating in the commercial, agricultural, and even industrial developments that were revolutionizing English society. They were involved in mining and capitalist agriculture, invested heavily in overseas companies, and were in no way fundamentally hostile to the industrial system.[33]

This aristocracy might even be described as bourgeois in economic outlook. Although, in the political and social realm, it sought to monopolize as much power and privilege as possible, it did not constitute a legal caste; nor was it necessary in England to be an aristocrat in order to wield significant political power. Thanks to the growth in the power and influence of the House of Commons and the city of London in English political life, the middle class was able to translate economic power into political influence even before passage of the great reform bill. It is banal but in all probability accurate to say that the historical evolution of England over the 200 years prior to the nineteenth century had created conditions in which the English middle class could feel, with some degree of certainty, that they breathed freer air than did their continental brethren.

In a very real sense, the existing freedom of the middle class and the opportunities that it enjoyed for working through the system made radical alternatives unappealing and wasteful. For the emerging middle-class capitalist and professional man, danger to their vision of the future came not from the aristocracy, but from the lower class, who might not understand the potential benefits to be derived from the new economic organization once its imperfections had been ironed out.

Because of England's peculiar historical evolution, its aristocracy and prosperous middle class together confronted what Robert Palmer called the "Age of the Democratic Revolution," to characterize the period between 1760 and 1801. For Palmer, the age witnessed a plethora of "agitations, upheavals, intrigues, and conspiracies" which constituted a general movement "reflecting a crisis in western society." Although drawing inspiration from France, the local disturbances were not the result of the importation of French ideas, but sprouted naturally from local causes.[34]

Palmer is not alone in the recognition of the transitional

nature of the late eighteenth and early nineteenth centuries. Jacques Godechot has argued that the age was characterized by an "Atlantic Revolution" rooted in the dynamic of historical development in the Atlantic world, including western Europe, North America, and the Caribbean.[35] Eric Hobsbawn devoted more attention to economic developments than did either Palmer or Godechot. His conception is of a "Dual Revolution" in which the transformation of European economic life led to rapid changes in society and polity.[36]

Palmer is more attuned to the significance of political and cultural developments, more instructive on the impact of the revolutionary threat on the establishment. While the French upper orders quarreled among themselves, the English upper and middle classes closed ranks against potential revolution in what Palmer ingeniously styled "The Leveé en masse of the people of quality," a mobilization that took the form of counter-revolutionary organization and propaganda.[37]

The Palmer thesis, revised by the more global views of Jacques Godechot, provides a window through which to look at the rise of benevolent reform movements in England, and anti-slavery in particular, from an empire-wide perspective. They can be seen as part of the conservative counterattack by which the English upper classes sought to win the ideological war against radical philosophies at home and abroad.

If, as Palmer argues, the democratic revolution is descriptive of a plethora of "agitations, upheavals, and conspiracies," then we must include the West Indies in that movement as well, for as we have seen, slave society there was marked by such phenomena. What we have, then, is a movement that arose at the end of the eighteenth century in response to the threat of radical social movements in England and Europe and to the danger of instability in the empire deriving from its multi-ethnic and multi-cultural character. That movement was characterized by the attempt to fashion the basis for a cultural community that would be strong enough to withstand the radical onslaught and equitable enough to provide a sound foundation for imperial security.[38]

The campaign against slavery was one of a host of projects undertaken by humanitarian activists in their efforts to reform the social system. A sampling of their enterprises would include the Society for Bettering the Condition of the Poor, the Church Missionary Society, London Society for the Promotion of Christianity Among the Jews, the Cheap Repository Tract project, and the Sierra Leone Company. [39] Characteristically, these missionary enterprises were directed primarily at either the poor or the "heathen."

Although anti-slavery was the most famous enterprise of the Clapham Sect, it was not their only concern, and aside from hostility to slavery, the Saints were united by a common set of beliefs. Clapham evangelicalism was not a religion that led to renunciation of the world or abandonment of established careers in business and government. On the contrary, it was quite compatible with the demands and opportunities of life in the upper middle class.[40] By turning to the serious Christianity that came to mark the Clapham Sect, Wilberforce and the members of his circle were selecting a means of resolving their personal spiritual crises that enhanced the quality and security of their middle-class life.

From the moment of conversion, Clapham evangelicals viewed the world and its problems through their own special evangelical paradigm. If it was a view that entailed special responsibilities, it also conferred certain blessings. Sir James Stephen, son of the abolitionist author, was one of the most renowned second-generation evangelicals. Stephen grew up in the Clapham environment and was intimately familiar with its particular world view. Living among the Saints, he had the opportunity to observe the humanitarians in their daily lives. He explained that for these men who moved easily among the powerful in the worlds of business and government, religion had become proof against seduction by the attractions of the world, so that they could remain in it without "being held in bondage" by its temptations.[41] Wilberforce confirmed this interpretation, when shortly after his conversion to serious Christianity in 1785 he confided to his journal that he must be ever vigilant against the snares of society. "Pride is my greatest stumbling block." He was fearful lest the fear of failure or the desire for praise should lead him astray.[42]

Such fear of social failure is easy to understand when set

against the moral atmosphere of the privileged classes in eighteenth-century England, where a well-to-do young man could easily lose himself in a dissolute life. Before his conversion to evangelicalism, even Wilberforce had participated fully in this social life and was intimately acquainted with its dangers.

The need for powerful guiding principles in life was felt by James Stephen as well. Stephen had, one might think, an even more pressing need than Wilberforce for the spiritual and emotional support of a religious faith. He had experienced real privation in his youth, even living for a while in jail, where his father, who seemed incapable of properly providing for his family, was imprisoned for debt. As a young man, Stephen had been involved in an illicit affair with a woman that resulted in the birth of a child out of wedlock.[43] That he managed to survive the temptations, hardships, and diseases of the late eighteenth century to become an established lawyer and a respected member of the middle class was, in Stephen's mind, proof of the workings of divine Providence. If success in the world was an indication of the hand of the Almighty, then for Stephen, it was also proof of right conduct, where heaven rewarded good and punished evil.[44] To live the moral life, as the evangelicals saw it, was to increase one's chances for temporal success as well.

Another self-made man agreed with Stephen, although Thomas Fowell Buxton, with a less remarkable past, was much more at ease with himself. In 1806, Buxton experienced a powerful religious rebirth, and his state of mind at that time reflects the concerns of a young man eager to rise in the world of business. "I never before felt," he wrote, "so assured that the only means of being happy, is from seeking the assistance of a superior Being, or so inclined to endeavour to submit myself to the direction of principle."[45] Buxton's introduction to benevolence seemed to coincide with his entrance into Truman's Brewery, about 1808. By 1811, he had begun a lively interest in evangelical reform. "From the time of my connection with the Brewery in 1808-1816," Buxton explained, "I took part in all the charitable objects of that distressed district, more especially those connected with education, the Bible Society, and the deep sufferings of the weavers."[46] Buxton's benevolent activities grew as did his success, until he eventually took over the leadership of the parliamentary fight to abolish slavery from an aged Wilberforce.

Buxton's mother, a Quaker, impressed her son with a sense of duty towards those less fortunate than himself. His benevolence, therefore, had a hereditary component, and one may speculate that a religious nature shaped from earliest childhood may have been an important edge in his business life, giving him a ready-to-hand rationale for sacrifice and hard work. It also may have made him susceptible to the attractions of evangelicalism.[47]

Submission to a higher authority, surrender of one's conventional and narrow individuality in order to attain the release of spiritual power, is as old as Christianity itself. The recognition of the apparent insignificance of the individual in a hostile world peopled by seemingly inexorable forces is elementary and universal. It is a spring that feeds all religions. Although it allows us to understand some of the attractions of evangelicalism to the upper middle class, it does not explain its social significance in the period of abolition and emancipation.

Whatever the reason for individual conversions, and the important problem of the appeal of religion to the individual goes far beyond the scope of the present work, the fact is that a group of such religious people, who quite naturally associated with one another, were able to achieve a profound influence on the culture and imperial policy of nineteenth-century Britain. The explanation for this is, I believe, related to the concept and program of benevolence, which, as David Brion Davis has brilliantly taught us, was a striking and unique characteristic of the transformation of religious life in the eighteenth century.[48] By embracing the obligation of benevolence, the evangelical humanitarians demonstrated in their behavior a belief in the brotherhood of man that seemed to dispense with the significance of class and status as categories for understanding the nature of society. Although benevolence reinforced an interpretation of social inequality as the operation of Providence, it could have the additional attraction of persuading the lower orders of the sincerity and moral worthiness of their rulers. In addition, because the targets of benevolence were generally lower class behavior and alien culture, it could serve to propagate what the humanitarians regarded as proper social values among those orders most in need of instruction.

To the benevolent, creation by God constituted the common link between people and compelled action to improve the condition of those who lived in ignorance and misery. But the existence of benevolence was premised on an acceptance of the inherent inequality of social relations, which was simply seen as a reflection of God's inscrutable plan. The benevolent person acts to ameliorate the condition of the less fortunate, and almost by definition the less equal, but never to destroy socioeconomic inequality, an enterprise that is thought to be beyond the limited capacity of man.

The question of inequality is never posed as a problem in benevolence because it is seen to be of divine origin. It is also important to bear in mind that since benevolence is an expression of the privileged classes, for the most part towards the lower orders or aliens, that is, a mode by which the rulers, or a section of them, relate to the ruled, there is little motivation for raising the issue of inequality except to explain why it is not a legitimate issue. On the contrary, speculation on the social origins of inequality and the means by which it might be removed is seen as dangerous and ought to be discouraged. Because evil in the world is the product of a human nature that is fundamentally corrupt, it can never be destroyed once and for all by changing society. This, the Clapham group believed, was a cardinal error of the French revolution. Instead, the arena of combat against evil is shifted to the soul, where the effects of evil can be tempered by cultivating the Christian virtues needed for salvation. The pursuit of spiritual salvation will necessarily tend to promote behavior productive of a better world.

Wilberforce presented the case for serious Christianity and the duty of benevolence in his tremendously popular book *A Practical View of the Prevailing Religious System of Professed Christians*. . . . This ideological guidebook for "serious" Christians argued that it was the duty of every Christian to cultivate the virtues demanded in the struggle against the very real devil at work in the world. At the same time, one was obliged to do everything possible to see that others had the opportunity to perfect their Christian duty.[49] Wilberforce was certain that if his contemporaries followed his advice, society would come to be increasingly governed by Christian precepts, making it more orderly, just, and productive.[50]

Such sentiments reflected the rising tide of evangelical fervor, and it is easy to see in them the expression of the conservative cultural needs of the men who welcomed the new commercial and industrial system but who wanted to limit its disruptive social consequences. It was Wilberforce, after all, in his *Practical View*, who emphasized the value of Christianity for ameliorating but clearly preserving the class structure by teaching each class the lessons proper to their station. The wealthy would be taught to "be liberal and beneficent" and the poor "to be dilegent, humble, patient."[51]

As Ford K. Brown demonstrated in his brilliant and much maligned study, *Fathers of the Victorians,* the evangelicals were keen to counter-act the potential influence of radical ideas on the lower class.[52] This ideological offensive is to be seen in classic expression in Hannah More's project for the publication of Cheap Repository Tracts. The enterprise, which became a Clapham affair, was definitely a response to radical ideology and most particularly to the ideas of Tom Paine. In the 1790s, when the *Rights of Man* was being read, More, a well-known writer and by now a Clapham associate, received numerous requests to pen a response to counter Paine. She replied with *Village Politics,* one of her most successful tracts.[53]

When Paine's *Age of Reason* appeared, Bishop Porteus wrote to ask her to compose something like an ideological manual on elementary Christianity as an antidote to Paine. But by now, More was engaged in planning a more extensive enterprise and was unable to comply with the bishop's request. Instead of writing the Christian manual that the Bishop of London had suggested, Hannah More eventually performed a much greater service as the moving light behind the Cheap Repository Tracts. Henry Thornton became treasurer of the publishing venture, which gained rapid success. By March of 1796, more than 2 million tracts had been sold.[54] The Bishop of London wrote to her in 1797 to explain his joy at "the sublime and immortal 'Cheap Repository.'"[55]

As has often been pointed out, the education of the poor was one of the evangelicals' most important programs. They were active in the Sunday school movement in England, as well as in the provision of religious instruction for Caribbean slaves and Indian peasants.[56] One of Hannah More's more cherished projects was the establishment of schools for the poor at Mendip. An 1801 letter to the Bishop of Bath and Wells reveals her pedagogic principles. "I allow no writing for the poor. My object is not to make fanatics, but to train up the lower classes in the habits of industry and piety." In order to influence the children more completely, provision was made for adult education on the basis of the Cheap Repository, thus ensuring instruction in proper thinking.[57]

Hannah More, Wilberforce, Buxton, and their associates were imperial humanitarians because they defined their humanity by reference to a set of assumptions and values that served the larger interests of empire and the stability of the domestic social system, while not always having a religious base. Their assumptions were not often clearly expressed, but when they were revealed, it was sometimes in a remarkably honest manner. In 1818, Wilberforce wrote:

It is on the basis of religion alone that the prosperity of political communities, no less than individuals, must be founded. All the wise legislators of antiquity have held this doctrine, as well as the greatest writers of modern times. . . . The Roman state, which at last established its dominion over all the rest, was declared by the wisest and best . . . of its citizens, Cicero, to owe all its superiority to the fear of the gods; and it was not till the decay of this grand principle of religion that the decline of the state began. . . . And it is the glory of the religion which we English men profess, that it is friendly to true liberty—liberty combined with law and order.

Wilberforce was even more specific about the value of religion as a political tool when he concluded that "as the well being of every political community is intimately connected with the state of its morals so religion is the only sound and stable basis of morality."[58]

Words like law and order, which are used to clarify the definition of liberty, suggest that despite his belief in the personal value of Christianity, Wilberforce saw it as an absolutely vital support for the social system. The values that Christianity would inculcate were those that Hannah More taught to the poor at her Mendip schools: obedience, content- ment with one's station in life, honesty or obedience to law, chastity, diligence, and abstinence, all of which would deflect criticism away from the established order and towards the individual. The purport of this teaching was that it was better to resolve contradictions in the soul, not in the political arena, better for the individual and better for society.

As I have argued, this heavy attention paid to moral propaganda was essential to a relatively small upper class without the benefit of a professional police force or a standing army. Aside from being expensive, those institutions could always lead to the abuse of power by the people controlling them. The upper and middle classes wanted to control the lower orders, but they did not want to create threats to their own liberty at the same time. One approach to the problem of social control was the creation of a climate of opinion favorable to, or at least non-resistant to, aristocratic social and political goals.

The success of moral support for what was, in effect, a conservative counter-revolution seemed to Claphamites to rest heavily on the good example of the aristocracy. Wilberforce worried that the tremendous increase in the wealth and power of England in the late eighteenth century would lead to the moral atrophy of society's natural leaders and prove a dangerous example to the lower class. He saw the signs of such decay in morality all about him, and his *Practical View* was designed to combat it.[59] But the problem was worse than that the poor would copy the bad habits of the wealthy.

Edmund Burke was certainly no evangelical, but he was un- questionably concerned that the moral state of the people who counted reflect well on their God-given trust of rulership. In his attack on the French revolution, Burke had warned that the decline of religion in the natural leaders of society could prove contagious. They must be sincere in their faith. A religious pose, designed simply to keep the lower class in check, would be transparent and "would defeat the politic purpose they have in view." Besides, the great were in vital need of religion as a restraint on the greater opportunity for corruption that came with their station in life.[60]

Wilberforce, like Burke, worried that Britain's growing wealth might destroy the sound morality that had made it possible in the first place. The very success of the middle class, which was the backbone of the nation, put it in danger of spawning the traditional vices of the aristocracy. Contrasting the present age with an idealized past, Wilberforce complained: "Everywhere we may actually trace the effects of increasing wealth and luxury, in banishing one by one the habits, and new-modelling the phraseology, of stricter times; and in diffusing throughout the middle ranks those relaxed morals and dissipated manners, which were formerly confined to the higher classes of society."[61] The natural defense against the moral and social dangers of new wealth was that same Christianity that offered individual salvation. Its adherents proclaimed that it secured the individual's spiritual welfare to the extent that it was seriously cultivated, but incidentally, the more seriously it was followed in thought, word, and deed, the more convincing would its example appear. The more fervently the evangelical clung to the Christian life, the greater the proof that his actions were governed by moral principle rather than by material self-interest. This could have the ironic, and even unintentional, benefit of confusing social critics and promoting respect for the existing social order. By aiming at a spiritual goal, one could sometimes more truly strike a temporal target.

In prescribing a return to "serious" Christianity as a sound foundation for social health, the evangelicals believed that they were contributing to the creation of a healthier society. They defined the problems of the day in religious terms and saw their solution as naturally involving a return to vital religion. Despite its negative potential for the lower class, it was a positive, that is to say a constructive, project. But the humanitarians refused to do anything about the political and social origins of inequality; neither were they interested in the views or aspirations of the poor so far as they diverged from their own vision of the problems and responsibilities of the lower class. Poor folk could not possibly voice original, or even legitimate, political ideas. Valid political thought could only be that taught to them by their social betters, and working people who articulated ideas of their own were seen as desperate and dangerous.

Still, English reformers like William Cobbett missed the mark when they accused the humanitarians of hypocrisy for concerning themselves with the plight of the slaves in the distant Caribbean while ignoring the poor at home. Claphamites could be deeply moved by the plight of the English poor. Wilberforce was particularly active in this regard, engaged in the provision of some of the more basic needs of the indigent. During distress caused by poor harvests, Wilberforce was active dispensing food in his native Yorkshire. In 1796, he was one of a number of people who sponsored a soup kitchen in the parish of St. Marylebone. In the same year, he was involved in founding the Society for Bettering the Condition and Increasing the Comforts of the Poor.[62]

Reformers like Hannah More and the Clapham group hardly ignored the poor. They took vigorous action on their behalf, but while willing to relieve what they defined as honest suffering, they were concerned to discourage reliance on charity. Relief was to enable the temporarily distressed to get back on their feet, not a mechanism for redressing the wrongs of an inequitable system.[63] They were also in favor of a moderate measure of parliamentary reform, if only in order to avoid more radical measures in the future. What Cobbett objected to was their disregard for the political causes of lower-class distress and the patronizing approach to the working class that was inseparable from their benevolence.[64]

There were windows and gaps in humanitarian social attitudes that place their total sincerity in question. Despite their refusal to deal significantly with the socioeconomic roots of poverty, there were cases that demonstrated that abolitionists were capable of appreciating the connections between what they considered anti-social behavior and oppressive social conditions. They could realize that the social order could actually produce evils, but their appreciation was limited to what they regarded as exceptional cases in which society had malfunctioned. Generally, this was seen to be the result of a failure to apply enlightened views drawn from the plain truths of Christianity and the observation of human nature as revealed by philosophers such as John Locke.[65]

English anti-slavery exemplifies the Anglo-American belief in the sanctity of the individual as a corporate entity. This is a belief that unites Christian thinking with natural rights philosophy. If Christianity has so strong an appeal to the politically active middle class, one reason was that it seemed to coincide so well with their political, social, and scientific ideas. John Locke saw society as the combination of free agents in a union for mutual security. Each person limited his own absolute freedom in exchange for a certain protection against the depredations of others. Implied in his views was the assumption that the individual was the basic unit for political analysis. As a free agent, the individual was capable of understanding and complying with the demands of self-interest. Christianity presented much the same view in the doctrine of creation and free will. Man, as a free agent, had the ability and responsibility to determine to live in accordance with the rules of God, which were, of course, in his own self-interest. While the temptations of the devil could lead a person astray, that did not excuse him from deservedly suffering the consequences of his behavior.[66]

On the other hand, even Wilberforce recognized that there were exceptions to the rule of laissez-faire. There were cases in which society had created unnatural conditions that interfered with the individual's ability to be responsible. One of the most outstanding such examples was that of the criminal whose crimes could, in part, be laid at the door of social irresponsibility.

Thomas Fowell Buxton believed that everyone shared responsibility for the behavior of a certain class of criminal. In his *Inquiry Whether Crime and Misery Are Produced or Prevented by Our Present System of Prison Discipline* he explained that the existing system created criminals rather than the reformed citizens which it ought to produce. Picturing a youth imprisoned for a mild offense and subjected to the harsh regime of the English prison, where he is schooled in vice by fellow inmates, he wrote:

In this state of mind and body, at the expiration of his term of confinement, you throw him at once upon the town without a shilling in his pocket, his next meal depending upon the dexterious application of those lessons of fraud which have been his only recent acquirement. He must starve, or must rob; you have taken from him the means of honest labour, but you have initiated him into other and more gainful arts.[67]

While insisting that it is immoral to steal no matter what the circumstances—"true morality would tell them it is better to starve than to rob"—he clearly believed that such lofty moral behavior was virtually impossible for the lower orders.[68]

Repeat offenders like Buxton's youth could represent an exception to the law of corporate individuality because the anti-social acts that they committed were largely conditioned by the socially created institutions which further corrupted their characters. It followed that the only effective way to alter the behavior of ex-offenders was to alter the prison system.[69]

The abolitionists' reaction to slavery was similar to their reaction to prisons. An artificial environment because it was based neither on natural nor divine law, the prison was perhaps the closest thing in England to slave society. Even more than prisoners, slaves could not be expected to abide by notions of corporate individuality. They possessed no autonomy. It was unquestionable that society was to blame for their misery. Therefore, there could be no legitimate moral defense of the system. Like the prison, it rested on force and force alone.

The danger of ex-offenders committing violent acts was ever present in the disturbed conditions of early industrial England. Buxton saw the prison as a factory for the production of monsters who could at any moment destroy the hard-won security of good middle-class citizens by acts of violence. So much more justification and potential for violence existed in the Caribbean. There slaves rebelled again and again throughout the eighteenth century, on an average of every three years in the British Caribbean.[70] Evidence of their discontent and alienation existed as well in the slave societies of Spain and Portugal, a fact which is frequently ignored when considering the impact of insurrection on the imperial authorities. Evidence of the instability of slave society was hemispheric.

Who was to blame for all this insecurity? To blame the planters alone and to forget the imperial guns, ships, and wealth that backed them would be as unjust as it would be to blame the corruption of young prisoners on their jailers, forgetting that the judicial and legal establishment and the public will supported them. Britain and every Englishman living there shared in the guilt of slavery, and they would go on sharing in it until slavery was destroyed.

We should now be able to appreciate that slavery was attacked by English reformers for reasons similar to those that led them to attack vice, irreligion, and immorality in society at home. Like all of these weaknesses, slavery produced a dangerously unstable and immoral society. Like the prison, it rested exclusively on force and created deformed characters by educating them in immorality. The problem was that these characters were capable of armed revolt against the planters and, ultimately, Britain. For this reason, the Caribbean was a prime candidate for the counter-revolution.

NOTES

1. Clyde Kluckhohn, *Culture and Behavior* (New York: The Free Press, 1962), p. 73.

2. My discussion of culture draws on the following works, among others, A. L. Kroeber and Clyde Kluckhohn, "Culture: A Critical Review of Concepts and Definitions." Harvard University. Papers of the Peabody Museum of American Archaeology and Ethology, vol. 47; Alfred Kroeber, *Configurations of Culture Growth* (Berkeley: University of California Press, 1944); and the same authors', *The Nature of Culture* (Chicago: University of Chicago Press, 1952); Leslie White, *The Evolution of Culture* (New York: McGraw-Hill, 1958); J. Steward, *Theory of Culture Change* (Urbana: University of Illinois Press, 1955); Marvin Harris, *The Rise of Anthropological Theory* (New York: Thomas Y. Crowell, 1968); Rom Harre, *Social Being* (Totowa, N.J.: Littlefield, Adams, 1980); Ludwig Wittgenstein, *Philosophical Investigations* (New York: Macmillian, 1958); Wilfrid Sellars, *Science, Perception and Reality* (New York: Humanities Press, 1984).

3. Writing of the influence of evangelicals around the turn of the century, Sidney Checkland observed that "it may be that as part of an inherent tendency of a society to preserve itself, significant minorities will be generated who will assert the principles necessary for such reforms as are required for social coherence." *British Public Policy 1776-1939* (Cambridge: Cambridge University Press, 1983), p. 43.

4. On the Enlightenment, see Norman Hampson, *The Enlightenment* (Baltimore: Penguin Books, 1968); Ernst Cassirer, *The Philosophy of the Enlightenment* (Princeton, N.J.: Princeton University Press, 1951); Peter Gay, *The Enlightenment: An Interpretation*, 2 vols. (Princeton, N.J.: Princeton University Press, 1966); Ira O. Wade, *The Structure and Form of the French Enlightenment*, 2 vols. (Princeton, N.J.: Princeton University Press, 1977).

5. The literature on the civil rights movement is immense. Perhaps the best starting place is the classics by John Hope Franklin, *From Slavery to Freedom* (New York: Alfred A. Knopf, 1967); Robert H. Brisbane, *The Black Vanguard* (Valley Forge, Pa.: Judson Press, 1970); same author, *Black Activism* (Valley Forge, Pa.: Judson Press, 1974); C. Vann Woodward, *the Strange Career of Jim Crow* (New York: Oxford University Press, 1974); Robert L. Allen, *Black Awakening in Capitalist America* (New York: Doubleday, 1970).

6. Clarkson certainly saw the abolition movement as a campaign by an enlightened group to change the way people thought and acted. The faith behind Clarkson's efforts was the belief, common to the philosophes, that ignorance was the enemy of justice. One must simply make people aware of a problem and they would naturally act to resolve it. Thus Clarkson wrote that "I was sure that it was only necessary for the inhabitants of this favoured island to know it [the evil of the slave trade] to feel a just indignation against it." *The History of the . . . Abolition of the African Slave Trade . . . ,* 2 vols. (London: Frank Cass & Co., 1968), 1:320-321.

7. See Granville Sharp, A Declaration of the People's Natural Right to a Share in the Legislature (New York: Da Capo Press, 1971).

8. See R. R. Palmer, *The Age of Democratic Revolution,* 2 vols. (Princeton, N.J.: Princeton University Press, 1971); Roger Norman Buckley, *Slaves in Red Coats. The British West India Regiments, 1795-1815* (New Haven, Conn.: Yale University Press, 1979); J. W. Fortesque, *A History of the British Army,* 13 vols. (London: Macmillan, 1899-1930), 4:pt. 1.

9. Ian R. Christie, *Wars and Revolutions. Britain, 1769-1815* (Cambridge, Mass.: Harvard University Press, 1982), p. 158; J. Holland Rose, A. P. Newton, E. A. Benians, *The Cambridge History of the British Empire* (Cambridge: Cambridge University Press, 1940), vol. 2, *The Growth of the New Empire, 1783-1870,* pp. 2-5; V. T. Harlow, *The Founding of the Second British Empire 1763-1793,* 2 vols. (Cambridge: Cambridge University Press, 1964), 2:783-784.

10. Ibid., 1:648; 2:785, 795, 799-800, 129; Grenville to Dorchester, 20 Oct. 1789, in Holland Rose et al., *Cambridge History,* 1:21.

11. Ibid., p. 129. For a negative view, see V. G. Kiernan, *The Lords of Human Kind* (Harmondsworth, England: Penguin Books, 1972).

12. See Paul E. Lovejoy, *Transformations in Slavery: A History of Slavery in Africa* (Cambridge: Cambridge University Press, 1983), chap. 8; A. G. Hopkins, *An Economic History of West Africa* (New York: Columbia University Press, 1973); Philip D. Curtin, *Economic Change in Pre-Colonial Africa,* 2 vols. (Madison: University of Wisconsin Press, 1975).

13. Viscountess Knutsford, *Life and Letters of Zachary Macaulay* (London: Edward Arnold, 1900), pp. 19-20; Christopher Fyfe, *A History of Sierra Leone* (London: Oxford University Press, 1963); Folarian Shyllon, *Black Slaves in Britain* (London: Oxford University Press, 1974).

14. Thomas Fowell Buxton, *The African Slave Trade: The Remedy* (London: Frank Cass & Co., 1968), pp. 301-339.

15. Ian Bradley, *The Call to Seriousness* (London: Jonathan Cape, 1976), pp. 74-75.

16. See especially Samir Amin, *Unequal Development* (New York: Monthly Review Press, 1976); the same author, *Neocolonialism in West Africa* (New York: Monthly Review Press, 1973); and Walter Rodney, *How Europe Underdeveloped Africa* (Washington, D.C.: Howard University Press, 1981) for a formulation of this thesis.

17. See Chapter 2.

18. Eric Stokes, *The English Utilitarians and India* (Oxford: Oxford University Press, 1959), pp. 27, 28, 158-159; C. H. Philips, *The East India Company 1784-1834* (New York: Barnes & Noble, 1961); James Mill, *The History of British India,* abr. William Thomas (Chicago; University of Chicago Press, 1975).

19. Ainslie Thomas Embree, *Charles Grant and British Rule in India* (New York: Columbia University Press, 1962), pp. 118-119, 142.

20. William Wilberforce, *Substance of the Speeches of William Wilberforce, Esq. on the Clause in the East India Bill for Promoting the Religious Instruction and Moral Improvement of the Natives of the British Dominions in India, on the 22 of June, and the 1st and 12th of July* 1813 (n.p., n.d.), pp. 55, 78.

21. Stokes, *English Utilitarians,* pp. 31-34.

22. Robert Isaac Wilberforce and Samuel Wilberforce, *The Correspondence of William Wilberforce,* 2 vols. (London: n.p., 1840), 2:343. See the passage from Charles Trevelyan's *The Education of the People of India,* quoted by Stokes in *English Utilitarians,* pp. 46-47, where Trevelyan argues that the only effective way to secure the Indian empire was to Europeanize the population.

23. Robert Isaac Wilberforce and Samuel Wilberforce, *Correspondence* 2:341.

24. This section is based on the works of the Clapham humanitarians cited in the bibliography. I have also found the following modern studies to be helpful: Bradley, *Call to Seriousness,* (London: Jonathan Cape, 1976). G. R. A. Balleine, *A History of the Evangelical Party in the Church of England* (London: Longmans, Green, 1933); M. Hennell, *John Venn and the Clapham Sect* (London: Lutterworth Press, 1958); Earnest

Marshall Howse, *Saints in Politics* (Toronto: University of Toronto Press, 1952); Elizabeth Jay, *The Religion of the Heart* (Oxford: Oxford University Press, 1979).

25. Howse, *Saints,* p. 15.

26. Robin Furneaux, *William Wilberforce* (London: Hamish Hamilton, 1974), p. 117.

27. Howse, *Saints,* pp. 15-16; Anthony Armstrong, *The Church of England: The Methodists and Society 1700-1850* (London: University of London Press, 1973), pp. 131-132; Standish Meacham, *Henry Thornton of Clapham 1760-1815* (Cambridge: Mass.: Harvard University Press, 1964), pp. 27-48.

28. Howse, *Saints,* pp. 16-17; Ainslie Thomas Embree, *Charles Grant and British Rule in India* (New York: Columbia University Press, 1964), pp. 27-48.

29. Howse, *Saints,* pp. 19-21; Elizabeth Jay, *The Evangelical and Oxford Movements* (Cambridge: Cambridge University Press, 1983); Denis Gray, *Spencer Perceval* (Manchester: Manchester University Press, 1963).

30. Elie Halevy, *England in 1815* (London: Ernest Benn, 1960).

31. This section draws on the following works: S. Maccoby, *English Radicalism 1786-1832* (London: George Allen & Unwin, 1955); Malcolm I. Thomis, *Threats of Revolution in Britain 1789-1848* (Hamden, Conn.: Shoe String Press, Archon Books, 1977); Carl B. Cone, *The English Jacobins* (New York: Charles Scribner's Sons, 1968); Norman Gash, *Aristocracy and People. Britain 1815-1865* (Cambridge, Mass.: Harvard University Press, 1979); Robert R. Dozier, *For King, Constitution, and Country: The English Loyalists and the French Revolution* (Lexington: University Press of Kentucky, 1983); Albert Goodwin, *The Friends of Liberty: The English Democratic Movement in the Age of the French Revolution* (Cambridge, Mass.: Harvard University Press, 1979); Christie, *Wars and Revolutions.*

32. George LeFebvre, *The French Revolution,* 2 vols. (New York: Columbia University Press, 1965); Palmer, *Democratic Revolution.*

33. Francois Crouzet, *The First Industrialists* (Cambridge: Cambridge University Press, 1985), chap. 5.

34. Palmer, *Democratic Revolution,* 1:4-7.

35. Jacques Godeschot, *France and the Atlantic Revolution of the Eighteenth Century, 1770-1799* (New York: The Free Press, 1965). Unlike Palmer and Hobsbawm, Godeschot includes the Caribbean in the Age of Revolution. See pp. 142-144.

36. Eric J. Hobsbawm, *The Age of Revolution 1789-1848* (New York: Mentor Books, 1962).

130   Moral Imperium

37. Palmer, *Democratic Revolution,* 1:485.

38. E. R. Norman, *Church and Society in England 1770-1970* (Oxford: Clarendon Press, 1976), chap. 1; Armstrong, *Church of England,* pp. 150-152; R. A. Soloway, *Prelates and People* (London: Routledge & Kegan Paul, 1969), p. 56; Martin J. Wiener, ed., *Humanitarianism or Social Control* (Houston: Rice University), Rice University Studies, vol. 67, no. 1 (Winter 1981).

39. Bradley, *Call to Seriousness,* pp. 74-77, 97; Armstrong, *Church of England,* p. 127.

40. Pollock, *Wilberforce,* p. 38.

41. Sir James Stephen, *Essays in Ecclesiastical Biography* (London: Longman, Green, Longman, & Roberts, 1860), pp. 484-485.

42. Robert Isaac Wilberforce and Samuel Wilberforce, *The Life of William Wilberforce,* 5 vols. (London: John Murray, 1839), 1:91-92.

43. James Stephen, *The Memoirs of James Stephen* (London: Berington Hogarth Press, 1957), pp. 84-135, 26; Bradley, *Call to Seriousness,* pp. 54-55.

44. Stephen, *Memoirs,* pp. 271, 280-283, 297.

45. Charles Buxton, ed., *Memoirs of Sir Thomas Fowell Buxton* (Philadelphia: Henry Longstretch, 1849), p. 32.

46. Ibid., pp. 40, 37-47.

47. Ibid., pp. 15, 21.

48. See the discussion in Chapter 1. See also David Brion Davis, *Slavery and Human Progress* (Oxford: Oxford University Press, 1984).

49. William Wilberforce, *A Practical View of the Prevailing Religious System of Professed Christians . . .* (Dublin: n.p., 1801), pp. vii, 40.

50. Ibid., pp. 291-300.

51. Ibid., pp. 291-300.

52. Ford K. Brown, *Fathers of the Victorians* (London: Cambridge University Press, 1961), p. 141.

53. William Roberts, *Memoirs of the Life and Correspondence of Mrs. Hannah More,* 2 vols. (New York: Harper & Bros., 1842), 1:345, 346.

54. Ibid., 2:366, 367-368; M. G. Jones, *Hannah More* (Cambridge: Cambridge University Press, 1952), pp. 138, 142.

55. Wilberforce, *Life,* 1:94.

56. Bradley, *Call to Seriousness,* p.46.

57. Roberts, *More,* 2:72-73.

58. Wilberforce, *Correspondence,* 1:370-371; A. Aspinall, ed., *The Latter Correspondence of George III* (Cambridge: Cambridge University Press, 1960), 3:418; Wilberforce, *Life,* 2:360-365; Halevy, *England in 1815,* pp. 435-436; J. Steven Watson, *The Reign of George III 1760-1815* (London: Oxford University Press, 1964), pp. 353-355.

59. Wilberforce, *Practical View,* pp. 270-271.

60. Edmund Burke, *Reflections on the Revolution in France* (Baltimore: Penguin Books, 1969), pp. 200-201, 186-187, 372.

61. Wilberforce, *Practical View,* pp. 268, 271; Wilberforce, *Life,* 1:219, 220.

62. Pollock, *Wilberforce,* pp. 141-142.

63. Soloway, *Prelates and People,* pp. 19-20, 56; Norman, *Church and Society,* p. 25; E. P. Thompson, *The Making of the English Working Class* (New York: Vintage Books, 1963), p. 56.

64. Wilberforce, *Life,* 5:414-416. For Cobbett's views on Wilberforce and the Clapham Sect, see William Reitzel, ed., *The Autobiography of William Cobbett* (London: Faber & Faber, 1967), pp. 94, 109-110; George Spater, *William Cobbett,* 2 vols. (Cambridge: Cambridge University Press, 1982), 1:203, 370; Daniel Green, *Great Cobbett* (London: Hodder & Stoughton, 1983), p. 219; G.D.H. Cole, *The Life of William Cobbett* (London: W. Collins Sons, 1927), p. 275.

65. See John Locke, *Of Civil Government* (London: J. M. Dent & Sons, 1947).

66. Wilberforce, *Correspondence,* 2:346.

67. Thomas Fowell Buxton, *An Inquiry Whether Crime and Misery Are Produced or Prevented by Our Present System of Prison Discipline* (London: John Hatchard, 1818).

68. Ibid., pp. 70-71.

69. Ibid., p. 54.

70. Mary Reckord, "The Jamaican Slave Rebellion of 1831," *Past and Present* no. 40, July 1968, pp. 108-125.

5

The Dangers of Slavery

One of the ways by which we confirm a positive image of ourselves as Western people is the celebration of the triumph of
reason and knowledge over ignorance, superstition, and cruelty.
For all of our increased sophistication over our ancestors, we
continue to be tinged with the enlightenment's faith in the
compelling power of knowledge. We like to think that once we
are made fully aware of injustice, we act with all reasonable
speed to remove its source.

By this simple faith we renew our self-image as rational and
humane people. Because this is often an accurate picture, we
may sometimes forget what being made aware of a social
problem means. Social knowledge is not like knowledge to the
solution to a problem in logic. Social knowledge partakes of the
political. It is not particularly susceptible to objectification, but
must be appreciated in terms of the social environment from
which it emerges. Injustice is not an objective entity, but the
conception of a social process. Although it is commonplace to
observe that one man's injustice is another man's good, it is
nonetheless true. Justice is a question of perspective, on which
there is often disagreement.

When one personally suffers an injustice, there is an
immediate and clear rationale for action to resolve it. The

problem of injustice arises when one attempts to convince others that an injustice has been done and that one deserves their support in the effort to address it. To do this entails persuading them to see things from one's own point of view. This can be done by presenting them with cogent arguments supported by mutually accepted evidence, but it is frequently necessary to draw attention to what is being argued by some sort of action. This is particularly the case when the injustice involves a political group. Here it is essential, first of all, to get people to listen, and the fallacy in our popular image of how we end up responding to wrong is that it assumes an automatic sympathy between the wronged and the respondent.

More typically, our attention is drawn to a problem by some unpleasantness associated with it. Thus, to use the analogy of the civil rights movement, black Americans began the movement by vigorous action against the policy of segregation. This "civil disobedience" led to arrests, violence against blacks, and media coverage, which eventually gained a hearing for the views that black activists were propounding. The constitutional arguments, which appealed to some of the fundamental principles on which the nation was built, convinced many of the need for reform. But it is essential to keep in mind that congressional action, made possible by the construction of a public consensus, was only ensured by maintaining constant pressure on the government.

The conviction that something in society is unjust, therefore, is more complex than a simple springing to mind of a vivid impression on hearing of a wrong. It involves the seeing of some portion of social reality in a new way and often occurs only because we have been "forced" to do so in order to deal effectively with a threat to ourselves, either material or cultural. One of the traditional reasons for celebrating the English anti-slavery movement was that it seemed to ignore this pattern. So, for generations of historians and idealists, Wilberforce and the wider anti-slavery campaign have been seen as disinterested reformers whose interest in the Caribbean and slavery was sparked by their intense religious faith, forgetting, of course, that religious faith is related to society. What made it even more remarkable is that there is so little evidence for any such occurrence anywhere else in history. But instead of suggesting the need for a fresh interpretation of anti-slavery, this has tended to reinforce the view that it represented the triumph of disinterested benevolence. The interpretation rests on accepting at face value the professions of altruism made by sophisticated upper-middle-class reformers. In addition, it misses the opportunity to look closely at the sociopolitical dimensions of altruism and benevolence. We can, however, begin with what the humanitarians said they believed, and believed that they were doing, and still end up with an interpretation of anti-slavery that sees it as a cultural response to a sociopolitical problem.

Early anti-slavery activity in England did not occur in Clapham, but was the concern of a Clapham associate. Granville Sharp represented, in a sense, the intersection of two worlds. A known and respected member of society, he was also a patron of the black poor of London. It was, in fact, his intervention on their behalf that got him directly involved in anti-slavery activity. Like Lisbon and Madrid in the sixteenth century, London had its population of blacks that had grown up out of the English involvement with the slave trade and slavery.[1] For the most part, these black Englishmen lived among the poor, followed similar occupations, and sometimes intermarried with the English.[2] Few ever achieved notoriety. Those like Gustavus Vassa, who published his autobiography, and Ottobah Cugoano, author of an anti-slavery tract, were outstanding exceptions to the rule of general anonymity. These men were, not surprisingly, leaders of the black community and, as such, early leaders in the struggle for civil rights and equality.

It was from this Afro-English community that one of the strongest pressures for anti-slavery action first emerged. It was blacks who had escaped from their masters and lived at large in London in a precarious freedom who brought the issue of slavery from the intellectual plane to the political stage. It is here, as well, that we see the intersection of black activism and the cultural predisposition of some Englishmen to act against slavery.

One of the earliest formulations of an anti-slavery thesis by an Englishman was made by Granville Sharp. Most of Sharp's work was abstract and directed to influencing judicial opinion in cases pending before the bench. Just such a piece is the historically important tract *A Representation of the Injustice and Dangerous Tendency of Tolerating Slavery in England* (1796). This classic of abolitionist literature was based on extensive research into the history of slavery in English law and marks a stage in the development of English anti-slavery. What is infrequently noted is that Sharp composed the essay while in the midst of defending himself against a heavy lawsuit.

In 1765, Jonathan Strong, the slave of one David Lisle of Barbados, sought out the medical services of William Sharp, a London surgeon. Strong had been subjected to continual violent assaults by his master, who had beaten him on the head with a pistol. Strong was cared for by both William and Granville Sharp, who did not then seem to be aware that he was a slave. Sometime after Strong had regained his health, he was spotted by Lisle, who had him seized and placed in custody. Remembering the benevolent brothers who had helped him once before, Strong sent for Granville, who investigated the situation and eventually was able to secure Strong's release.

This action by Granville Sharp depended, of course, on his predisposition towards benevolence, but it was most emphatically initiated by Jonathan Strong in his quest for freedom and in his wisdom in calling on Sharp, who responded as Strong had hoped he would.[3] But it was a further complication that pushed Sharp into print, when some days after Strong's release, David Lisle charged him in a heavy suit.

Sharp was called upon on other occasions as well. In 1768, he aided the black Hylas, whose wife had been kidnapped and was to be shipped to the West Indies and sold as a slave.[4] In 1770, he was called on to assist in the freeing of the black Thomas Lewis. Lewis, who was attempting to live in London as a free man, was dragged on board a ship bound for Jamaica. Friends of the victim alerted anti-slavery sympathizers, and Sharp, who by now had a reputation for aiding Africans, was applied to. The slave was eventually released.[5] The 1783 case of the ship *Zong* on which slaves were murdered in an attempt to gain the insurance on them, moved the humanitarian network to action but not before the African community had brought the atrocity to their attention. Thus Sharp noted in his diary for March 19: "Gustavus Vasa, a Negro, called on me, with an account of one hundred and thirty Negroes thrown alive into the sea, from on board an English slave ship." Sharp moved on the next day to bring the culprits to justice.[6]

It was a complication arising out of the Jonathan Strong affair that pushed Sharp into print against slavery, when sometime after Strong's release, David Lisle charged Sharp for damages.[7] At the beginning of his defense efforts, Sharp sought legal advice on what he regarded as the key issue, the legality of slavery in England and was referred to the traditional widsom since 1729 that slaves arriving in Great Britain or Ireland from His Majesty's plantations did not thereupon become free men. What made matters appear worse was that Lord Chief Justice Mansfield, who would try the case, was of the same opinion.

In order to prepare an adequate defense, Sharp undertook extensive researches into English law. His painstaking work led him to conclude that, contrary to accepted wisdom, the law of England did not support slavery. There was, he believed, neither statute nor precedent in favor of human bondage. Sharp argued that, on the contrary, the judiciary had customarily acted on the principle of presumptive freedom. Throughout English history, justices of the peace had generally acted in favor of those claiming wrongful enslavement. "Therefore, it must appear," he wrote, "that slavery is by no means tolerated in this island, either by the law or custom of England." Unless the master had a written contract indicating voluntary bondage, he had no power over the person of the slave which was recognized in law.

Anticipating the argument that English law did not apply to the African race, Sharp answered significantly that the law of England did not mention race or color, only subjects:

So that, though he may have been a slave, and (according to the custom of the colonies) accounted the private property of his master, before he came to England, yet these circumstances make no alteration in his human nature; for every Negro slave, being undoubtedly either man, women, or child; he or she, immediately upon their arrival in England, becomes the King's property in the relative sense before mentioned, and cannot, therefore, be "out of the King's protection."[8]

Citing statute, he argued that all men of whatever estate have the right to the benefit of the king's justice. There is no distinction drawn between black men and white men or between slave and free. To Sharp, the significant point was that the statute mentioned only men; therefore, blacks were included.[9]

Sharp was clear that blacks were as fully human as were Europeans. He is "undoubtedly either man, woman, or child," of the same species as Englishmen. As English law did not specifically exclude Negroes from its protection, their enslavement could not be upheld by it.

Sharp believed that the English constitutional tradition guaranteed English liberty. Slavery represented a distortion of that tradition, the introduction of an alien element into the English commonwealth. Slavery could continue to exist only if its contradiction to English law were ignored. But eventually, the acceptance of slavery for blacks could establish a precedent in which liberty was sacrificed to tyranny. A *Representation* centered on this danger to English liberty inherent in the tolerance of slavery.

For Granville Sharp, the unrestrained rule of one man over many undermined the principles of individual responsibility on which British society was built. Therefore, in slave societies, human beings were reduced to the level of animals. They were allowed no purpose beyond service to their masters. This state of affairs was directly opposed to the English conception of liberty as a state in which one was free to accommodate oneself to one's environment in the most beneficial manner. That freedom was guaranteed by impartial laws which protected each person against coercion by the will of others. Neither the mob nor a wealthy elite could prevail against the power of the law.[10]

Sharp was afraid that if slavery were allowed to exist in England, a bias would come to be formed in its favor. If it were ever to flourish under the protection afforded by race prejudice, slavery might soon overwhelm the commonwealth. "The evil may take root; precedent and custom will too soon be pleaded in its behalf." Appeal to the precedent of the enslavement of black men might be used as justification for the enslavement of whites.

The toleration of slavery would lead to the rise of a class of men who were withdrawn from the control of government and law but who were directly controlled by their masters. This situation could promote the formation of a master class, whose power base was removed from public regulation. Such an unrestrained power, similar to the late Medieval barons with their private retainers, could upset the foundations of royal government and create "a general bondage of the common people" to the powerful.[11]

In Sharp's formulation, then, slavery threatened danger to the liberty of Englishmen. But it also threatened to corrupt their characters, of which liberty was an essential support. For Sharp, the most important foundation of English society was Christianity, a religion which the abolitionists believed taught the integrity, responsibility, and unquestionable value of each individual. They believed that Christianity mandated a social system which enshrined its vision of man, a vision in which there was no room for slavery.

The trial of the slave Somersett provided the opportunity for the elaboration of Sharp's views on the relationship between slavery and Christianity. An essay by Thomas Thompson, *The African Trade for Negro Slaves Shown to Be Consistent with Principles of Humanity and with the Laws of Revealed Religion*, drew from Sharp a critique designed to forestall its use in support of arguments against Somersett's bid for freedom. After completion of his argument against Thompson, Sharp went on to search the scriptures for material which could be construed as a defense of slavery. The result of his efforts was published in 1776 in the form of four tracts constituting a defense of Christianity against the imputation that it was pro-slavery.[12]

In *An Essay on Slavery,* Sharp challenged Thompson's contention that slave trading was consistent with the law of nature because it was recognized by the Jewish constitution. Sharp objected that the Jewish constitution itself was not entirely consistent with the law of nature, but in some aspects ran counter to moral law and natural equity. He pointed out that the allegation that the Jewish constitution supported slavery was based on a supposed divine permission to Hebrews to enslave strangers.[13] But this claim could have no relevance for

Christians because the Christian dispensation which taught universal benevolence abrogated Jewish law. The demands of benevolence negated the significance of ethnicity or nationality and entailed the inclusion of all men in a community of spirit.

Sharp dismissed Thompson's attempt to use the authority of St. Paul in support of slavery, explaining St. Paul's failure to develop a thoroughgoing condemnation of slavery by the fact that it was protected by the state. He argued that under this circumstance, condemnation might have caused unrest among the slaves, encouraging them to strive after temporal rather than spiritual rewards.[14]

In *The Law of Passive Obedience,* Sharp emphasized his point that slavery and Christianity could not be reconciled. He maintained that, although early Christianity had taught the slave to obey his master, teaching was unintelligible unless it was placed in historical perspective. Sharp contended that the early Christians were not concerned with social reform or with suffering in a world they believed would soon pass away, but with the cultivation of the immortal soul. In this context, slaves taught to obey their masters were instructed in nothing more than the vital Christian doctrine of the liberating power of returning love for hate. Such teachings enhanced the slave's humanity.[15] On the other hand, Sharp argued, the master who claimed to be a Christian committed a gross sin in attempting to enforce a right of ownership over a being belonging to God.[16] Masters were as obliged as were slaves to return love for hate. But because slavery could not exist without the physical and psychological coercion of slaves by their masters, Christians could not really be slaveholders.

In *The Law of Liberty, or, Royal Law by Which All Mankind Will Certainly Be Judged!* Sharp summed up his argument on slavery and Christianity. Slavery violated the golden rule. "We cannot say of any slave holder that he doth not to another what he would not have done to himself."[17] This rule is at the heart of Christianity. Its violation diminished one's right to be called a Christian. Because England supported slavery and the slave trade, Sharp was fearful that its sin would in time provoke divine retribution.[18] The only way to attain national reformation was by abolition.

Sharp's visions of a national guilt deriving from the slave trade was shared by William Wilberforce. Probably the best-known abolitionist, Wilberforce led the parliamentary campaign against the British and foreign slave trade. He was a leader in evangelical circles, gaining a reputation for piety and humanity by his exemplary life and support for worthy causes.[19] Wilberforce's social activism was so extensive that at one time he was a contributor to sixty-nine societies, a patron of one, vice-president of twenty-nine, treasurer of one, governor of five, and a committee member of five.[20]

Not content with work on behalf of reform societies, Wilberforce sought to influence public opinion by writing and speaking. In 1823, he published his most substantial denunciation of slavery, *An Appeal to the Religion, Justice, and Humanity of the Inhabitants of the British Empire on Behalf of the Negro Slaves in the West Indies.* In this work, Wilberforce called on all Englishmen with respect for justice and feelings of humanity to support the mitigation and gradual elimination of slavery.

Because planters had accused abolitionists of radicalism, Wilberforce was concerned to demonstrate that abolition had nothing to do with ideas of the *Rights of Man* variety. He argued that it would be wrong to associate the emancipation of the slaves with the release of the subject from the obligations of loyalty, the ties of law, and social deference. The freeing of the slave is, on the contrary, only a matter of extending the blessings of English law and constitution to cover English colonial subjects. Discussing the conservative proposals of Secretary Dundas for gradual emancipation, he wrote: "And by whom was this proposal made? Was it by some hot-headed enthusiast some speculative votary of the rights of man? No: by the late Lord Melville, then Mr. Dundas, . . . to whom no one ever imputed an extravagant zeal for speculative rights or modern theories."[21] To bolster his claim that anti-slavery was safe, Wilberforce marshalled out the authority of Edmund Burke. Pointing out that Burke was an abolitionist and in fact developed a plan for gradual emancipation, he concluded that "his authority will at least absolve those who now undertake the cause of the Negro slaves, from the imputation of harshly and unwarrantably disturbing a wholesome and legitimate system of civil subordination."[22] Having identified himself and anti-slavery with conservative principles, Wilberforce formulated his critique of slavery.

In the past, abolitionists had concentrated almost exclusively on the treatment of the slaves. Wilberforce explained that this was because in the beginning, their objective was to destroy the slave trade, in the belief that the treatment of slaves would improve once the planters were deprived of the African slave market. However, abolition did not bring amelioration, and it was now important to realize that over and above the question of treatment per se, "there exists essentially in the system itself, from various causes, a natural tendency toward the maximum of labor, and the minimum of food and other comforts." Wilberforce found that even worse than the physical degradation was the intellectual and moral decline of the black because this undermined the basis for a healthy society. Emphasizing his belief that slavery rested on a foundation of ignorance and superstition, Wilberforce reminded his readers that, ironically, this most outrageous symptom of the system was used as one of its defenders' favorite arguments in support of the alleged inferiority of Africans. But the environment, not heredity, was at work here. The system of slavery worked inexorably to depress the slaves "below the level of human beings" so that even an educated man like Edward Long could, with some seriousness, compare them with orangutans.[23]

Wilberforce placed major blame for the degenerate condition of slave society on its laws. Because those laws regarded blacks as chattels, they removed from the blacks all hope for the development of a settled life and destroyed all incentive for the slaves to form attachments to the communities in which they lived. These laws rested on the assumption that blacks could not be governed by "hope of reward, or the fear of punishment," as others were, but only by the threat and application of physical force. For that reason, the whip became the emblem of authority, and slaves were driven to work like animals. But to Wilberforce, such an approach to social control was clearly counterproductive. It tended to foster progressive social degeneracy, which was not a sound basis for a healthy society. If their present treatment continued, blacks would never achieve moral or intellectual improvement.[24]

In this connection, the greatest wrong perpetrated by the slave regime was the suppression of religion, which alone was sufficient to call down the condemnation of heaven on the slave owners and their supporters. Wilberforce argued that the laws passed by the island assemblies, which ostensibly aimed at the cultivation of religion, in fact did little more than camouflage its serious neglect. He pointed out that Sunday, which is supposed to be reserved for religious instruction, is the only day allowed the slaves for work on their provision grounds. Even the dedicated missionaries who went out to the colonies to spread truth and light were persecuted by planters, who were determined to discourage, rather than to spread, Christianity among their people.[25]

Nor did the metropolis escape its share of responsibility for the sins of slavery. Wilberforce insisted that, although the planters might be the perpetrators, all Englishmen were responsible for the state of affairs in the Caribbean, which they have allowed to continue under the support of Britain.[26]

Ironically, the abolitionists bore a particular blame from Wilberforce's perspective because their initial strategy led indirectly to the perpetuation of slavery. An incorrect assessment of the situation in the islands led them to select the slave trade, rather than the institution of slavery itself, as the target of anti-slavery activity in the 1780s. Their assumption that the destruction of the trade and the consequent drying up of the supply of African laborers would lead the planters to improve the condition of the remaining stock proved wrong, when after 1807 little was done to mitigate the harshness of the institution.[27] "And is it to societies consisting of such elements as these," Wilberforce asked, "that a humane and enlightened legislature can conscientiously delegate its duties as to religious and moral reforms?"[28] In full awareness of this state of affairs, it is the responsibility of the imperial government to assume the duty of re-ordering colonial society, so as to bring it in line with the principles of sound policy.

Sensitive to the charge of idealism, Wilberforce insisted that virtue and national interest coincided in the reform of slave society. British West Indian society was corrupt, and therefore a source of weakness to the empire. The colonies must be reformed not only for the benefit of the slaves, but also for the good of

England. Wilberforce explained the coincidence of interest and virtue when he wrote:

At such an enlightened period as this, when commerce herself adopts the principles of true morality, and becomes liberal and benevolent, will it be believed that the almighty has rendered the depression and misery of the cultivators of the soil in our West-Indian Colonies necessary, or even conducive, to their prosperity and safety? No surely . . . ultimately, the comfort of the labourer, and the well-being of those who have to enjoy the fruits of his labour will be found to be coincident.[29]

God had so constructed the world that the interests of the material welfare of England would not be harmed, but secured by the amelioration of slavery.

Wilberforce's religious language can hide much of the social significance of his formulations. Fortunately, he also demonstrated that there were clear political and military reasons for reforming slave society as soon as possible. The slaves of the British colonies were surrounded by similar communities of Africans in Brazil, Cuba, and Puerto Rico. The instability of these societies contributed to the danger of rebellion in the English colonies. Wilberforce thought that this problem was exacerbated by the proximity of Haitian blacks, who were skilled in the use of arms and had a revolutionary tradition. Pointing to the Haitian example and to the example of emancipation in many of the northern states of the United States, as well as in parts of South America, he asked his countrymen, "Is this a time, are these the circumstances, in which it can be wise and safe, if it were even honest and humane, to keep down in their present state of heathenism and almost brutish degradation, the 800,000 Negroes in our West-Indian colonies?"[30]

Here was a clear connection between social degradation in the sugar colonies and social instability. To leave the African in his "brutish" state was to court the danger of servile war. Wilberforce argued that the way to build secure communities in the Caribbean was through reforms that would elevate the Negroes to a condition in which they would be fit for freedom. The English should give the slaves something worth working and fighting for, "implant in them the principle of hope—let free

scope be given for their industry, and for their rising in life by
their personal good conduct—give them an interest in defending
the community to which they belong."[31] This fostering of hope
would be accompanied by instruction in the principles of the
Christian religion, which, as we have seen, Wilberforce regarded
as the foundation of social health. In lines which might have
been written by Burke, he wrote that "taught by Christianity,
they will sustain with patience the sufferings of their actual lot."
In this way, the slaves would pass from being the weakness, and
at times the terror, of their communities to become "the
strength of the communities in which they live."[32]

Wilberforce concluded with a warning, which, as we shall see,
expressed his conception of the relationship of ruler and ruled.
"Power," he wrote, "always implies responsibility; and the
possessor of it cannot innocently be neutral, when by his exertion
moral good may be promoted, or evil lessened or removed."[33] The
responsibility of which he wrote turned out in practice to be the
guiding of colonial social development in a direction consistent
with imperial goals.

One of the most prolific anti-slavery writers was Thomas
Clarkson. His abolitionist activity pre-dated that of Wilberforce,
Stephen, Buxton, and Macaulay, and he remained active in the
field well into the 1840s. Clarkson composed perhaps the best
known of all abolitionist tracts, *An Essay on the Slavery and
Commerce of the Human Species*. It was originally a Latin
dissertation which won first prize at Cambridge University.
Later, in the midst of the struggle against the slave trade,
Clarkson decided on its publication as a weapon in the campaign
for abolition. It appeared in revised form in 1786, a year before
the formation of the Society for Effecting the Abolition of the
Slave Trade.[34]

Clarkson began by summarizing the traditional justification
for slavery. Arguing that ancient usage had always had a
tendency to establish a bias in favor of the presumed justice of
custom, he explained that the antiquity and universality of
slavery lent it the justification of tradition. In the case of human
bondage, however, we are led by native sensibility to question
the justice of the institution on reflecting that the enslaved are
people like ourselves, capable of sensation and aspiration. Our

natural feelings of humanity are aroused to sympathy for the slave and come into contradiction to custom, so that with slavery, convention and natural sentiment are directly opposed.[35]

It was Clarkson's belief that modern slavery differed qualitatively from its ancestral forms. Plantation slavery was alleged by its defenders to be based "in great measure on the principles of antiquity." But the slavery into which the African had been plunged could not be justified by any of the traditional rationales for bondage. African slaves in the plantations were not legitimate prisoners of war, nor debtors, nor criminals produced by legitimate judicial processes. On the contrary, this modern form of slavery led to social disruption in Africa instead of serving as a mechanism by which to vent undesirable social elements.

"The great taste, which the Africans have acquired for European commodities particularly spirits," wrote Clarkson, "and the ready sale, which is found for the human species through the whole of their extensive continent have tempted the strong to seize upon the weak, the cunning, to lay snares for the unwary, and the rich to circumvent the poor."[36] Wars between African peoples were now simply another means of obtaining slaves. Enslavement became a common sentence for crimes. Laws were designed to make infractions unavoidable in order to increase the pool of potential slaves, and raiding for the production of captives became a way of life.[37]

Clarkson maintained that Europe was ultimately responsible for the degradation of Africa caused by the slave trade. Europeans had offered the African the opportunity for wealth based on the capture and sale of human beings, thus tempting them into a commerce which Christian Europe knew to be sinful and which, Clarkson implied, was beyond the moral character of the African to resist. Yet, from Clarkson's perspective, the knowledge that only European demand perpeturated the slave trade was perhaps an even greater condemnation of the civilized continent than the already barbarous act of having initiated it.

Clarkson was led to indict Europe for the distruption of African society because he shared the belief common to abolitionists that, as Wilberforce put it, "power always implies responsibility." If Europe had the power to alter the life of primitive communities, then it also had the responsibility to do so in a morally progressive and politic manner. Nevertheless, Europe had pursued the opposite course, and its actions raised the question of whether it was a civilized society after all.

In the view of the humanitarians, the greatest crime for which Great Britain could be blamed was a by-product of the slave trade. By blocking normal social development in Africa, the slave trade frustrated the growth of Christianity there, which one could expect to emerge in the course of social evolution. For Clarkson, this outcome represented the perversion of the behavior that Christianity enjoined on its adherents. While Christian nations ought to lead less civilized societies out of their pagan darkness and into the way of light, the English had joined their Iberian predecessors in forcing Africa into an ignorance and savagery even more profound than the state in which the Europeans had found it.[38]

Clarkson made it clear that the slave trade was merely the tip of the iceberg and its abolition, only the opening act in the drama of full emancipation. The selection of the trade as the target for the first anti-slavery crusade was explained in terms familiar to Wilberforce, "for what was more reasonable than to suppose that, when masters could no longer obtain slaves from Africa or elsewhere, they would be compelled individually, by a sort of inevitable necessity, or a fear of Consequences, or by a sense of their own interest to take better care of those whom they might then have in their possession."[39] That hope was shattered after 1807, when the condition of the slaves remained essentially unchanged.

From Clarkson's viewpoint, the most significant failure of the amelioration campaign was that the slave's status in point of law remained virtually the same, so that the arbitrary power of the master remained. Good masters treated slaves well, bad masters, with cruelty; all was caprice in which no mechanism existed to enforce a common pattern of acceptable conduct. Accordingly, the most pressing need was for a change in the legal condition of the bondsmen. Caribbean society must be reformed so that the rule of law "binding upon all, by means of which the Negroes in our islands shall have speedy and substantial redress," will take the place of the arbitrary will of the master.[40] Such reformation could not be left up to the virtues of a self-interested master class, but is properly the duty of the imperial government.

As with Wilberforce, Clarkson believed that more than virtue was involved in amelioration; the very stability of slave society was threatened by the continued ignorance and immorality of the African slave. These social ills were the natural accompaniments of the suppression of liberty. Clarkson warned his countrymen that historically, tyranny had always been met by resistance. Pointing to the history of the West Indies between the seventeenth century and the close of the eighteenth century, he wrote that one "must have read it very superficially, not to know that there have been various insurrections of the slaves there, within this period."[41] Clarkson claimed that the slave trade was ultimately responsible for these revolts because it fed the islands with discontented African bondsmen. But it is clear from his writings that slavery was the real culprit. Clarkson wrote that because of the trade,

thousands are annually poured into the islands, who have been fraudulently and forcibly deprived of the rights of men. All these come into them of course with dissatisfied and exasperated minds; and this discontent and feeling of resentment must be further heightened by the treatment which people coming into them under such a situation must unavoidably receive; for we cannot keep people in a state of subjection to us, who acknowledge no obligation whatever to serve us, but by breaking their spirits and treating them as creatures of another species.[42]

Clarkson made the common assumption that abolition would bring amelioration and that the Creole generation would, accordingly, develop a healthy attachment to the colonies. But how could one explain planter persistence in a course of action that had historically produced unstable societies?

In an attempt to answer this question, Clarkson raised the issue of race prejudice. For Clarkson, the slavery of the African originated in violence and had for its justification only the force which deprived them of their liberty. It violated scripture, natural reason, and the principles of the British constitution. Deprived of any rational ground for their position, Caribbean planters rested their case in large measure on the argument of black inferiority. They claimed that blacks would simply refuse to work consistently unless coerced and were disqualified by nature for civilized life in free communities. "I have no doubt," wrote Clarkson, "that this prejudice has been one of the great causes why the improvement of our slave population by law has been so long retarded, and that the same prejudice will continue to have a similar operation, so long as it shall continue to exist."[43]

Clarkson's explicit grappling with the problem of race was unique among abolitionists. He saw a giant irony in the invention of color prejudice. Race bias was an exteriorizing of those character traits that Europeans had come to consider evil, ugly, repugnant, and fixing it as a moral blackness on the actual blackness of the African's skin. The result was confusion of character and appearance, in what amounted to a step backward in the science of social distinctions.

Clarkson was not opposed to social distinctions so long as they were natural. Slavery, however, introduced distinctions of an artificial nature.

Indeed, men in civilized society are reduced to the necessity of making personal distinctions, both on the principle of expediency and of duty, or men would have no right notions of justice, nor could the world be kept in order without them. Now, what have been, and what are, these personal distinctions at the present day? What entitles a man, where the world is as it should be, to respect among his fellow-citizens? I answer, his virtues only, his amiable qualities, his talents rightly directed, his usefulness in society. And what, on the other hand, subjects him to degradation and contempt? I answer his black character, his black deeds, but not his black skin. The Americans, then, by making virtue and vice, and good and bad treatment, to depend upon the color of the skin, show themselves . . . not fit to be reckoned among the civilized nations of the world; for they set at naught, . . . the laws of civilized society, by setting up a new principle of morality of their own.[44]

Clarkson traced the origin of this peculiar and perverse moral system to slavery.

It was the almost necessary and legitimate offspring of slavery . . . and that slavery, and nothing else, was the true cause of all the infamy attached to blackmen, is true from the consideration that, if the first slaves introduced into America had been blue, or yelloe, or crimson, and if their present posterity were not of these same colors, namely blue, yelloe or crimson, these colors would be as much a mark of reproach with the American citizen as black is now and as much as occasion for ill-treatment.[45]

Race bias was thus a mere convention. But race was real for Clarkson and the other humanitarians, who believed that it constituted a directly perceptible phenomenon. What disturbed Clarkson was not that a distinction was drawn between black and white, or that whites were held to be culturally superior to Africans, but that in the Caribbean and the United States, race was used as the rationale for exploitation. Clarkson's objection was that this obscured the true nature of social reality. He believed that Africans were backward, indeed, but not because they happened to be black. Their backwardness reflected their lower stage on the ladder of social evolution. All abolitionists could agree with this notion. No one thought of advancing the thesis of social or cultural equality between Africa and Europe. None of the abolitionists were cultural relativists; on the contrary, they were strongly against any such ideas, as demonstrated in the Clapham Sect's reaction to the Clive-Hastings policies in India. The problem with the idea of race as it had developed around black slavery was that a biological category had been perverted into a basis for social distinctions. Because such a system destroyed the similarity of fact and ideology, there were natural aristocrats, men of sterling characters living lives of mean desperation while they were often ruled over by people whose status would be in question in a free society.

In conditions such as these, it was up to those with under-standing of humanity and the laws of social progress to put Caribbean society on the right track. The imperial government must intervene and do what the colonials were incapable of doing, develop a social structure in which status and rank would be related to ability.

Clarkson was convinced that amelioration would be immensely successful. The black slave, rather than the stubborn, inherently lazy individual portrayed by the master, was an excellent subject for such social engineering. "The Negro Character is malleable at the European will," he wrote. "There is, as I have observed before, a singular pliability in the constitutional temper of the Negroes, and they have besides a quick sense of their own interest which influences their conduct."[46] Blacks, that is, were able to understand and participate in a society based on the free contract and individual responsibility. They would respond like Europeans to the law of laissez-faire.

As an illustration of the potential for the improvement of blacks through successful amelioration, Clarkson pointed with approval to the experiments of Mr. Joshua Steele of Barbados. Steele had tried assigning his slaves task work, set up Negro courts, and established copyhold tenure. He claimed to have had great success and to have cut his expenses as well. Clarkson's knowledge of Steel's experiment came from Dr. Dickson's *The Mitigation of Slavery* (1814). In a letter to Clarkson, Dickson discussed what he saw as the fundamental weakness of the slave system in the age of revolution.[47] Reinforcing what Sharp, Wilberforce, and James Stephen had warned, he maintained that "the true seat of government is in the affections of the governed; and these never will or can be gained by the barbarous policy of the Slave system, and the more barbarous practices which it authorizes."[48]

By 1814, the British West Indies existed in a sea of new world slave societies, most of which were still growing, fed by the annual addition of new Africans. These were people who did not form part of the Western cultural community and did not constitute as they were a secure cultural affiliation with Britain. Those in the French islands were perhaps still moved by the revolutionary spirit, with the Jacobin principles that had led to the revolution in St. Domingue. Knowledge of revolutionary ideas could not be kept from the slaves in the British Caribbean any more than it could be kept from the lower class at home. The only sure remedy was to reform decadent social orders wherever they existed in the hope of removing the sources of revolt, while generating the sound Protestant principles of diligence, respect for authority, but invariably respect for individual freedom. The slave must be given a stake in the community which he would be called on to defend. Dickson concluded with a warning:

The present Slave-system is not made for stability; nor indeed can it be safely continued for a single day, without some material modifications of the nature of those put in practice by Mr. Steele. Absolute Slavery and tolerable security are moral and political Contradictions; and idiocy alone will expect contradictions to be reconciled, in order to gratify absurdity. A system which never was rationally defensible, on any grounds of morality, religion, or policy, is now become dangerously incompatible with the new and portentious state of things. "The existence of a black power" in the vicinity of an important but "weak and feeble" British island, standing on a mine of explosive materials, may well make those whose language we quote "shrink with horror."[49]

Dickson was not the only writer with knowledge of the Caribbean who expressed anti-slavery sentiments which pointed to the danger to social security presented by the unassimilated African. Robert Renny was an acute observer of colonial manners. His *History of Jamaica* provides insight into slave society as it was just after the turn of the century. No enemy of Jamaica's plantocracy, whom he believed treated their slaves with humanity, he nevertheless saw in that society threats to continued stability. The continuing importation of Africans led to a greater disproportion in the ratio of blacks to whites, which would eventually produce evil consequences. Pursuing a familiar theme, he argued that abolition, by making the slave more valuable to the master, would tend to bring about the amelioration of slavery. The improvement in the condition of the Negroes would tend to "secure the attachment of the slaves to their masters, and prevent their power from increasing to a still more dangerous and alarming extent." Given a house, a piece of ground, and a family to defend, the Negro could be relied on to preserve the security of the islands.[50]

In 1801, Clement Caines, an owner of sugar estates in St. Christopher, had warned his fellow planters that the continuation of the trade in slaves filled their island with lurking assassins whose outward behavior, as James Ramsay had warned, could not be relied on as indication of inward disposition. The fate which waited to reward planter intransigence could be examined close at hand in St. Domingue. Clearly, "the sword of Dionysius was not suspended by a slighter hair, than the mischiefs which await the unthinking West Indian amidst his crowd of blacks."[51]

The young Henry Brougham shared this perspective. He felt
that the one thing which more than anything else marked the
West Indies off from other colonies was the great disproportion
of slave to free, which served to exacerbate the inherent
inferiority of satellite colonies to independent nations. "How
vastly is the difference augmented," he wrote, "by the existence
of a foreign nation in the heart of the colony, held by force and
intrigue, in subjection to the handful of white inhabitants, who
by violence or fraud, have transported them from their native
country."[52]

Brougham cautioned that the antagonistic nature of the
master-slave relationship rendered the security of the colonies
especially precarious in time of war, when the colonists were
forced to keep a continual watch over their bondsmen. He
contrasted colonial slavery, in this respect, with that which had
prevailed in the Roman Empire. There, the Germanic bondsmen
were assimilated into the society of their masters, developing
attachment to the polity in which they were given a stake. The
African slave of the British subject, on the other hand, forced
into a permanent caste by race slavery, could have no interest in
the society in which he found himself. The only means of motiva-
ting the slave in such circumstances was the threat or
application of physical force.[53]

Brougham warned that the contradictions in slave society
could explode in revolt. Because planters insisted on using
archaic and ruinous labor-intensive methods of production, the
prevailing system demanded the importation of ever larger
numbers of Africans. This demographic flow fed the rapid rise of
an African community which could have no other goal than the
destruction of European hegemony. Drawing what he saw as the
lessons of the past, Brougham reminded his countrymen, "But
the example of Spain, both in the old and new World, and of
France herself, in Europe, may convince us, that political
importance and national strength, are not so much proportioned
to the national resources and capability of a country, as to the
state of its society and the nature of its institutions."[54] These
lessons were reinforced and given immediate importance by the
catastrophe at St. Domingue. Once the jewel in the French
colonial diadem, it now lay in ruins, and a recent British attempt
at conquest had failed at great cost in life and money.[55]

Brougham read the St. Domingue revolution to mean that even the greatest terrors of slavery had proven unable to prevent what they were ultimately designed to avoid, servile war. On the contrary, violence had merely served to confirm the blacks in their hostility to European rule. When force was unable to keep the slaves in order any longer, the native "barbarism" of the African fed the flames of revolution. The savage destroyed his chains, and chaos and social decay ensued. "The destruction of negroe slavery has been followed by its natural consequence, the complete overthrow of the European power, and the establishment of an independent African Commonwealth in the noblest settlement of the new world."[56]

For Brougham, the St. Domingue rising had major significance for the English colonies. The freed slaves of Haiti would seek their fortunes by preying on neighboring islands, where they would find ready allies in the blacks who suffered under the British lash. Brougham was convinced that British slaves were well informed about events in St. Domingue. House slaves served as informants to those laboring in the fields, bringing news gleaned from the careless conversations of whites. In this way the progress of the St. Domingue revolution came to be known to the slave populations of the English islands. The example of the white master succumbing to the black slave in St. Domingue would undermine the notion of white invincibility, which Brougham believed was essential to the maintenance of slavery, and would plant the seeds of future revolt.[57]

Brougham's vision of an alien community coming to birth in the womb of the British Empire and threatening the existence of the plantation colonies was a clear formulation of growing concern with the disruptive potential of the African slave.[58] If slavery was a problem, then one clear reason was that it was a dangerously immoral system that undermined all reasonable basis for a stable society, turning the Caribbean into a cauldron with explosive potential.

No one argued with more force than James Stephen that the immorality and impolity of the slave system made the British West Indies a degenerate and insecure society. Stephen, who remained a staunch abolitionist all of his life, had been to the West Indies as a young man. About 1775, he obtained a position as "bookkeeper" on a Jamaican estate. Unaware of what the designation bookkeeper meant, he assumed that it was an administrative position that would enable him to become proficient in the arts of plantation management and put him on the path of quick wealth from sugar production. He was surprised to learn that his "duties would be to superintend the work of two or three hundred wretched human beings driven to their labour by a driver's lash."[59]

Fortunately, Stephen was spared the need to go and work in this capacity. Before he was able to depart, his brother returned from St. Christopher and impressed on him the negative features of the task he was about to assume, and his father came up with a plan to fund his study of the law. To the devout evangelical like Stephen, Providence had saved him from becoming directly implicated in the sin of slave driving. Stephen did eventually go to the Caribbean, but it was as a barrister, in which capacity he served there between 1783 and 1794. His Caribbean residence allowed him to observe the peculiar workings of the system at close hand, and he drew on this knowledge in his later anti-slavery work.[60]

In 1791, the slaves of St. Domingue rose in an extensive rebellion, which was to gain them mastery of the island. They successfully fought off a French attempt at reconquest and a British attempt to conquer them and achieved full independence by 1804. Haiti, as the new republic was named, became a warning to slaveholders throughout the Americas.[61]

We have seen how the St. Domingue problem was conceived by Brougham to represent a threat to the continued security of the British islands. Stephen, as well, was aware that the existence of a free African state on the borders of the British Caribbean would have to be treated with special care if the integrity of the British colonial system in the Caribbean was to be preserved.

In the *Crisis of the Sugar Colonies,* published in 1802, Stephen outlined the dangers and opportunities presented to the British Empire in the Caribbean by the new black state. The fate of St. Domingue drew together and symbolized for Stephen the dangers which slavery posed for England's colonial interests, The occasion for composition of the essay was an intended

French expedition to the West Indies.[62] The object of the yet-to-depart expedition was a matter of speculation. To some, the issue appeared to be the simple matter of a metropolis subduing a revolted colony, a struggle between Toussaint and Napoleon, "the Consul of St. Domingo, and the Consul of France." Stephen believed this to be a gross misconception. Reminding his readers that a sugar colony is nothing without a labor force, he argued that the real purpose of the French expedition could only be the restoration of slavery.[63]

How would the reimposition of slavery in St. Domingue affect the British sugar colonies? This is the question that Stephen set out to answer. He recognized the existence of a public sentiment favorable to the success of the French expedition. Those who regarded the mere existence of an independent Negro state as a grave threat to the security of the British islands would regard St. Domingue as a center from which revolutionary ideas would be spread throughout the Caribbean, and from whence armies of liberation would go forth to the overthrow of slavery in foreign islands. Stephen believed that this view was a simplistic prejudgment of a situation pregnant with a rich potential. He argued that a careful consideration of the possible impact of the French design on the true colonial interests of Great Britain first entailed an understanding of the nature of slavery before the revolution in St. Domingue. We must first know what the state of slavery in that island was before the meaning of its attempted restoration could be determined.[64]

But here, meaning had a dual dimension. The attempt to restore slavery has meaning for Great Britain but only because of its meaning for the freed blacks of St. Domingue. This is because, for Stephen, the reaction of the ex-slaves is the factor which will determine the significance of the French expedition. This is why it becomes vital to appreciate what the French would be attempting to reimpose. The significance of this observation is that Stephen is advocating that we see things from the perspective of the slave. This is an expression of the slave's impact on the thought of abolitionists. The important thing, however, is not the slave's perspective in and of itself, but that it indicates a threat, the slave's potential to be something for himself, something beyond control, and therefore alien. Putting it in terms of real politick, the action of these ex-slaves must be anticipated precisely so that it may be frustrated. The black must not be left unmade, if only because, in the British view, he will do a poor job of self-construction.

To Stephen, slavery was the antithesis of what man's state should be in a just political order. Drawing on his personal knowledge of bondage and his wide and famous learning in colonial affairs, Stephen outlined what he considered to be the main features of slavery. The leading characteristic of that system was the forced labor of "chattels personal." The Negroes were the absolute property of their masters. The slaves were worked and maintained at their discretion and were driven like beasts at their labors in the field.

Ominously, Stephen claimed that St. Domingue's past could be glimpsed today in the British colonies. In those societies, the laborer was bent to his task by the application of an artificial or external compulsion, rather than by an internal compulsion. But because this destroyed the connection between work and reward, life and labor, and replaced that nexus by force, the slave master relinquished his responsibility and in fact lost his capacity to shape the character of the slave. In this case, the planter was still acting on the Negro but in a negative way. He was forcing the black into further savageness instead of tutoring him in the arts of civilization. His abdication of responsibility for the moral growth of the slave could only weaken society by producing men who were less capable of moral commitment and less susceptible to rational argument, which would entail the increasing application of force. The end of this circular process could only be the barbarization of society.

Because of this creation of a cultural vacuum, the Negro, denied spiritual development, was the creation of the European, who bore full responsibility for his degenerate condition. "In the Negro," Stephen instructed his readers, "the self-dependency of a rational being, the close connection between his conduct and his nature, or social welfare are ideas perfectly new."[65] The normal lessons of life and labor have been perverted, since in the past, encrease of labour, has by impairing his health and strength, diminished his bodily comforts without adding to his external enjoyments. His subsistence, has been proportioned to his imbecilities, rather than to his powers of exertion: when able to do least for the master, he has received the most from him; and inaction, when sickness produced a respite from his labours, has been the parent rather of plenty, than of want.[66]

Inevitably, slave society must disintegrate into a reign of terror. Beaten, tortured, driven to work like cattle, the slaves were depressed even below the state of ignorance and superstition in which they came from their African homeland.

But how could such a society be maintained by force alone, in view of the high slave-to-free ratios there? Stephen's answer, like that of the black abolitionist Frederick Douglass, refers us to psychology. Stephen believed that slavery produced a "fortunate prejudice" in the slave cultivated, no doubt, by the white elite, which accounted for the security of slave societies, such as it was. He recognized that beyond the application and threat of physical terror lay the psychology of servility, an attitude so pervasive that even the idea of resistance to a white man evoked the darkest dread in the Negro. It was this irrational force that held slave society together. "Without the solution which this principle affords, the passive submission of the West India Negroes to a very small and often unarmed minority of white men, and the extreme rarity of any act of individual vengence on a master, would be wholly inexplicable."[67] Anticipating the theoretical work of Third World scholars like Frantz Fanon and Albert Memmi on the psychocultural effects of European colonialism, Stephen claimed that the pent-up, tormented emotions of the slaves were discharged on themselves.[68] Stephen had isolated a major danger of slavery. If the system rested on a psychology of fear, what would happen once that fear were removed?

This was exactly what had occurred in St. Domingue. In that island, the planter regime had pushed the slaves over the brink of tolerance by a slavery famous for its cruelty. At the same time, the slaves' "native ignorance" was replaced by revolutionary doctrines. Thus the moral and intellectual vacuum which planters had cultivated, thinking it a necessary support for their regime, had been filled by the principles that Britain struggled to combat in Europe and at home. In place of ignorant slaves there were now, in the words of C.L.R. James, "Black Jacobins."

In St. Domingue, the dispossessed had arisen, slain the oppressor, struck off the head of the master class. The act of rebellion was cathartic. Once the fear of the master was uprooted, it could never be replaced. This fear, unlike the respect earned for themselves by a virtuous ruling class, was founded on ignorance, perpetuated by deception and force. It could never withstand the graphic demonstration of its false-hood brought about by the military victories of the black armies. For Stephen, this process was conclusive. "I consider this change in the ideas of the negroes as the most invincible of bars to the permanent restitution of the slave system in the French Islands."[69] The experience of freedom would make slavery, deprived of its psychological prop, intolerable.[70]

The prospect of French success was dim. Stephen was positive that the ex-slaves would fight to the death to avoid the reimposition of the tyranny from which they had only lately escaped. The French would meet not slaves, but determined freedom fighters, defending a homeland they knew in intimate detail, and who were immune to many of the diseases that would decimate the French armies. Even should the French somehow achieve their goal and reimpose their rule over the black majority, the maintenance of slavery under present conditions would mean the permanent settlement of a large army of occupation, waging perpetual war against a determined opponent.[71] Clearly, the example of St. Domingue was proof that a society held together by fear in the absence of any common interest between master and slave was built on tenuous foundations.

The most important question remained, what attitude should the British take toward the French venture? Stephen's answer was that England must take that position which best secured the safety and welfare of its colonies. The way to accomplish this certainly did not lie through aid to the French or hostility to the now-free blacks of St. Domingue, which would only turn them into permanent enemies of the British. The British colonies could be secured by constructing a healthy social fabric, one which did not rest on the false bottom of fear and ignorance. Because the defense of the sugar islands depended on the loyalty of black troops and workers, the English must reform the social system so that disenchanted slaves became loyal laborers, peasants, and soldiers. As we have seen, this had, in fact, been the approach of Dundas with the West India Regiment. Were the French to fail in their attempt at reconquest, and, even more, should they succeed and then seek to foment revolt in the English islands, the remedy was the same. The revolution in St. Domingue demanded that the British ameliorate the condition of the slaves in their islands in order to secure the safety of their plantations.[72] Amelioration would "substitute internal strengths and security for internal weakness, before the approaching danger arrives." The destruction of chattel slavery would remove the temptation for British blacks to revolt in concert with the French.[73] This is how the English should meet the French threat.

In *The Dangers of the Country*, Stephen pursued the theme of the relationship between slavery and social decay. Published in 1807, on the eve of the vote on the abolition of the slave trade, it was written, no doubt, to influence the outcome. Despite its obvious propagandistic quality, it contains much which is central to abolitionist thinking. This work reflects the atmosphere of impending danger and crusade surrounding abolitionist activity in the age of revolution. Stephen's intensity stems from his concern to warn the public of approaching doom. "The dangers of the Country I fear have not been so much despised as forgotten." Stephen pointed out that history is littered with the examples of improvident societies. The overthrow of Alexander, the fall of Carthage and Rome, all of which were great empires, were heralded by numerous signs of the approaching decay which were ignored to the detriment of those societies. He thought that contemporary Britain manifested similar signs of decay. In danger of conquest by French arms, his countrymen seemed to lack the will to put petty jealousies aside and look carefully to the defense of their precious liberties.[74]

The signs that Stephen set out to interpret for his countrymen indicated threats to what he believed was the greatest society ever produced. Stephen shared with all humanitarians the belief that British society was the measure of all human social organization. The essence of that society consisted of individual legal and political freedom guaranteed by a constitution which put law above rank, power, or racial background. "That inestimable blessing, chiefly consists, in the supremacy of known and equal laws, in their upright administration, and in the security of the individual, against the oppression of the civil magistrate, or the state."[75]

If as Stephen believed English justice was the most perfect that had ever existed, developing from the time of the Henries and arriving at a state of excellence that might never be surpassed, the whole of this great heritage would be destroyed by a French conquest.[76] The subversion of individual liberty which was sure to follow the extension of the French autocracy to England would inevitably bring the collapse of England's commercial and industrial pre-eminence, which depended on nothing so much as the freedom of thought and contract, and the integrity of the English character bred by the civil liberties that Englishmen took for granted. As the destruction of the roots brings about the death of the tree, so the decay of the English character would quickly follow the suppression of civil liberty.[77]

Stephen's reading of the signs of the times convinced him that a national reformation was needed to save the English way of life. This was not an unusual view. Indeed, we can consider the Association movement, as well as the whole of what Palmer called the Leveé en masse of the people of quality, as a movement for national reformation in the face of the revolutionary threat from abroad. What must have appeared odd to many, however, was that Stephen argued that reformation must begin with the abolition of the slave trade. Involvement in the trade and slavery spoiled an otherwise enviable record of humanity and respect for individual liberty. To emphasize this point, Stephen briefly reviewed social conditions in England and elsewhere in the empire.[78]

In nineteenth-century England, the danger of tyranny was now distant, and where imperfections existed, they could be remedied, given sufficient time. Stephen wrote of England that "in no part of the globe, are the poor and helpless so well

protected by the laws, or so humanely used by their superiors."
Even in its relations with Ireland, its oldest imperial possession,
England could be accused of neglect rather than abuse or
unrighteousness, "nor does the fault arise from any of those
unrighteous principles, or from that oppressive use of power,
which are so peculiarly offensive to Heaven."[79] In India as well,
Stephen was willing to stand on the British record

I know there are many who suppose us to be merciless oppressors in the
East Indies, as well as the West. But if the suspicion be applied to our
treatment of the poor or the great mass of the people; it is utterly
unfounded. There is no slavery in the dominions of the East India
Company, unless the condition of a few domestic life servants may
deserve the name; and even these are so treated, that their bondage can
scarcely be distinguished from freedom.[80]

Convinced that the great majority of Indian laborers were free
to work their own land, for which they paid a moderate and fixed
rent, Stephen was satisfied with the overall state of British rule
in India. No doubt improvements could be made, especially in
the area of education and religious instruction, but all in all, he
was confident that "in no part of India are they so happy" in the
secure enjoyment of land ownership, which meant economic
security, "as within the British territories."[81]

In Stephen's view, the English could not be reproached for
misconduct in any area of their dominions where it could be
shown that the people were free. Liberty prevailed in England,
Ireland, and India, where the record of British rule was
unblemished. As long as personal freedom, guaranteed by
impartial laws, existed, there was no cause for either reproach
or alarm; there was no danger of social decay or divine
retribution. Where liberty prevailed, one could improve, but the
basic structure of society was sound.

In Stephen's picture of the British Empire, the Caribbean was
a glaring exception to the pattern of social health. It was the
only area in which liberty was purposely suppressed in order to
provide the normal economic foundation for society. It was the
only British domain in which men were turned into commodities,
thus losing all stake in the society in which they lived and

worked. Lacking positive ties to their island homes, the slaves in the Caribbean could not be relied on to defend them in time of war, and they would prove a continual threat to their internal security in either war or peace.[82]

The slave trade and slavery presented an additional danger that was directly related to the Anglo-French struggle. Stephen placed concern for the slave squarely within the context of the "Age of the Democratic Revolution" when he argued that the existence of the slave trade provided a powerful propagandistic device in the hands of the leadership of the international revolution. The slave trade and Caribbean slavery gave the French the opportunity to portray the English as the real enemies of freedom, in order to rouse popular passions against them. Thus the immediate abolition of the trade would remove a powerful weapon from the enemies' arsenal and help to open the minds of the French people to "our true character."[83] Persistence in the infamous traffic would constantly handicap English efforts to develop an effective counter-revolution to the Napoleonic challenge.

It would tend much to preclude our effectual interposition, at some future and auspicious season, between his ambition, and the remnant of Europe that has yet escaped his sword, if he could succeed in persuading the world, that we are a sordid, selfish, and unprincipled people, whose gold is their god, and who would spread desolation through the earth, for the sole purpose of extending their commerce. It might also further his present plan, of engaging the powers still neutral, in a confederacy against our maritime rights.[84]

Stephen clearly recognized the importance of an ideology of mass appeal in an age of total war and the leveé en masse. The English commitment to liberty must be demonstrated to be greater than their concern for profit if they were to convince the world that theirs was a better system than that of the French. This could never be done while England continued to condone the slave trade.

But it was not a temporal danger alone that threatened to befall England. Stephen warned that failure to abolish the slave trade would call down divine retribution. "Like Pharaoh, we promised for a moment to let the people go; but like him, we speedily relapsed, and persevered in following the counsels of national avarice, in defiance of that voice of conscience, which is the undoubted messenger of God."[85] Like most abolitionists, Stephen believed that the slave trade had already provoked God's wrath in the form of the Napoleonic wars, which had unleashed suffering in Europe. Stephen explained that

induced by a common temptation, the lucrative oppression of the African race, many nations start together in a new race of guilt; a strange source of unprecedented evil immediately burst forth and suddenly overwhelms them all. A cruel and unlimited slavery is the subject of their crimes: a lawless and ferocious liberty is made their common scourge. Not only France, but Europe, becomes a second Africa. Order security, public morals, the sacred principles which mitigate the horrors of war, and regulate the intercourse of nations, have vanished, from this civilized quarter of the globe. . . . The public law of the slave coast may soon be upon a level with that of polished Europe.[86]

Strangely enough, Stephen argued that the peace and growing prosperity of the United States, the one nation that had abolished the trade, was proof of the reality of divine justice.[87] The notion that God would spare one of the major slave nations was one of the few lapses in Stephen's otherwise impeccable logic, and impressive integrity.

As we have seen, the abolitionists were of one mind in the belief that abolition would lead the planters to ameliorate the condition of their labor force and were disappointed when it did not achieve that result. Twenty years after abolition, slavery was still going strong in the British colonies. Consequently, for James Stephen, England's burden of sin remained. In 1826, he published a work with the quite revealing title of *England Enslaved by Her Own Slave Colonies*. It enables us to glimpse the evolution of his thought and to take the pulse of humanitarian reform in the 1820s.

In this work, Stephen revealed an increasing impatience with West Indian intransigence in the face of abolitionist pressure and goes on the offensive. It is not slavery that is wrong, he now argues, but the entire old colonial system that slavery supports.

In short, West Indian political and economic organization reveals all the faults and dangers of all arbitrary and despotic polities.

The root of the problem was the existence of a master class that the imperial government had permitted to enjoy despotic powers over what one had to regard as British subjects. The islands operated under "constitutions preposterously called English" but which were in effect dictatorships of self-interest that had no legitimate claim to self-government. Because the mass of the Caribbean population remained unrepresented in any form and subjected to a special law, the island governments violated every constitutional principle.[88] There could be no justification for tolerating this aberration of normal English practice; only the expediency of a narrow economic interest could be marshalled out in its behalf.

Ironically, however, even in regard to economic self-interest, the colonial situation was indefensible. The sound principle that colonies are established for the good of the mother country had been perverted in the case of the West Indies, where instead the planters gain was England's loss. Colonials were allowed to receive supplies from rival nations and to ignore, if they chose, the manufactures of Great Britain. Their sugar could go to non-British ports, even while it enjoyed protection in the home market, as opposed to cheaper foreign sugar.[89]

While this perverse colonial system secured the welfare of a small group of West Indian planters and merchants, it operated to restrict the market for British manufactures and to discourage the development of the potentially much more valuable market in East India.[90] East Indian trade would have been an immeasurable spur to the increase of the national wealth and maritime power, "but all these potent considerations fell before West Indian influence."[91]

Thus the need for artificial props for a system which was internally weak was already beginning to hinder imperial economic development. Despite metropolitan support, the planters were bringing ruin on themselves by refusing to adopt sensible industrial practices. They ruined the soil by substituting human power for animal power, while at the same time they lost the fertilizing value of manure. They insisted on using slave

labor, universally recognized to be inferior to free labor, and
made their situation worse by refusing to introduce the plough,
the most rudimentary of modern agricultural implements. As a
consequence, they were perpetually engaged in the heavy
expense of purchasing and supporting a labor force that
accounted for the major draw on their capital. Given such a
ruinous system, it was only improvidence that persuaded men to
invest in the enterprise of sugar cultivation. Like Bryan
Edwards before him, Stephen compared sugar cultivation to the
national lottery.[92] Since indemnification was not granted to
those who risked their money in gambling, why, then, should the
nation guarantee West Indian planters in their foolish speculations? "I am at a loss," Stephen complained, "to conceive on
what grounds, except the preponderating weight of their
political influence, our sugar planters are entitled more than any
other adventurers in hazardous and losing speculations, to cast
the burden of their distress or ruin on the shoulders of their
fellow-subjects in Europe."[93]

The sacrifice of national welfare to the narrow special interest
of sugar-growing slave drivers was evident in strategic as well
as economic matters. As in the *Crisis*, so in 1826 Stephen took
up the case of Haiti and its meaning for Great Britain. The
history of the island was both an example and a warning. The
recent history of the British in the Caribbean revealed the
distortions in imperial policy attributable to the "narrow views
and potent influence of the Colonial Party." At a crucial moment
in the war against Napoleon, England weakened its fighting
force by pursuing an impossible attempt to conquer St. Domingue
"to restore the cart-whip government, lest it should be
subverted also in our own islands."[94] The rational course of
action would have been to make an alliance with the St. Domingue
blacks and establish commercial relations with them. This would
have secured England's interests in the region. But once again,
the dictates of reason and national interest were subverted by
the racism of the West Indian interest. "The pestilent vapours
of Creolian prejudice obscured the true interests of our country,
as the fatal influence of the Colonists betrayed them."[95]

Stephen's thought derived its force from the powerful vision
of the moral as well as the economic and political connections

between domestic and overseas imperial problems. For Stephen, as for Wilberforce and Clapham, whatever was wrought in the name of Britain and British law would impact on the moral structure of English culture and would ultimately affect the way people thought of and reacted to the empire.

Stephen thought that slavery bred contempt for authority and restraint, which was harmful to the preservation of the empire. Observing that "you found it to your cost in America," Stephen cautioned that "you find it now in the West Indies."[96] He believed that the relationship of master and slave presented the unique and archaic example of a power unlimited by the interposition of a public power. Between the lord and the serf, argued Adam Smith, the king had gradually intruded his authority, tending eventually to the extinction of slavery and serfdom in Europe. Between king and subject the law arbitrates, subjecting all to its commands. But in the sugar colonies, one could observe the unmitigated authority of one man over multitudes of other men, where virtually no outside authority interfered with the exercise of this personal domain. In this sense, the master was above the law of England and, in this particular, even above the king of England. "The pedestals of the British throne are law, justice, and well-regulated freedom; all which this institution of private slavery subverts."[97] Stephen saw the issue clearly. Should England continue in slavery to a band of petty tyrants, or abolish the danger which threatened its temporal and spiritual welfare.[98]

In *The Slavery of the British West India Colonies Delineated,* Stephen expanded his attack on slavery. The work was divided into two parts, the first volume appearing in 1824, the second, in 1830. They were published in the midst of abolitionist agitation, and the dates of publication indicate the high points of the anti-slavery movement. The explanation of the work's object confirms this conclusion. Its publication was designed to prove to the government that the amelioration plans introduced in 1823 had not been effective. The strategy was to overwhelm the political community with a wealth of detailed information on every aspect of slavery as an economic and legal system, destroying by sheer weight of evidence all support for the system.[99]

Abolitionists had traditionally written of the injustice, sinfulness, and cruelty of slavery, which was, of course, a good way to drum up public support, and Stephen was no exception. But he certainly objected to the spiritual deprivation of the bondsmen as well. In a "Christian country, the first and most sacred duty of the legislature is to provide for the religious instruction of the people under its government, whether bond or free." This public religious training was provided with vital reinforcement by the private instruction of children by parents and clergymen, so that in Christian lands, the spiritual care of the young was well provided for. But even here, the "most serious minds" believed that perfection had not yet been achieved.[100]

If religious training was necessary in Christian countries, the situation in the islands demanded an even closer application to the inculcation of proper religious values. However, the natural education provided by familial instruction could not be relied on, since the family had been destroyed by slavery and the adult population was ignorant, for the most part, of even the rudiments of religion. "A great portion of the Adults had notoriously been brought from a country, where, with the exception of a few Mohammedans, there are none but pagan inhabitants."[101]

Despite the crying need for religious instruction, the policy of the planters was to discourage religion entirely. "The only education of the newly-arrived African was his seasoning." No education of any sort was provided to the young. Nothing was done that would in any way interfere with the labor regime. Not content with this shameful negligence of religion, the colonial establishment even placed obstacles in the way of the missionaries, "who for conscience sake have become [the slave's] voluntary teachers."[102]

Stephen found that the suppression of moral instruction was reflected in the distortion of sound principles of justice as they applied to the Negro. In order to emphasize the danger that this presented, he clarified the reciprocal nature of a just political order. "It is regarded as an axiom in political morality, that allegiance and protection are reciprocal obligations; and local allegiance, by which alone the captive African could be supposed to be bound in our colonies, can be referred to no other principle."[103] Consistently hammering away at a theme that runs through all of his writing, Stephen maintained that there could be no legitimate social bond in the absence of legal and moral equality.

The case may be illustrated by that of an alien enemy, entering the realm as such, by open invasion, in time of war. He is not entitled to the protection of the law; but for that very reason he cannot be treated as a traitor, though taken in the perpetration of an act which would be treason in a subject . . . for he owes not even a temporary allegiance to that state, which owes him no protection. The difference in the case of the African captive was, that he entered the country, not by choice, but constraint; not with any hostile intention on his part, but by an act of harsh hostility upon ours; a distinction which can hardly be thought to have imposed upon him moral obligations to which the alien enemy is not subject.[104]

Where a free contract was based on consent, engaging a moral obligation on the part of the laborer, slavery is an external compulsion, which, of course, negated any conceivable notion of consent. The slave's labor, even his good behavior, could not, therefore, be taken as indication of his true feelings. As James Ramsay had noted, for the slave, "the circumstances that brought him within his adversaries' power might, in his opinion, be treachery or violence. He will therefore submit to the consequences only till he can help himself."[105]

The argument that slavery was immoral had been made many times, but morality is seldom a persuasive reason for state action. The humanitarians recognized that they would have to appeal to the economic and political self-interest of the governing elite as well. Thus Stephen performed a unique and valuable service for anti-slavery when he examined slavery's claim to legitimacy as a labor system. Stephen argued that in order to wring maximum profit from the cultivation of sugar in a tropical climate, the planter turned of necessity to the African slave. Negroes, who could work more effectively in the tropics than whites, came to replace Europeans as the labor force. Yet, even the African could not work at full capacity in the Caribbean and was not as productive there as the Englishman was at home.

The problem was that in the tropics, the sustained labor which was necessary for the production of sugar "is extremely noxious to the human frame." Therefore, repugnance to such work was natural, not racial. The whip was a necessary incentive because it was the only way to compel men to engage in self-destruction for the benefit of others.[106]

Introducing the major concern of the second volume, Stephen wrote that "the best criterion of the good or bad condition of the labouring classes in any country, may be found in the increase or decline of their numbers."[107] It was a historical truth that the slave population in the sugar colonies was unable to maintain itself through natural increase, a problem that Stephen blamed on the negative effects of sugar cultivation on the human constitution. He insisted that slavery alone was not a sufficient explanation for the decline of the Caribbean population. In the Bahamas, for example, where sugar cultivation was absent, the African population grew by natural increase. Even in the United States, where slavery flourished, there was a natural increase of between 2 and 2.5 percent per year, due to the less debilitating work of cotton cultivation. Meanwhile, in Haiti, the much maligned Negro state, the population has almost doubled in the past thirty years of freedom.[108]

Stephen thought that the case of the liberated African population of Trinidad was of particular interest in this regard. Composed, for the most part, of the fugitive slaves of American masters taken aboard British ships during the last war, these people had settled in semi-freedom in Trinidad. Between November of 1815 and January of 1821, 774 blacks were delivered into the island. Living in a state not much distinguished from slavery, they were free in one essential condition; they were not driven to work in the cultivation of sugar, but were able to cultivate their own grounds. By the end of 1824, they had achieved a natural increase of 147. In the same period, the field slave population of Trinidad had suffered an annual decline. Lest this terrible mortality be laid at the door of the disproportion of sexes, Stephen was quick to point out that such disproportions no longer existed. In fact, the old colonies appeared to have an oversufficiency of women. The point was brought home when Stephen revealed that in the free population, where natural increase did take place, there were far more men than women.[109]

To demonstrate in a most effective way the excessive demands that sugar cultivation made on the slave, Stephen analyzed planter statements, drawn, for the most part, from parliamentary papers. Examining arguments against James Ramsay's classic *Treatment and Conversion of African Slaves in the British Sugar Colonies* (1784), he concluded that by the admissions of the planters themselves, the length of the working day varied from eighteen hours out of every twenty-four in the five months of crop time, to sixteen and one-half hours for the remainder of the year.[110] Stephen found that such excessive labor was ruinous to the life of the slave.

Stephen's effort demonstrated powerfully that slave labor in the sugar colonies was a system developed in response to the peculiar needs of sugar cultivation for a capitalist market. In order to produce commodities capable of competing on the world market, British merchants and planters turned to African slavery, which allowed them to overcome the natural resistance of free men to the debilitating conditions of labor on tropical plantation units. Without the slave trade, the labor force could not be maintained unless the condition of the slave were drastically modified. Thus, to the ethical and political objections to slavery, Stephen added those based on careful researches into the economics and demography of the system.

James Stephen was a prolific writer, and his work provides a reasonable method of identifying some of the major issues of concern to imperial humanitarians. The titles of Stephen's books give a pretty good idea of what he understood the problems of slavery to be: *The Crisis of the Sugar Colonies, The Dangers of the Country, England Enslaved by Her Own Slave Colonies*, and *The Slavery of the British West India Colonies Delineated*. With the exception of the last work, all of these essays suggest danger. Without a doubt, they were designed to do just that in order to generate public concern. Not only the titles, but also the works themselves stress danger. Thus they are not calls to abolish the slave trade and slavery on humanitarian grounds alone, but they stress as well a concern for the danger to Great Britain and the empire that involvement in slavery threatened.

The Crisis of the Sugar Colonies argues the dangers presented by unreformed slave societies in the age of revolution. Although Stephen's subject here was the French expedition to St. Domingue, it is only a vehicle for demonstrating what he believed to be the vulnerability of colonial society. His message is simply that the danger to the British sugar colonies is presented not so much by the threat of invasion as by the internal weakness that slavery creates. It is the danger that the slaves may rise in support of a foreign invasion or in response to the example of the blacks in St. Domingue. Stephen insisted that the only way to avoid disaster was to remove the source of weakness by the reform of slave society.

His point is virtually the same in his other works. *The Dangers of the Country,* for example, derives from a weakness in the imperial fabric. That chink in the British armor is caused by the slave trade and slavery. Persistence in the violation of the right to liberty of thousands of Africans weakens England's ability to wage successful ideological war against France, while the existence of slavery weakens the security of colonial society. Furthermore, England's involvement in slavery violated the religious principles on which social health is founded and threatened to provoke divine retribution.

England Enslaved by Her Own Slave Colonies and *The Slavery of the British West India Colonies Delineated* revealed the dangers of economic decay which slavery created. Stephen warned that bondage to the interests of the plantocracy prevented England from expanding its trade in the East Indies and South America. In addition, the human and ecological wastefulness of sugar production with slave labor frustrated the development of a viable economy in the West Indies.

We can see, then, that for Stephen, slavery threatened dangers not so much for the slave as for England, the enslaver. His gaze was firmly fixed on the interests of the metropolis, and although there is certainly no reason to doubt his sincere concern for the welfare of the African slave, that must be seen in the context of his passion for the welfare of his own nation. Thus his formulation of the dangers of slavery is governed by his concern for the interests of England. This is, I will argue, a significant characteristic of anti-slavery thought; concern for the African slave is mediated through the prism of Britain's welfare as a free society and as an empire.

Granville Sharp, whom I characterized as one of the first writers to formulate an anti-slavery argument, was led, in the first place, to formulate a condemnation of slavery as part of his effort to defend himself against a lawsuit. Ironically, his attempt to apply English law by securing the release of Jonathan Strong from wrongful imprisonment placed Sharp in a position of financial jeopardy. This was not a symbolic, but a very real situation in which slavery appeared to threaten the integrity of the very laws which were supposed to protect the liberty of the English. Sharp's response was a protracted effort to demonstrate that slavery was not supported by English law after all. His success, which came in the Somersett decision, removed the danger that the existence of personal property in men would subvert the integrity of the law.

It is apparent here that although escaped slaves living in England could benefit from the Somersett decision, the goal was to protect English law and English freedoms. That this was Sharp's overriding goal is apparent from a review of his non-abolitionist writings. Such tracts as *The People's Natural Right to a Share in the Legislature* were arguments in defense of English constitutional freedoms. Clearly, Granville Sharp was at pains to protect English democracy from all dangers.

The bulk of Sharp's abolitionist writings were arguments that slavery and Christianity were incompatible. Sharp was at pains to show that Christianity enjoined conduct on the faithful which could not be followed by slave owners. Here, persistence in slavery endangered the religious and moral basis of the English nation. As with slavery and English law, so with slavery and Christianity; the two could not coexist; one must destroy the other.

Sharp's arguments were thus essentially moralistic. Slavery threatened to plunge England into moral decay by subverting the twin pillars of English liberty—the integrity of impartial laws and the Christian religion. Once this subversion was accomplished, English liberty would be unable to survive, and with that liberty would vanish the morality and culture, the humane and enlightened civilization that Sharp believed England possessed.

Wilberforce was much more concerned with slavery in the sugar colonies. In his formulation, those colonies suffered from instability generated by slavery. Like Sharp, Wilberforce was worried about the state of religion, but his concern was rather with its absence than with its destruction. Because he regarded Christianity as a necessary foundation for social health, Wilberforce argued that its suppression in the Caribbean frustrated the development of sound social virtues, leaving unmediated the conflict of master and slave.

But Wilberforce condemned slavery itself as a source of social instability. With all power and reward on one side and all misery and labor on the other, there could be no community of interest between the master and the slave. Slaves could not have any real interest in the societies where they were held captive. Their one fondest dream must be the overthrow of the master class.

Clarkson and Brougham agreed with this assessment. Their arguments were, in no uncertain terms, that slaves had no interest in the protection or welfare of the societies in which they lived. They could be prevailed on by potential invaders to rebel, and they did, and would continue to rebel on behalf of their own freedom.

All of these writers, including James Stephen, condemned slavery on moral grounds. It was sinful, contradictory to Christianity, and could lead to the moral decay of the slave owner and his society. But there is no doubt that the moral dangers of slavery related to what was an apparent political danger, the threat of servile war and revolution. Thus the elite humanitarian concern with slavery was not motivated exclusively, and I would argue not even primarily, by a compulsion to right wrongs wherever they were to be found. It was a highly selective compulsion and appears to have been activated by cases in which the political, economic, and military security of either the empire or English society was at stake. Thus the Clapham Sect was silent on the very real exploitation of the Irish or the general tendency of English rule to undermine the integrity of Indian society. Their loud complaints about the inhumanity of slavery concerned social conditions in a segment of the empire in which the population showed every inclination of eventually achieving the capability of shattering British rule.

NOTES

1. Paul Edwards and James Walvin, *Black Personalities in the Era of the Slave Trade* (Baton Rouge: Louisiana State University Press, 1983, p. 19.
2. Ibid.
3. Prince Hoare, ed., *Memoirs of Granville Sharp* (London: n.p., 1802), pp. 32-35.
4. Ibid., pp. 47-48.
5. Ibid., pp. 52-61.
6. Ibid., p. 236.
7. Ibid., p. 35.
8. Granville Sharp, *A Representation of the Injustice and Dangerous Tendency of Tolerating Slavery in England* (London: n.p., 1769), pp. 19-21.
9. Ibid., pp. 25, 28.
10. Ibid.
11. Ibid., pp. 91-92, 99, 104-105.
12. Granville Sharp, *Tracts on Slavery* (London: n.p., 1776).
13. Hoare, *Memoirs of Granville Sharp*, p. 263.
14. Ibid., pp. 32-35, 37-38.
15. Granville Sharp, "The Law of Passive Obedience," *Tracts on Slavery*, pp. 12-14, 18.
16. Ibid.
17. Granville Sharp, "The Law of Liberty, or, Royal Law by Which All Mankind, Will Certainly Be Judged," *Tracts on Slavery*, pp. 33, 48-50.
18. Ibid.
19. Robin Furneaux, *William Wilberforce* (London: Hamish Hamilton, 1974), pp. 54-55.
20. Ibid., p. 217.
21. William Wilberforce, *An Appeal to the Religion, Justice, and Humanity of the Inhabitants of the British Empire . . .* (New York: Negro Universities Press, 1969), pp. 6-7.
22. Ibid.
23. Ibid., pp. 8-11.
24. Ibid., pp. 12-13.
25. Ibid., pp. 19-21.

176   Moral Imperium

26. Ibid.
27. Ibid., pp. 25-26.
28. Ibid., p. 39.
29. Ibid., p. 51.
30. Ibid., pp. 52-53.
31. Wilberforce, *Appeal*, pp. 53, 54.
32. Ibid.
33. Ibid.
34. Thomas Clarkson, *The History of the Rise, Progress, and Accomplishment of the Abolition of the African Slave Trade by the British Parliament*, 2 vols. (London: Frank Cass & Co., 1968), 1:209-217.
35. Thomas Clarkson, *An Essay on the Slavery and Commerce of the Human Species* (New York: AMS Press, 1972), pp. 1-2.
36. Ibid., pp. 119, 36, 40-42; Thomas Clarkson, *A Summary View of the Slave Trade* (London: L. T. Phillips, 1787).
37. Ibid.
38. Clarkson, *Essay on Slavery*, pp. 161-163.
39. Thomas Clarkson, *Thoughts on the Necessity of Improving the Condition of the Slaves in the British Colonies* (New York: n.p., 1823).
40. Ibid., pp. 7-9, 10.
41. Thomas Clarkson, *The True State of the Case Respecting the Insurrection at St. Domingo* (London: n.p., 1792), pp. 2-3.
42. Ibid., p. 3.
43. Clarkson, *Thoughts*, pp. 16-17, 19, 10-11.
44. Thomas Clarkson, *Letters to a Friend on the Treatment of the People of Color in the United States . . .* (Boston: New England Anti-Slavery Tract Association, 1814), pp. 66-67.
45. Ibid., p. 68.
46. Clarkson, *Thoughts*, p. 46.
47. Ibid., p. 11.
48. Ibid., pp. 38-47.
49. William Dickson, *Mitigation of Slavery* (London: Longman, Hurst, Rees, Orme & Brown, 1814), pp. 363-365, 368.
50. Robert Renny, *History of Jamaica* (London: n.p., 1807), pp. 213-214, 182-183, 185, 186-187.
51. Clement Caines, *Letters on the Cultivation of the Otaheite Cane . . .* (London: Robinson & Co., 1801), pp. 287, 185-186.
52. Henry Brougham, *An Inquiry into the Colonial Policy of the European Powers*, 2 vols. (New York: Augustus M. Kelley, 1970), 2:167.
53. Brougham, *Colonial Policy*, 2:14.
54. Ibid., p. 99.
55. On the revolution in St. Domingue, see C.L.R. James, *The Black*

Jacobins (New York: Vintage Books, 1963). On the British attempt at conquest, see James, chap. 9, and J. W. Fortesque, *A History of the British Army*, 13 vols. (London: Macmillan, 1915), vol. 4, pt. 1, 1789-1801, pp. 565-566, for the costs of war.

56. Brougham, *Colonial Policy*, 2:141.

57. Ibid., 2:149-153, 154-155.

58. See John Woolman, "Considerations on Keeping Negroes," in Phillip T. Moulton, *The Journal and Major Essays of John Woolman* (New York: Oxford University Press, 1971), pp. 227-228.

59. James Stephen, *The Memoirs of James Stephen* (London: Bevington Hogarth Press, 1954), p. 166.

60. William Green, "James Stephen and British West India Policy, 1834-1847," *Caribbean Studies*, vol. 13, no. 4, pp. 33-56.

61. See James, *Black Jacobins*.

62. James Stephen, *The Crisis of the Sugar Colonies* (New York: Negro Universities Press, 1969).

63. Ibid., pp. 6-7.

64. Ibid., pp. 78-80.

65. Ibid., p. 54.

66. Ibid.

67. Ibid., pp. 72-73.

68. Ibid., p. 74.

69. Ibid., pp. 75-76.

70. Ibid.

71. Ibid., pp. 55-70, 70-72.

72. Ibid., pp. 82-83, 121, 124-125.

73. Ibid., pp. 125-126.

74. James Stephen, *The Dangers of the Country* (London: J. Butterworth and J. Hatchard, 1807), pp. 226, 3.

75. Ibid., p. 14.

76. Ibid., p. 15.

77. Ibid., p. 22.

78. Ibid.

79. Ibid., pp. 186-187.

80. Ibid., p. 186.

81. Ibid.

82. Ibid., pp. 168-169.

83. Ibid., pp. 174-175.

84. Ibid., pp. 170-171.

85. Stephen, *Dangers*, pp. 199-203.

86. Ibid., p. 122.

87. Ibid.

`178   Moral Imperium`

88. James Stephen, *England Enslaved by Her Own Slave Colonies* (London: n.p., 1826), pp. 8-12.

89. Ibid., p. 13.

90. Ibid., p. 14.

91. Ibid., p. 16. See also Anonymous, *East India Sugar or an Inquiry Respecting the Means of Improving the Quality and Reducing the Cost of Sugar Raised by Free Labor in the East Indies* (London: Pritchard & Sons, 1824), and John Gladstone and James Cropper, *The Correspondence Between John Gladstone and James Cropper, on the Present State of Slavery in the British West Indies . . .* (Shannon: Irish University Press, 1972), pp. 2-13.

92. Stephen, *England Enslaved,* pp. 32-33, 40.

93. Ibid.

94. Ibid., p. 31.

95. Ibid., pp. 18-19; Fortesque, *British Army,* vol. 4, pt. 1, pp. 565-566.

96. Stephen, *England Enslaved,* p. 19.

97. Ibid., p. 84.

98. Ibid., pp. 86-88.

99. James Stephen, *The Slavery of the British West India Colonies Delineated,* 2 vols. (New York: Kraus Reprint Co., 1969), 1:xi-xxxiii; 2:7-10, 42.

100. Stephen, *Slavery,* 1:203-205.

101. Ibid., p. 206.

102. Ibid., pp. 206-207, 234.

103. Ibid., p. 277.

104. Ibid.

105. James Ramsay, *Objections to the Abolition of the Slave Trade with Answers* (Miami: Mnemoyne Publishing Co., 1969), p. 45.

106. Stephen, *Slavery,* 2:xxvii, 44-60, 52-53.

107. Ibid., p. 76.

108. Ibid., pp. 78-79.

109. Ibid., p. 80.

110. Ibid., p. 153.

Conclusion

The subject of St. Domingo is a very difficult one; it clearly exceeds all the bounds of expense we had resolved upon, and what the country either can or will bear.[1]

The lesson that Henry Dundas learned in St. Domingue was an extremely costly one for Britain. Disregarding the advice of James Stephen, William Pitt went ahead and involved the nation in what amounted to a vain attempt to conquer the revolted colony. Some hundred thousands of pounds and thousands of lives later, the British abandoned the reckless enterprise, leaving the island to the blacks. Lack of mature reflection on the balance between desire and capability in part explains the tragedy; simple arrogance completes the picture.

About the same time, Canning was writing to Windham, explaining why he was prepared to argue for abolition. Side-stepping the question of morality, he pressed Windham to consider that the extension of British slavery to the recently acquired Trinidad would be one more sacrifice of security to the desire for quick profits. "We have our choice," he wrote, "whether to make Trinidad a new sugar growing, negro driving colony, productive indeed, but weak, and exposed, and inviting attack in proportion—or to create there a place of military strength, a fortress for the defence of our other colonies; and to lay the foundation of a new system of colonization for future military purposes."[2]

Canning's recognition of limits is implied in his argument.

Slavery would weaken Trinidad precisely because slaves could not be relied on to defend it against a French attack or be trusted to keep the peace in times of trouble. They had given every indication that they would rise whenever sufficient opportunity presented itself. But this was only a problem because, as Dundas learned in St. Domingue, Britain did not have the means of defending such a colony at such a distance for any length of time. It was better, then, much more statesmen-like, to build societies that could live on their own with a minimum of assistance from the mother country.

Canning was thinking in strategic terms and for the good of the empire as a whole. His argument was political and military, consciously avoiding the moral high ground, not because it was unimportant, but because as a policymaker, he knew that it would not have much appeal for Windham. The evangelical humanitarians did not labor under such constraints. True, they formulated arguments designed to appeal to economic interest, but the thrust of their campaign was moral, and they got away with it, in a manner of speaking, because they were quite self-consciously the party of morality.

The great campaign to abolish the institution of slavery in the British Empire marked the coming of age of Britain as a self-conscious imperial power with responsibilities for the welfare of the people living within the bounds of the empire. It represented the realization that must come to all those who would govern and preserve, as well as accumulate, an empire, that the two enterprises frequently involved vastly different talents. The callous daring of a Robert Clive or a Stamford Raffles was not the art requisite to the careful day-by-day care of a going concern that must be balanced on the interests of multitudes of people from different races.

If the foundation of empire is always laid in blood, sweat, and tears, and if its history is frequently the story of brute force, destruction, and human waste on the one hand and material splendor and progress on the other, then we must not forget that the towering edifice is held in place by something as delicate as human thought, attitudes, expectations, and fears. By the 1780s, the British Empire had become too vast and too complex to remain an affair of private traders and merchants. Even in

India, the bastion of private control, the state of things was under attack. Central direction was needed to ensure that the interests of posterity were not sacrificed to the drive for immediate gain.

This required vision. It called for the courage of those who were willing to base action for the future on principles drawn from reflection on the nature of political order, as well as the particulars of imperial political, economic, and military issues. These qualities were seldom found in career politicians who were worried about re-election and political advancement. They were qualities that were traditionally found among the intelligentsia. But generally, this group had little impact on political affairs. This is what made the anti-slavery movement so striking; it represented the direct intrusion of intellectuals into policy-making.

The imperial humanitarians of Clapham and their associates called on their countrymen in high moral terms to renew the sense of mission and the high ethical purpose that they believed had made England great. They were able to exert the great influence that they did because the times demanded a new model for imperial rule, and they had both the genius to develop one and the selflessness to pursue it in the political arena, regardless of the consequences for career. This was not because they were foolish men. By and large, they were immensely successful in business and finance. On the contrary, they had gone into politics and active humanitarian work out of a sense of religious calling. Their careers were centered on doing good, and they calculated their success in terms of how well they secured the humanitarian goals at which they aimed.

The model that they advocated was appealing because like all successful cultural innovations, it combined elements of the existing culture in a fresh and exciting way. Thus it was able to indicate a new way of relating to subject races overseas that promised to secure them to the empire, while at the same time, because it was presented as the very finest of English cultural values, it could re-inforce a positive self-image of Britain.[3] The evangelicals were not calling for an innovation, but for a return to what were supposed to be ancient English values. In the minds of Wilberforce and his friends, there was a virtual identity between vital Christianity and the highest values of the English nation. If English civilization had achieved for the English the highest moral and material state of any nation known to history, then that was simply because English civilization was Christian civilization.

These observations allow us to appreciate how it was that the Clapham humanitarians could be both altruistic reformers and cultural imperialists. In advocating Christianization of the East Indies and the conversion and education of Caribbean slaves as the way to create social health and discharge moral responsibility, they were not trying to seduce Afro-Caribbeans or Indian peasants away from attention to their own self-interest in order that the empire might more effectively exploit them, but to provide them with the means of truly discovering and pursuing their "real" interests. The means being extended were Protestant religion and English culture. Ironically, as the Bishop of Calcutta had suggested to Wilberforce, in receiving this gift, the alien and now pagan races would inevitably become sympathetic to the imperial mission because for the first time, they would be able to see the world in "objective" terms. By freeing them from the bonds of superstition and ignorance, Christianity would make them capable of choosing for themselves the values most beneficial for guiding their lives. In the free market of world culture, however, the value of a civilization could be judged by the attainments of its people, just as in the realm of individual lives, success in life often demonstrated inward righteousness. Because Britain was the nation par excellence, it was inconceivable that anyone who had an open mind would fail to live by English values, just as in the economic realm, one purchased English goods because they were cheaper and of superior craftsmanship.

Clearly, neither Wilberforce nor Buxton, nor even the libertarian Granville Sharp, ever questioned for a moment the absolute superiority of true English values. For the Clapham Sect, Africans and Asians were at an objectively lower level of cultural development; that is what made them potentially dangerous subjects. In their original state, under the sway of native ideas, they could misinterpret their own self-interest and struggle against Britain, when, in fact, their interests lay in assimilating to the British model. This would be a tragedy for them, as well as a problem for the empire. They must be given the opportunity of choosing rightly. There would always be some who were insolent and would refuse to follow the correct path, even when it was opened to them. These could be dealt with justly, but only once the ground for free choice had been laid. Under slavery, one could not blame the slave for acting in a barbarous manner, and therefore, one could not expect to exercise much control over him. But once a moral basis for rule had been laid, action to compel would be based on appeal to a common code of values.

In the final analysis, then, slavery had to go because it prevented alien races from entering and participating in the English cultural heritage that ought to undergird the empire. Slavery, like the policy of dual control in India, stood in the way of progress because it frustrated the expansion of the highest modern cultural values which happened also to be the necessary cultural basis for imperial rule. Members of the Clapham Sect were not against empire. It did not have for them the negative connotations that it has for Americans reared in the illusion that we have never engaged in the purposeful direction of other people's lives. For them, it could be something honorable, a high calling. What they insisted on was that Britain must exercise a moral imperium, not simply a wanton hegemony, over other people. This perception drew on their cultural heritage, true, but it was stimulated, catalyzed, by the refusal of Afro-Caribbean people to exist as slaves. It represents, therefore, a political solution to the problem of governing at least one part of a large empire, a solution which wisely paid attention to the signs of power and humanity emanating from the Caribbean. In this sense, the imperial humanitarians symbolized the very best of that type of culture that is organized around the domination of other people. They met the responsibilities that logically emerged from their self-imposed way of life with vigor, high purpose, and, most important, a refusal to accept the cynical premise that empire did not allow for humanity. They did not call for the dismantling of the imperial project, but they did insist on its humanity, at least as they conceived of it.

But finally, we must observe that the need for humanity did

not emerge by itself from some cultural realm detached from what happened in the world outside. It was called into being because Afro-Caribbeans, for their own reasons and their own purposes, sometimes spectacularly but usually in painful daily resistance, defined the boundaries beyond which any hegemonic power would move at its peril. And so it is with all empires. They live by compromise with the oppressed who defend as much of their integrity as they can with their blood. But imperial elites never admit of any such compromises; instead they celebrate concessions made to humanity as evidence of moral superiority, and therefore as proof of the justice of their rule.

NOTES

1. Henry Dundas to Lord Grenville in a private communication, *Historical Manuscripts Commission. Thirteenth Report Appendix,* Pt. 3. *The Manuscripts of J. B. Fortesque,* vol. 1, pp. 390-391.

2. Canning to Windham, 23 May 1802, in William Windham, *The Windham Papers,* 2 vols. (London: Herbert Jenkins, 1933), 2:191-192.

3. See D. B. Davis, *The Problem of Slavery in the Age of Revolution* (Ithaca, N.Y.: Cornell University Press, 1975), where Davis argues that one purpose of anti-slavery was to validate the integrity of the English constitutional tradition. (See chapters eight and nine.)

Selected Bibliography

Anonymous. *East India Sugar or an Inquiry Respecting the Means of Improving the Quality and Reducing the Cost of Sugar Raised by Free Labor in the East Indies.* London: Pritchard & Sons, 1824.

Barclay, Alexander. *A Practical View of the Present State of Slavery in the West India Colonies.* Miami: Mnemoyne Publishing Co., 1969.

Benezet, Anthony. *Some Historical Account of Guinea.* Philadelphia, 1977.

Bleby, Henry. *Death Struggles of Slavery.* London, 1868.

Blome, Richard. *The Present State of His Majesties Isles and Territories in America.* London: H. Clark, 1967.

Bridges, G. W. *The Annales of Jamaica.* London: Frank Cass & Co., 1968.

Brougham, Henry. *An Inquiry into the Colonial Policy of the European Powers.* 2 vols. New York; Augustus M. Kelley, 1970.

Bryant, Joshua. *Account of an Insurrection of the Negro Slaves in the Colony of Demerara.* Georgetown, Demerara: A. Stevenson, 1824.

Burke, Edmund. *Reflections on the Revolution in France.* Baltimore: Penguin Books, 1969.

————. *Works,* 6 vols. London: G. Bell, 1887-1890.

Buxton, Charles, ed. *Memoirs of Sir Thomas Fowell Buxton.* Philadelphia: Henry Longstretch, 1849.

Buxton, Thomas Fowell. *An Inquiry Whether Crime and Misery Are*

Produced or Prevented by Our Present System of Prison Discipline. London: John Hatchard, 1818.

_____. *The African Slave Trade. The Remedy.* London: Frank Cass and Co. Ltd., 1968.

Caines, Clement. *Letters on the Cultivation of Otaheite Cane.* London: Robinson & Co., 1801.

Calendar of State Papers, Colonial Series. Great Britain: Public Records Office. 38 vols.

Carmichael, Mrs. *Domestic Manners and Social Conditions of the White, Colored, and Negro Population of the West Indies.* 2 vols. New York: Negro Universities Press, 1969.

Carr, Cecil T., ed. *Select Charters of Trading Companies 1530-1707.* Selden Society, vol. 28, 1913.

Casas, Bartolome de las. *The Devastation of the Indies: A Brief Account.* New York: Seabury Press, 1974.

Child, Sir Josiah. *Brief Observations Concerning Trade.* London, 1668.

Clarendon, Edward, Earl of. *The History of the Rebellion and Civil Wars in England.* 6 vols. London: Oxford University Press, 1958.

Clarkson, Thomas. *An Essay on the Slavery and Commerce of the Human Species.* New York: AMS Press, 1972.

_____. *A Summary View of the Slave Trade.* London: L. T. Phillips, 1787.

_____. *A Letter to the Friends of the Slaves on the New Orders in Council.* Ipswich: King & Garrod, 1926.

_____. *Letters to a Friend on the Treatment of the People of Color in the United States.* Boston: New England Anti-Slavery Tract Association, 1814.

_____. *Strictures on a Life of William Wilberforce.* Freeport, N.Y.: Books for Libraries Press, 1971.

_____. *The History of the Rise, Progress, and Accomplishment of the Abolition of the African Slave Trade by the British Parliament.* 2 vols. London: Frank Cass & Co., 1968.

_____. *The True State of the Case Respecting the Insurrection at St. Domingo.* London, 1792.

_____. *Thoughts on the Necessity of Improving the Condition of the Slaves in the British Colonies.* New York, 1823.

Coke, Roger. *A Discourse of Trade.* London, 1670.

Collins, Dr. *Practical Rules for the Management and Medical Treatment of Negro Slaves in the Sugar Colonies.* Freeport, N.Y.: Books for Libraries Press, 1971.

Cugoano, Ottobah. *Thoughts and Sentiments on the Evil of Slavery.* London: Sawsons, 1969.

Cundall, Frank, ed. *Lady Nugent's Journal*. New York: Adan & Charles Black, 1907.

Dallas, R. C. *History of the Maroons*. 2 vols. London: Frank Cass & Co., 1968.

D'Avenant, Charles. *The Political and Commercial Works of Charles D'Avenant*. Edited by Sir Charles Whitworth. 7 vols. London, 1771.

Davy, John. *The West Indies Before and Since Slave Emancipation*. London: Longman, Hurst, Rees, Orme & Brown, 1814.

Donnan, Elizabeth. *Documents Illustrative of the History of the Slave Trade to America*. 4 vols. New York: Octagon Books, 1965.

Douglass, Frederick. *My Bondage and My Freedom*. New York: Dover Publications, 1969.

Eaden, John, trans. *The Memoirs of Pere Labat 1693-1705*. London: Frank Cass & Co., 1970.

Eburne, Richard. *A Plain Pathway to Plantations*. Ithaca, N.Y.: Cornell University Press, 1962.

Edwards, Bryan. *The History, Civil and Commercial of the British West Indies*. 3 vols. London, 1819.

Equiano, Oloudah. "The Life of Oloudah Equiano, or Gustavus Vasa, the African." In *Great Slave Narratives*. Edited by Arna Bontemps. Boston: Beacon Press, 1969.

Firth, H., ed. *The Narrative of General Venables*. New York: Longmans, Green, 1900.

Gardner, W. T. *History of Jamaica*. London: Frank Cass & Co., 1971.

Gladstone, John, and James Cropper. *The Correspondence Between John Gladstone and James Cropper, on the Present State of Slavery in the British West Indies*. Shannon: Irish University Press, 1972.

Griggs, Earl, ed. *Henri Christophe and Thomas Clarkson: A Correspondence*. Westport, Conn.: Greenwood Press, 1968.

Hakluyt, Richard. *The Principle Navigations, Voyages, Traffiques and Discoveries of the English Nation*. 8 vols. London: J. M. Dent & Sons, 1926.

————. *Discourse of Western Planting*. In *The Original Writings and Correspondence of the Two Richard Hakluyt*. Hakluyt Society, 2d series, no. 76, 1935.

Hilton, John. "The Relation of . . . John Hilton." In *Colonizing Expeditions to the West Indies and Guiana, 1623-1667*. Edited by V. T. Harlow. Hakluyt Society, 2d series, no. 56, 1925.

Historical Manuscripts Commission. Thirteenth Report. Appendix, Pt 3. *The Manuscripts of J. B. Fortesque.*

Hotten, John Camden. *The Original Lists of Persons of Quality . . . Who*

Went from Great Britain to the American Plantations 1600-1700.
Baltimore: Genealogical Publishing Co., 1968.

Humbolt, Alexander von. *Personal Narrative of Travels to the Equinoctial Regions of America.* 3 vols. London: Henry G. Bohn, 1853.

Jeaffreson, John Cardy, ed. *A Young Squire of the Seventeenth Century.* 2 vols. London: C. Hurst & Blackett, 1878.

Knutsford, Viscountess. *Life and Letters of Zachary Macaulay.* London: Edward Arnold, 1900.

Lewis, M. G. *Lewis Journal of a West India Proprietor 1815-1817.* Edited by Mona Wilson. New York: Houghton Mifflin, 1929.

Ligon, Richard. *A True and Exact History of the Island of Barbados.* London, 1703.

Long, Edward. *The History of Jamaica.* 3 vols. London: Frank Cass & Co., 1970.

Madden, R. R. *A Twelve Months' Residence in the West Indies.* 2 vols. New York: Negro Universities Press, 1970.

Marshall, Woodville, K., ed. *The Colthurst Journal. Journal of a Special Magistrate in the Island of Barbados and St. Vincent, July 1835-August 1838.* Millwood, N.Y.: KTO Press, 1977.

Misselden, Edward. *The Circle of Commerce, or the Ballance of Trade.* New York: Augustus M. Kelley, 1971.

Montejo, Esteban. *The Autobiography of a Runaway Slave.* Edited by Miguel Barnet (New York: Pantheon Books, 1968).

Moulton, Phillip P. *The Journal and Major Essays of John Woolman.* New York: Oxford University Press, 1971.

M'Queen, J. *The West India Colonies.* New York: Negro Universities Press, 1969.

Mun, Thomas. *England's Treasure by Foreign Trade.* Oxford: Basil Blackwell, 1949.

Nisbet, Richard. *The Capacity of Negroes for Religious and Moral Improvement Considered.* New York: Negro Universities Press, 1970.

Oldmixon, John. *The British Empire in America.* 2 vols. New York: Augustus M. Kelley, 1969.

Parliamentary Papers, 1831-1832. Shannon: Irish University Press, vol. 47.

Phillippo, James M. *Jamaica, Its Past and Present State.* London: Davidson of Pall Mall, 1969.

Pinckard, George, M.D. *Notes on the West Indies.* 3 vols. New York: Negro Universities Press, 1970.

Postlethwayt, Malachy. *Britain's Commercial Interest Explained and Improved.* 2 vols. New York: Augustus M. Kelley, 1968.

Poyer, John. *The History of Barbados.* London: Frank Cass & Co., 1970.
Prichard, M. F. Lloyd, ed. *Original Papers Regarding Trade in England and Abroad.* New York: Augustus M. Kelley, 1967.
The Proceedings of the Governor and Assembly of Jamaica, in Regard to the Maroon Negroes. Westport, Conn.: Negro Universities Press, 1970.
Raleigh, Sir Walter. *Observations Touching Trade and Commerce. The Works of Walter Raleigh.* New York: Burt Franklin, 1829.
Ramsay, James. *An Essay on the Treatment and Conversion of African Slaves in the British Sugar Colonies.* London: James S. Phillips. 1784.
_____. *Objections to the Abolition of the Slave Trade with Answers.* Miami: Mnencesyne Publishing Co., 1969.
Raynal, Abbe. *A Philosophical and Political History of the Settlement and Trade of the Europeans in the East and West Indies.* Trans. by J. O. Justomond. 5 vols. New York: Negro Universities Press, 1969.
Renney, Robert. *History of Jamaica.* London, 1807.
Riley, Edward Miles, ed. *The Journal of John Harrower, an Indentured Servant in the Colony of Virginia 1773-1776.* New York: Holt, Rinehart & Winston, 1963.
Roberts, William. *Memoirs of the Life and Correspondence of Mrs. Hannah More.* 2 vols. New York: Harper & Bros., 1845.
Robertson, William. *The History of the Discovery and Settlement of America.* New York: Harper & Bros., 1842.
Roughley, Thomas. *Jamaica Planters Guide.* London, 1823.
Scott, William R. *The Constitution and Finance of English Scottish and Irish Joint Stock Companies to 1720.* 3 vols. New York: Peter Smith, 1951.
Senior, Bernard. *Jamaica, as It Was, as It Is, and as It May Be.* New York: Negro Universities Press, 1969.
Sharp, Granville. *A Declaration of the People's Natural Right to a Share in the Legislature.* New York: Da Capo Press, 1971.
_____. "An Essay on Slavery." In *Tracts on Slavery.* London, 1776.
_____. *A Representation of the Injustice and Dangerous Tendency of Toleration Slavery in England.* London, 1769.
_____. "The Just Limitation of Slavery in the Laws of God." In *Tracts on Slavery.* London, 1776.
_____. "The Law of Liberty, or Royal Law by Which All Mankind Will Certainly Be Judged." In *Tracts on Slavery.* London, 1776.
Sloane, Sir Hans. *A Voyage to the Islands, Medera, Barbados Nieves, St. Christopher, and Jamaica.* 2 vols. London, 1707.
Smith, Adam. *The Wealth of Nations.* New York: Random House, 1965.

Southey, Captain Thomas. *Chronological History of the West Indies*. 3 vols. London: Frank Cass & Co., 1968.

Stedman, Captain J. G. *Narrative of a Five Years' Expedition Against the Revolted Negroes of Surinam*. Amherst: University of Massachusetts Press, 1971.

Stephen, Sir George. *Anti-Slavery Recollections*. London: Thomas Hatchard, 1854.

Stephen, James. *England Enslaved by Her Own Slave Colonies*. London, 1826.

_____. *The Crisis of the Sugar Colonies*. New York: Negro Universities Press, 1969.

_____. *The Dangers of the Country*. London: J. Butterworth & J. Hatchard, 1807.

_____. *The Memoirs of James Stephen*. London: Bevington Hogarth Press, 1954.

_____. *The Slavery of the British West India Colonies Delineated*. 2 vols. New York: Kraus Reprint Co., 1969.

_____. *War in Disguise; or The Frauds of the Neutral Flags*. London, 1806.

Stephen, Sir James. *Essays in Ecclesiastical Biography*. London: Longman, Green, Longman, & Roberts, 1860.

Stewart, James. *A View of the Past and Present State of the Island of Jamaica*. New York: Negro Universities Press, 1969.

Stock, Leo Francis, ed. *Proceedings and Debates of the British Parliaments Respecting North America*. 5 vols. Washington, D.C.: Carnegie Institution, 1924.

Substance of the Debate in the House of Commons. London: Dawsons of Pall Mall, 1968.

Thomas, Dalby. *An Historical Account of the Rise and Growth of the West India Colonies*. New York: Arno Press, 1972.

Tocqueville, Alexis de. *The Old Regime and the French Revolution*. New York: Doubleday, 1955.

Waddell, Rev. Hope Masterton. *Twenty-nine Years in the West Indies and Central Africa 1829-1858*. London: Frank Cass & Co., 1970.

Wallbridge, Edwin Angel. *The Demerara Martyr. Memoirs of the Rev. John Smith*. New York: Negro Universities Press, 1969.

Wilberforce, Robert Isaac, and Samuel Wilberforce. *The Life of William Wilberforce*. 5 vols. London: John Murray, 1839.

_____. *The Correspondence of William Wilberforce*. 2 vols. London, 1840.

Wilberforce, William. *An Appeal to the Religion, Justice, and Humanity of the Inhabitants of the British Empire on Behalf of the Negro*

Slaves in the West Indies. New York: Negro Universities Press, 1969.
_____. *A Letter on the Abolition of the Slave Trade.* London, 1807.
_____. *A Practical View of the Prevailing Religious Stystem of Professed Christians.* Dublin, 1801.
_____. *Substance of the Speeches of William Wilberforce.* London, 1813.
Windham, William, *The Windham Papers.* 2 vols. London: Herbert Jenkins, 1933.
Young, Sir William. *An Account of the Black Caribs in the Island of St. Vincent.* London: Frank Cass & Co., 1971.

MODERN WORKS

Allen, Robert L. *Black Awakening in Capitalist America.* New York: Doubleday, 1970.
Amin, Samir. *Neocolonialism in West Africa.* New York: Monthly Review Press, 1973.
_____. *Unequal Development.* New York: Monthly Review Press, 1976.
Andrews, Charles M. *British Committees, Commissions, and Councils of Trade and Plantations, 1622-1675.* Baltimore: Johns Hopkins University Press, 1908.
_____. *The Colonial Period of American History.* 4 vols. New Haven, Conn.: Yale University Press, 1948.
Andrews, K. R., ed. *English Privateering Voyages to the West Indies 1588-1595.* Hakluyt Society, 2d series, no. III, 1956.
Andrews, K. R., N. P. Conny, and P.E.H. Hair. *The Western Enterprise.* Detroit: Wayne State University Press, 1979.
Anstey, Roger. *The Atlantic Slave Trade and British Abolition, 1760-1810.* Atlantic Highlands, N.J.: Humanities Press, 1975.
Aptheker, Herbert. *American Negro Slave Revolts.* New York: International Publishers, 1974.
Armstrong, Anthony. *The Church of England, the Methodists and Society 1700-1850.* London: University of London Press, 1973.
Ashley, Maurice. *Financial and Commercial Policy Under the Cromwellian Protectorate.* New York: Augustus M. Kelley, 1962.
_____. *The Greatness of Oliver Cromwell.* London: Hodder & Stoughton, 1957.
Ashton, Robert. *The Crown and the Money Market 1603-1640.* Oxford: Oxford University Press, 1927.
Aspinal, Arthur. *Lord Brougham and the Whig Party.* London: Manchester University Press, 1927.

192   Selected Bibliography

Balleine, G.R.A. *A History of the Evangelical Party in the Church of England*. London: Longmans, Green, 1933.
Barbour, Violet. *Capitalism in Amsterdam in the 17th Century*. Ann Arbor: University of Michigan Press, 1966.
Beer, G. L. *British Colonial Policy 1754-1765*. New York: The Macmillan Co. 1907.
_____. *The Old Colonial System 1660-1688*. 2 vols. New York: The Macmillan Co. 1912.
_____. *The Origins of the British Colonial System, 1578-1660*. New York: The Macmillan Co. 1908.
Bell, Herbert C. "The West India Trade Before the American Revolution." *American Historical Review*, vol. 22, 1917, pp. 272-287.
Bennett, J. H. *Bondsmen and Bishops. Slavery and Apprenticeship on the Codrington Plantation of Barbados 1710-1838*. Berkeley: University of California Press, 1958.
Bethell, Leslie, "The Mixed Commissions for the Suppression of the Transatlantic Slave Trade in the 19th Century." *Journal of African History*, vol. 7, no. 1, 1966, pp. 79-93.
Black, Eugene C. *The Association*. Cambridge, Mass.: Harvard University Press, 1963.
Blassingame, John. *The Slave Community*. New York: Oxford University Press, 1972.
Bowman, William. *Bristol and America. A Record of the First Settlers in the Colonies of North America, 1654-1685*. Baltimore: Genealogical Publishing Co., 1967.
Boxer, C. R. *The Dutch Seaborne Empire: 1600-1800*. New York: Alfred A. Knopf, 1979.
Bradley, Ian. *The Call to Seriousness*. London: Jonathan Cape, 1976.
Brathwaite, Edward. *The Development of Creole Society in Jamaica 1777-1820*. London: Oxford University Press, 1971.
Bridenbaugh, Carl, and Roberta Bridenbaugh. *No Peace Beyond the Line. The English in the Caribbean, 1624-1690*. London: Oxford University Press, 1972.
Brinton, Crane. *A Decade of Revolution 1789-1799*. New York: Harper & Row, 1965.
Brisbane, Robert H. *Black Activism*. Valley Forge, Pa.: Judson Press, 1974.
_____. *The Black Vanguard*. Valley Forge, Pa.: Judson Press, 1970.
Brown, Ford K. *Fathers of the Victorians*. London: Cambridge University Press, 1961.
Bruce, P. A. *Economic History of Virginia in the Seventeenth Century*. 2 vols. New York: Peter Smith, 1935.

Buckley, Roger Norman. *Slaves in Red Coats. The British West India Regiments, 1795-1815.* New Haven, Conn.: Yale University Press, 1979.

Burn, William L. *Emancipation and Apprenticeship in the British West Indies.* New York: Jonathan Cape, 1937.

Cassirer, Ernst. *The Philosophy of the Enlightenment.* Princeton, N.J.: Princeton University Press, 1959.

Chandman, C. D. *The English Public Revenue 1660-1688.* London: Oxford University Press, 1975.

Checkland, Sidney. *British Public Policy 1776-1939.* Cambridge: Cambridge University Press, 1983.

Christie, Ian R. *Wars and Revolutions. Britain 1769-1815.* Cambridge, Mass.: Harvard University Press, 1982.

Cohen, David, and Jack Green. *Neither Slave nor Free. The Freedmen of African Descent in the Slave Societies of the New World.* Baltimore: Johns Hopkins University Press, 1972.

Cole, G.D.H. *The Life of William Cobbett.* London: W. Collins Sons, 1927.

Coleman, D. C., and A. H. John, eds. *Trade Government and Economy in Pre-Industrial England.* London: Weidenfeld & Nicolson, 1976.

Cone, Carl B. *The English Jacobins.* New York: Charles Scribner's Sons, 1968.

Coupland, Reginald. *The British Anti-Slavery Movement.* London: Frank Cass & Co., 1963.

Cowley, Malcom. *Black Cargoes.* New York: Viking Press, 1972.

Craton, Michael. *Sinews of Empire.* New York: Doubleday, 1974.

———. *Searching for the Invisible Man.* Cambridge, Mass.: Harvard University Press, 1978.

———. "The Passion to Exist: Slave Rebellion in the British West Indies 1650-1832." *Journal of Caribbean History,* vol. 13, December 1981. pp. 1-20.

———. "Slave Culture, Resistance and the Achievement of Emancipation in the British West Indies, 1783-1838." In *Slavery and British Society, 1776-1846.* London: Edited by James Walvin. Macmillan, 1982.

———. *Testing the Chains. Resistance to Slavery in the British West Indies.* Ithaca, N.Y.: Cornell University Press, 1982.

Craton, Michael, and James Walvin. *A Jamaican Plantation. The History of Worthy Park, 1670-1970.* Toronto: University of Toronto Press, 1970.

Crouzet, Francois, ed. *Capital Formation in the Industrial Revolution.* London: Methuen, 1972.

_____. *The First Industrialists*. Cambridge: Cambridge University Press, 1985.

Cunningham, W. *The Growth of English Industry and Commerce*. 3 vols. Cambridge: Cambridge University Press, 1912.

Curtin, Philip D. *The Atlantic Slave Trade*. Madison: University of Wisconsin Press, 1969.

_____. *Economic Change in Pre-Colonial Africa*. 2 vols. Madison: University of Wisconsin Press, 1975.

_____. *The Image of Africa: British Ideas and Action, 1780-1850*. Madison: University of Wisconsin Press, 1964.

Daaku, K. Y. *Trade and Politics on the Gold Coast, 1600-1700*. Oxford: Clarendon Press, 1970.

Davies, K. G., "The Origins of the Commission System in the West India Trade." *Transactions of the Royal Historical Society*, 5th series, vol. 3, 1952, pp. 89-107.

Davis, David Brion. *The Problem of Slavery in the Age of Revolution*. Ithaca, N.Y.: Cornell University Press, 1975.

_____. *The Problem of Slavery in Western Culture*. Ithaca, N.Y.: Cornell University Press, 1966.

_____. *Slavery and Human Progress*. Oxford: Oxford University Press, 1984.

Davis, Ralph. *The Rise of the English Shipping Industry in the Seventeenth and Eighteenth Centuries*. New York: Macmillan, 1962.

Deane, Phyllis. *The First Industrial Revolution*. London: Cambridge University Press, 1969.

Deer, Noel. *The History of Sugar*. 2 vols. London: Chapman & Hall, 1949-50.

Degler, Carl N. *Neither Black nor White: Slavery and Race Relations in Brazil and the United States*. New York: Macmillan, 1971.

DeVries, Jan. *The Economy of Europe in an Age of Crisis 1600-1750*. Cambridge: Cambridge University Press, 1976.

Dozier, Robert R. *For King, Constitution, and Country. The English Loyalists and the French Revolution*. Lexington: University Press of Kentucky, 1983.

Drescher, Seymour. *Econocide: British Slavery in the Era of Abolition*. Pittsburgh: University of Pittsburgh Press, 1977.

DuBois, W.E.B. *Black Reconstruction in America 1860-1880*. New York: Atheneum, 1975.

_____. *The Suppression of the African Slave Trade to the United States of America, 1638-1880*. New York: Atheneum, 1975.

Dunn, Richard S. *Sugar and Slaves*. New York: W. W. Norton, 1972.

Embree, Ainslie Thomas. *Charles Grant and British Rule in India*. New York: Columbia University Press, 1962.

Fortesque, John W. *A History of the British Army*. 13 vols. London: Macmillan, 1899-1930.

Franklin, John Hope. *From Slavery to Freedom*. New York: Alfred A. Knopf, 1967.

Freyre, Gilberto. *The Masters and the Slaves*. Trans. by Samuel Putnam. New York: Alfred A. Knopf, 1956.

Friss, A. *Alderman Cockayne's Project*. London: Oxford University Press, 1927.

Furneaux, Robin. *William Wilberforce*. London: Hamish Hamilton, 1974.

Fyfe, Christopher. *A History of Sierra Leone*. London: Oxford University Press, 1963.

Gash, Norman. *Aristocracy and People. Britain 1815-1865*. Cambridge, Mass.: Harvard University Press, 1979.

Gaspar, David Barry. *Bondsmen and Rebels. A Study of Master-Slave Relations in Antigua*. Baltimore: Johns Hopkins University Press, 1985.

Gay, Peter. *The Enlightenment: An Interpretation. The Rise of Modern Paganism*. New York: Vintage Books, 1968.

_____. *The Enlightenment: An Interpretation. The Science of Freedom*. New York: Alfred A. Knopf, 1969.

Geiser, K. F. *Redemptioners and Indentured Servants in the Colony and Commonwealth of Pennsylvania*. New Haven, Conn.: Tuttle Morehouse & Taylor, 1901.

Gemery, Henry A., and Jan S. Hogendarn, eds. *The Uncommon Market*. New York: Academic Press, 1979.

Genovese, Eugene. *From Rebellion to Revolution*. New York: Vintage Books, 1981.

_____. *Roll, Jordan Roll. The World the Slaves Made*. New York: Pantheon Books, 1966.

_____. *The Political Economy of Slavery*. New York: Pantheon Books, 1966.

Geyl, Peter. *The Netherlands in the 17th Century*. 2 parts. New York: Barnes & Noble, 1961.

Gill, Conrad. *Merchants and Mariners of the Seventeenth Century*. London: Edward Arnold, 1961.

Godeschot, Jacques. *France and the Atlantic Revolution of the Eighteenth Century, 1770-1799*. New York: The Free Press, 1965.

Goodwin, Albert. *The Friends of Liberty. The English Democratic*

Movement in the Age of the French Revolution. Cambridge, Mass.: Harvard University Press, 1979.

Goslinga, Cornelis, Ch. *A Short History of the Netherlands Antilles and Surinam.* The Hague: Martinus Nijhoff, 1979.

Goveia, Elsa. *Slave Society in the British Leeward Islands at the End of the Eighteenth Century.* New Haven, Conn.: Yale University Press, 1965.

———. "The West Indian Slave Laws of the Eighteenth Century." *Revista de ciencias sociales,* vol. 4, no. 1, March 1960, pp. 75-105.

Gray, Denis. *Spencer Perceval.* Manchester: Manchester University Press, 1963.

Green, Daniel. *Great Cobbett.* London: Hodder & Stoughton, 1983.

Green, William. *British Slave Emancipation.* London: Oxford University Press, 1975.

———. "James Stephen and British West India Policy, 1834-1847." *Caribbean Studies,* vol. 13, no. 4, pp. 33-56.

Gutman, Herbert G. *The Black Family in Slavery and Freedom 1750-1925.* New York: Pantheon books, 1976.

Halevy, Elie. *England in 1815.* London: Ernest Benn, 1960.

Hampson, Norman. *The Enlightenment.* Baltimore: Penguin Books, 1968.

Handler, Jerome S. *The Unappropriated People: Freedmen in the Slave Society of Barbados.* Baltimore: Johns Hopkins University Press, 1974.

Harlow, V. T. *History of Barbados 1625-1685.* New York: Oxford University Press, 1926.

———. *The Founding of the Second British Empire 1763-1793.* 2 vols. Cambridge: Cambridge University Press, 1964.

Harper, L. A. *The English Navigation Laws.* New York: Octagon Books, 1973.

Harre, Rom. *Social Being.* Totowa, N.J.: Littlefield, Adams, 1980.

Harris, Marvin. *The Rise of Anthropological Theory.* New York: Thomas Y. Crowell, 1968.

Helps, A. G. *The Conquerors of the New World and Their Bondsmen. Being a Narrative of the Principal Events Which Led to Negro Slavery in the West Indies and America.* 2 vols. London: William Pickering. 1848.

Hennell, M. *John Venn and the Clapham Sect.* London: Lutterworth Press, 1958.

Herrick, C. A. *White Servitude in Pennsylvania.* Philadelphia: John Joseph McVery, 1929.

Heskovits, Melville T. *The Myth of the Negro Past.* Boston: Beacon Press, 1958.

_____. *The New World Negro.* Bloomington, Indiana: Indiana University Press, 1966.

Higham, C.S.S. *The Development of the Leeward Islands Under the Restoration, 1660-1688.* Cambridge: Cambridge University Press, 1921.

Higman, Barry W. *Slave Populations of the British Caribbean 1807-1834.* Baltimore: Johns Hopkins University Press, 1984.

_____. *Slave Population and Economy in Jamaica, 1807-1834.* Cambridge: Cambridge University Press, 1976.

Hill, Christopher. *The English Revolution.* London: Lawrence & Wishant, 1949.

Hobsbawm, Eric J. *The Age of Revolution 1789-1848.* New York: Mentor Books, 1962.

_____. *Industry and Empire.* London: Weidenfeld & Nicolson, 1968.

Hoffman, Paul E. *The Spanish Crown and the Defense of the Caribbean 1535-1585.* Baton Rouge: Louisiana State University Press, 1980.

Holdsworth, Sir William. *A History of English Law,* 16 vols. London: Methuen, 1966.

Hopkins, A. G. *An Economic History of West Africa.* New York: Columbia University Press, 1973.

Hoskins, W. G. *The Age of Plunder. King Henry's England 1500-1547.* London: Longmans, 1976.

Howse, Earnest Marshall. *Saints in Politics.* Toronto: University of Toronto Press, 1952.

James, C.L.R. *The Black Jacobins.* New York: Vintage Books, 1963.

Jay, Elizabeth. *The Evangelical and Oxford Movements.* Cambridge: Cambridge University Press, 1983.

Jernegan, Marcus Wilson. *Laboring and Dependent Classes in Colonial America 1607-1783.* Chicago: University of Chicago Press, 1931.

Johnson, Samuel. *The History of the Yorubas.* 2 vols. Westport, Conn.: Negro Universities Press, 1970.

Jones, M. G. *Hannah More.* Cambridge: Cambridge University Press, 1952.

Judson, M. A. *The Crisis of the Constitution.* New Brunswick, N.J.: Rutgers University Press, 1949.

Kiernan, V. G. *The Lords of Human Kind.* Harmondsworth, England: Penguin Books, 1972.

Klingberg, Frank. *The Anti-Slavery Movement in England.* London: Oxford University Press, 1926.

Kluckhohn, Clyde. *Culture and Behavior.* New York: The Free Press, 1962.

Knight, Franklin. *Slave Society in Cuba During the Nineteenth Century.* Madison: University of Wisconsin Press, 1970.

Kroeber, Alfred. *Configurations of Culture Growth.* Berkeley: University of California Press, 1944.

———. *The Nature of Culture.* Chicago: University of Chicago Press, 1952.

Kroeber, A. L., and Clyde Kluckhohn. "Culture: A Critical Review of Concepts and Definitions." Harvard University. Papers of the Peabody Museum of American Archaeology and Ethnology, vol. 47.

Landes, David. *The Unbound Prometheus.* Cambridge: Cambridge University Press, 1970.

LeFebvre, George. *The French Revolution.* 2 vols. New York: Columbia University Press, 1965.

Levine, Lawrence. *Black Culture and Black Consciousness.* Oxford: Oxford University Press, 1978.

Lipson, Ephraim. *The Economic History of England.* 3 vols. London: A. & C. Black, 1948-1949.

Locke, John. *Of Civil Government.* London: J. M. Dent & Sons, 1947.

Lockyer, Roger. *Tudor and Stuart Britain, 1471-1714.* London: Longmans, 1969.

Lovejoy, Paul E. *Transformations in Slavery: A History of Slavery in Africa.* Cambridge: Cambridge University Press, 1983.

Lucas, C. P. *Historical Geography of the British Colonies.* 2 vols. Oxford: Clarendon Press, 1890.

Maccoby, S. *English Radicalism 1786-1832.* London: George Allen & Unwin, 1955.

Macinnes, C. M. *Bristol: A Gateway of Empire.* New York: Augustus M. Kelley, 1968.

Mann, J. de L. *The Cloth Industry in the West of England from 1640 to 1880.* Oxford: Clarendon Press, 1971.

———. *The Cotton Trade and Industrial Lancashire 1600-1780.* Manchester: Manchester University Press, 1931.

Mathieson, William. *British Slavery and Its Abolition, 1823-1838.* New York: Octagon Books, 1967.

McKee, Samuel. *Labor in Colonial New York 1664-1776.* New York: Columbia University Press, 1935.

Meacham, Standish. *Henry Thornton of Clapham 1760-1815.* Cambridge, Mass: Harvard University Press, 1964.

Metcalf, George. *Royal Government and Political Conflict in Jamaica, 1729-1783.* London: Longmans, 1965.

Mill, James. *The History of British India.* Chicago: University of Chicago Press, 1975.

Minchinton, W. E., ed. *The Growth of English Overseas Trade in the Seventeenth and Eighteenth Centuries.* London: Methuen, 1969.

Mullin, Gerald. *Flight and Rebellion*. London: Oxford University Press, 1972.

Newton, Arthur P. *The Colonizing Activities of the English Puritans*. New York: Kennikat Press, 1966.

Norman, E. R. *Church and Society in England 1770-1970*. Oxford: Clarendon Press, 1976.

Ogg, David. *England in the Reigns of James II and William III*. London: Oxford University Press, 1966.

Palmer, R. R. *The Age of the Democratic Revolution*. 2 vols. Princeton, N.J.: Princeton University Press, 1971.

Pares, Richard. *A West India Fortune*. New York: Longmans, 1950.

_____. *Merchants and Planters*. Cambridge: Cambridge University Press, 1900.

_____. *War and Trade in the West Indies 1739-1763*. Oxford: Clarendon Press, 1936.

_____. *Yankees and Creoles*. New York: Longmans, 1956.

Parker, J., ed. *Merchants and Scholars*. Minneapolis: University of Minnesota Press, 1967.

Parry, J. H. *The Age of Reconnaisance*. New York: Praeger, 1969.

Patterson, Orlando. *Slavery and Social Death*. New Haven, Conn.: Yale University Press, 1984.

_____. *The Sociology of Slavery*. Rutherford, N.J.: Fairleigh Dickinson University Press, 1969.

Pearl, Valerie. *London and the Outbreak of the Puritan Revolution*. London: Oxford University Press, 1924.

Penson, Lilian M. *The Colonial Agents of the British West Indies*. London: University of London Press, 1924.

Philips, C. H. *The East India Company 1784-1834*. New York: Barnes & Noble, 1961.

Phillips, U. B. *American Negro Slavery*. Baton Rouge: Louisiana State University Press, 1969.

Pitman, Frank W. "Slavery on British West India Plantations in the Eighteenth Century." *Journal of Negro History*, no. 11, 1926, pp. 584-668.

_____. *The Development of the British West Indies, 1700-1763*. New Haven, Conn.: Yale University Press, 1917.

_____. "The Settlement and Financing of British West India Plantations in the 18th Century." In *Essays in Colonial History Presented to Charles McLean Andrews by His Students*. New Haven, Conn.: Yale University Press, 1931.

Porter, Dale H. *The Abolition of the Slave Trade in England 1784-1807*. Hamden, Conn.: Shoe String Press, Archon Books, 1970.

Poyer, J. R. *Society and Pauperism. English Ideas on Poor Relief 1795-1834*. London: Routledge & Kegan Paul, 1969.

Price, Richard. *Maroon Societies*. New York: Doubleday, 1973.

Rabb, Theodore K. *Enterprise and Empire*. Cambridge, Mass.: Harvard University Press, 1967.

Ragatz, Lowell J. *The Fall of the Planter Class in the British Caribbean, 1763-1833*. New York: Appleton-Century-Crofts, 1928.

Ramsay, G. D. *English Overseas Trade*. London: Macmillan, 1957.

Rawick, George P. *From Sundown to Sunup*. Westport, Conn.: Greenwood Press, 1972.

Reckord, Mary "The Jamaican Slave Rebellion of 1831." *Past and Present*, no. 40, July 1968, pp. 108-125.

Reitzel, William, ed. *The Autobiography of William Cobbett*. London: Faber & Faber, 1967.

Rice, Charles Duncan. *The Rise and Fall of Black Slavery*. New York: Harper & Row, 1977.

Rodney, Walter. *How Europe Underdeveloped Africa*. Washington, D.C.: Howard University Press, 1981.

Rose, J. Holland, A. P. Newton, and E. Z. Benians. The Cambridge *History of the British Empire*. vol. 2, *The Growth of the New Empire, 1783-1870*. Cambridge: Cambridge University Press, 1940.

Rude, George. *Europe in the Eighteenth Century. Aristocracy and the Bourgeois Challenge*. New York: Praeger, 1973.

Scott, William R. *The Constitution and Finance of English, Scottish and Irish Joint Stock Companies to 1720*. 2 vols. New York: Peter Smith, 1951.

Sheridan, Richard B. *Sugar and Slavery, An Economic History of the British West Indies, 1623-1775*. Baltimore: Johns Hopkins University Press, 1973.

————. "The Wealth of Jamaica in the Eighteenth Century: A Rejoinder." *The Economic History Review*, 2d series, vol. 21, 1968, pp. 46-61.

Shyllon, Folarian. *Black Slaves in Britain*. London: Oxford University Press, 1974.

Smith, Abbot Emerson. *Colonists in Bondage. White Servitude and Convict Labor in America, 1607-1776*. Chapel Hill: University of North Carolina Press, 1947.

Smith, Gordon-Connel. *Forerunners of Drake*. Westport, Conn.: Greenwood Press, 1975.

Smith, M. G. *The Plural Society in the British West Indies*. Berkeley: University of California Press, 1965.

Smith, Warren B. *White Servitude in Colonial South Carolina*. Columbia: University of South Carolina Press, 1961.

Soloway, R. A. *Prelates and People*. London: Routledge & Kegan Paul, 1969.

Spater, George. *William Cobbett*. 2 vols. Cambridge: Cambridge University Press, 1982.

Stampp, Kenneth M. *The Peculiar Institution*. New York: Vintage Books, 1956.

Steward, J. *Theory of Culture Change*. Urbana: University of Illinois Press, 1955.

Stokes, Eric. *The English Utilitarians and India*. Oxford: Oxford University Press, 1959.

Supple, Barry. *Commercial Crisis and Change in England 1600-1642*. Cambridge: Cambridge University Press, 1959.

Sypher, Wylie. *Guinea's Captive Kings*. Chapel Hill: University of North Carolina Press, 1942.

Tawney, R. H., ed. *Studies in Economic History: The Collected Papers of George Unwin*. New York: Augustus M. Kelley, 1966.

Thomas, R. P. "The Sugar Colonies of the Old Empire: Profit or Loss for Great Britain." *The Economic History*, 2d series, vol. 31, 1968, pp. 30-45.

Thomis, Malcolm I. *Threats of Revolution in Britain 1789-1848*. Hamden, Conn.: Shoe String Press, Archon Books, 1977.

Thompson, E. P. *The Making of the English Working Class*. New York: Vintage Books, 1963.

Thornton, A. P. *West India Policy Under the Restoration*. Oxford: Oxford University Press, 1956.

Unwin, George. *Studies in Economic History: The Collected Papers of George Unwin*. Edited by R. H. Tawney. New York: Augustus M. Kelley, 1960.

Vlekke, B. *Evolution of the Dutch Nation*. New York: Roy Publishers, 1945.

Watson, J. Steven. *The Reign of George III 1760-1815*. London: Oxford University Press, 1960.

White, Leslie. *The Evolution of Culture*. New York: McGraw-Hill, 1958.

Wiener, Martin J., ed. *Humanitarianism or Social Control*. Houston: Rice University Studies, vol. 67, no. 1, Winter 1981.

Williams, Eric. *Capitalism and Slavery*. New York: G. P. Putman's Sons, 1966.

_____. *From Columbus to Castro*. New York: Harper & Row, 1973.

_____. "The British West Indian Slave Trade After Its Abolition in

1807." *Journal of Negro History,* vol. 27, 1945, pp. 175-191.

————. "The Golden Age of the Slave System in Britain." *Journal of Negro History,* vol 25, no. 1, pp. 60-106.

Williams, Gomer. *History of the Liverpool Privateers and Letters of Marque with an Account of the Liverpool Slave Trade.* London: n.p., 1897.

Williamson, J. A. *The Caribee Islands Under the Proprietary Patents.* London: Oxford University Press, 1926.

Wilson, Charles. *England's Apprenticeship 1703-1763.* London: Longmans, 1965.

————. *Profit and Power. A Study of England and the Dutch Wars.* New York: Longmans, 1957.

————. *The Dutch Republic.* New York: McGraw-Hill, 1977.

Woodward, C. Vann. *The Strange Career of Jim Crow.* New York: Oxford University Press, 1974.

Zins, Henryk. *England and the Baltic in the Elizabethan Era.* Translated by H. C. Stevens. Manchester: Manchester University Press, 1972.

Zook, G. G. *The Company of Royal Adventurers Trading into Africa.* New York: Negro University Press, 1969.

Index

Abolition of slave trade: and amelioration, 69, 142, 148, 152, 164; and conservative principles, 141-42; and the Creolization of society, 76-77; and demographic changes in slave population, 77, 78; discredited on the basis of slave characterization, 60-61; and economic decline in British West Indies, 2-4, 6-7, 78; as first step toward emancipation, 147; and the homogenization of Afro-Caribbean culture, 87-88; humanitarianism and, 9; and national reformation, 161; and the perpetuation of slavery, 143; and productivity in the colonies, 77; religion and, 163-64; slave rebellion as justification for, 79-81, 98-99, 156-57. *See also* Anti-slavery
Africa, 104-5

African company, 31
The African Trade (Thompson), 139
Afro-Caribbean culture: and anti-slavery, 2, 183-84; attempts to limit, 41, 64-65; homogenization of, 87-88; recognition of, 65-66; and slave rebellion, 76, 81-82, 85. *See also* Blacks; British West Indies
Altruism, 135
Amelioration, 147; abolition and, 69, 142, 148, 152, 164; and improvement of the black character, 151; and the security of the empire, 69, 160. *See also* Anti-slavery
America, as a source of raw material, 25. *See also* United States
Anti-slavery: Afro-Caribbean culture and, 2, 81, 183-84; Afro-English community and,

135-37; apparent altruism of, 134-35; Christianity and, 83-85, 139-40; and conservative principles, 142; context of moral judgements and, 12-13; and cultural change, 102; development of, 11-12; and the development of bourgeois ideology, 10; discredited on the basis of slave characterization, 60-61; economic and social changes and, 1-2; economic decline of islands and, 2-4; English law and, 137-38, 147-48; evangelicals and, 110; historiography of, 1; humanitarianism and, 8-9; and imperial security, 14, 143-44; and individualism, 123-24, 151; intelligentsia and, 181; literature of, 2; as a response to radicalism, 114; and the role of government, 102-3; scripture and, 139-40; slave rebellion and, 51, 68-69, 85-86, 148; social and cultural transformation as factor in, 8-9; and social stability, 98. *See also* Abolition of slave trade; Slavery

Antigua codes of 1702 and 1723, 54

An Appeal (Wilberforce), 141-45

Aristocracy: capitalist participation of, 112-13; and moral decline, 115-16, 121-22; resistance to radicalism, 113-14; sugar cultivation and, 34-35. *See also* Imperial government

Atkins, John, *A Voyage to Guinea, Brazil and the West Indies,* 72

Bahamas, 170

Baptists, 63, 84

Barbados, 26-29, 32, 51-52; code of 1661, 53, 54

Barclay, Alexander, *A Practical View of the Present State of Slavery,* 67

Benevolence, 116-18, 135

Bible, the, 139-40

Blacks, 75-76, 135, 142. *See also* Afro-Caribbean culture; Characterization of blacks/slaves; Slavery

Britain: absence of radicalism in, 112-14; benevolent imperial record of, 161-62; civil war in, 27-29; constitutional crisis, 26-27; Dutch competition in trade, 21-24; impact of slavery on, 167; intervention in St. Domingue revolution, 179; law of, 137-38, 147-48; as multi-ethnic empire, 99; poor blacks in, 135; Protestant civilization and, 108, 182; relations with subject races, 100, 102, 181; responsible for the savagery of Africa, 147; social and cultural transformations in, 8-9, 160; ment, 111-12. *See also* Imperial government

British Guyana, 80

British West Indies: aristocracy and concentration of holdings in, 34-35; dependence on British manufacture, 21; dependence on imperial government, 97; economic decline in, 2-4, 6-7; growing imperial control over, 32-33; growth of slave population, 52, 152-53; increase of trade, 5-6;

monopoly and, 4; and the national interest, 164-66; slavery in (*see* Slavery); sources of revolution in, 151, 154; type of society, 33, 35-36, 143. *See also* Colonization

Brougham, Henry, 153-54

Brown, Ford K., *Fathers of the Victorians,* 119

Burke, Edmund, 141; *Reflections on the Revolution in France,* 121

Buxton, Thomas Fowell, 116-17; *Inquiry,* 124-25

Caines, Clement, 152

Calais affair, 8

Canning, George, 179-80

Capitalism, 112; and class consciousness, 11; formulation of ideology, 10; mercantile/commercial vs. industrial, 4-5; participation of aristocracy in, 113; and social transformations, 9

Caribbean. *See* Afro-Caribbean culture; British West Indies *and names of specific islands*

Carlisle, first earl of, 27-28

Characterization of blacks/slaves: as anti-abolition argument, 58-61, 149; improved by amelioration, 150-51; as justification for management by force, 66-67; and slave codes, 53-56; slavery's effect upon, 157

Chartered companies, 30-31, 105

Cheap Repository Tracts, 119-20

Christianity: in Africa, 104-5; and individualism, 124; and anti-slavery, 83-85, 139-40; and cultural imperialism, 106-8,

182; as a means of managing slavery, 64-65; and slave rebellion, 63-64; slavery frustrating growth of, 147; and the social order, 120-22. *See also* Evangelicals; Religion

Chronological History of the West Indies (Southey), 79

Civil rights movement, 101-2, 134

Civil war, in Britain, 27-29, 37

Clapham group, 104; and cultural imperialism, 108, 181-83; establishment of, 110-11; and the moral dangers of upper-class life, 115-16. *See also* Evangelicals; Humanitarianism

Clarkson, Thomas, 146-50; *Essay on Slavery,* 145-46; *History,* 11-12

Class structure, 11; evangelical support of, 117-22. *See also* Aristocracy; Middle class

Cobbett, William, 123

Colonization, 21; beginning of, 25-26; chartered companies and, 30-31; civil war and, 27-29; constitutional crisis and, 26-27; growing imperial control over, 32-33, 97, 105; impetus for, 25; labor recruitment and, 37-40, 165-66; and the struggle between merchants and planters, 32-36; support for, 41-42. *See also* British West Indies

Commercial capitalism, 4-5

Concentration of agriculture, 34-35, 77

Constitutional crisis, in Britain, 26-27

Convicts, and labor recruitment, 37-38

Creoles, 56, 76, 87-88. *See also*
  Afro-Caribbean culture
Crime, 124-25
Crisis of the Sugar Colonies
  (Stephen), 155-60
Cugoano, Ottobah, 83; *Thoughts
  and Sentiments on the Evils of
  Slavery*, 84
Cultural imperialism, 106-8,
  181-83
Cultural revolution, 8-9, 100-102

D'Avenant, Charles, 41; *Political
  and Commerical Works*, 19-20
Dallas, R.C., *History of the
  Maroons*, 61
The Dangers of the Country
  (Stephen), 160-64
Davis, David Brion: *Problem of
  Slavery in the Age of Revolu-
  tion*, 12; *Problem of Slavery in
  Western Culture*, 9-11
Davis, Ralph, "English Foreign
  Trade, 1660-1700," 23
Davy, John, *The West Indies
  Before and Since Slave Eman-
  cipation*, 60-61
Demographics of slave popula-
  tion, 7, 52, 77-78, 87-88,
  152-53, 170-71
Dickson, William, 151-52
Diversification of trade, 22-23
Divine justice, 163-64
Douglass, Frederick, *My Bondage
  and My Freedom*, 70-71
Drescher, Seymour, *Econocide*,
  5-7
Duncan-Rice, Charles, *The Rise
  and Fall of Black Slavery*, 1-2

Economics: decline in the British
  West Indies, 2-4, 6-7, 78; transformation in British society,
  8-9
Emancipation, 7, 9, 76, 147.
  See also Anti-slavery
England Enslaved (Stephen),
  164-66
Enlightenment, 133
Essay on Slavery (Clarkson),
  145-46
Essay on Slavery (Sharp),
  139-40
Europe, 113-14, 146
Evangelicals, 104, 110; against
  radicalism, 119; apparent
  altruism of, 134-35; attitudes
  toward Hindu culture, 106-7;
  beliefs of, 108-10; and the
  development of British imperial
  culture, 110; notion of crime
  and social irresponsibility,
  124-25; and the question of
  social inequality, 117-23;
  support of industrial
  capitalism, 119. *See also*
  Christianity; Clapham group;
  Humanitarians
Evil, 118

Family, 109, 168
Fathers of the Victorians
  (Brown), 119
Fedon, Julien, 75
Financing of overseas trade,
  30-31
France, 74, 156, 159
Freedom, 138, 151. *See also*
  Emancipation
Free labor, 166. *See also* Labor
  recruitment
Free trade, 32. *See also* Trade
French revolution, 103, 112, 118,
  121, 164

Gay, Peter, *The Enlightenment,* 8
"Good" Negro, image of, 59, 89
Government, role of, 102-3. *See also* Imperial government
Grant, Charles, 106-7
Grenada, 75
Guiana, 25

Haiti, 170. *See also* St. Domingue revolution
Hakluyt, Richard, *Discourse of Western Planting,* 24-25
Hall, Thomas, 31
Hawkins, John, 30
Head Negro driver, 58-59
Hinduism, 106-7
Historiography, 1, 8
History of Jamaica (Renny), 152
History of the Discovery and Settlement of America (Robertson), 77-78
Homogenization of Afro-Caribbean culture, 87-88
Hughes, Victor, 74-75
Humanitarianism, 8-9; discredited on the basis of slave characterization, 60-61; and the domestic social system, 114-15, 120, 161; focus on "Third World" colonies, 104; and the founding of Sierra Leone, 104; ideology and, 6, 102-3; impact on imperial affairs, 100; against the management of slaves by force, 67; and moral judgements, 13, 180-82; slave rebellion and, 81; on slavery and Christianity, 147. *See also* Clapham group; Evangelicals
Human nature, 118

Ideology, 81; of industrial

capitalism, 10; of revolution, 102-3
Imperial government: growing control over colonies, 32-33, 97, 105; and the lessons of popular revolution, 103; and the master-slave relationship, 105; perception of subject races, 100; religious influence on, 117. *See also* Britain
Imperialism, 19-29; cultural, 106-8, 181-83
Indentured labor, 36-37, 39-40
India, 98, 105-8, 162
Individualism, 123-24, 151
Industrial capitalism, 4-5, 9-11, 112, 119
Inequality, 117-22
Injustice, 133-34
Inquiry (Buxton), 124-25
Intellectual transformations of British society, 8-9
Intelligentsia, 181
Ireland, 162
Islam, 64

Jamaica, 56, 58; growth of slave population, 52; maroonage in, 72-74; rebellion in, 63, 76, 78-79, 81-87
Jamaican Planters Guide (Roughley), 56-59
James I, king of England, 27
Journal of a West India Proprietor 1815-1817 (Lewis), 62
Judaism, 139-40
Justice, 168-69; divine, 163-64

Klingberg, Frank, *The Anti-Slavery Movement in England,* 8-9

Labor recruitment, 36-40, 165-66, 169-71
Law, English, 137-38; 147-48
The Law of Liberty (Granville Sharp), 140
The Law of Passive Obedience (Granville Sharp), 140
Lefebvre, George, 112
Legislation, slavery, 52-54
Lewis, M. G., *Journal of a West India Proprietor 1815-1817*, 62
Liberty, 138-39, 161. *See also* Emancipation
Literature, anti-slavery, 2
Locke, John, 124
London, poor blacks in, 135
Long, Edward, 55

M'Queen, James, *The West India Colonies*, 69
Management of slavery: through fear and awe of the master, 70, 158-59; by force, 65-68; through kindness, 62-63; by legislation, 52-54; psychological, 55-56, 57-58, 61-62, 158; through religious instruction, 63-65; scientific, 56-62
Manufacture, 20, 21
Maroons, 71-74, 89-90
Master-slave relationship, 69, 89; characterization of slave and, 60; cooperation, 78; imperial control and, 105; leading to social instability, 153; and management through fear, 70; and the psychological manipulation of slaves, 55-56, 61
Mercantile capitalism, 4-5
Merchants, 30-36
Middle class, 9, 11, 112-14, 122
Missionaries, 83, 109-10

Monopoly, 4, 31
Morality, 169; aristocracy and, 115-16, 121-22; socioeconomic context of, 12-13. *See also* Religion
Moravians, 64
More, Hannah, 119-20, 123
Mulattoes, 88. *See also* Creoles
My Bondage and My Freedom (Douglass), 70-71

Napoleonic wars, 164
Navigation acts, 29-30, 35
Netherlands, 21-24

Obeah, 64, 65
Oldmixon, John, *The British Empire in America*, 60
Overseers, 56

Paine, Thomas, 103, 119
Palmer, Robert, *Democratic Revolution*, 113-14
Parliament, 28
Pembroke, Philip Earl of, 27
Planters: labor problems of, 38-39; merchants and, 31-36
Poverty, 123, 135; and labor recruitment, 36-37
Poyer, John, *The History of Barbados*, 60
A Practical View (Barclay), 67
A Practical View (Wilberforce), 118-19
Prejudice, racial, 148-50. *See also* Characterization of blacks/ slaves
Prison, slavery compared to, 125
Prisoners, and labor recruitment, 37-38
Private enterprise, 105
Protestantism, 107, 182. *See also*

Christianity Psychological manipulation of slaves, 55-56, 57-58, 61-62

Racial prejudice, 148-50. *See also* Characterization of blacks/slaves
Radicalism, 111-14, 119
Ragatz, Lowell, *The Fall of the Planter Class 1763-1833*, 3-4, 78
Raleigh, Sir Walter, *Observations Touching Trade and Commerce*, 22
Re-export, 22-23
Rebellion, slave, 66; Afro-Caribbean culture and, 81-82, 85; anti-slavery and, 68-69, 85-86, 148; Christianity and, 63-64; Creole slaves and, 76, 87; in Jamaica, 63, 76, 78-79, 81-87; as justification for abolition, 79-81, 98-99, 156-57; maroonage, 71-74, 89-90; and raising of black regiments, 75-76; religion and, 82-85; ruling-class divisions and, 80-81; in St. Domingue, (*see* St. Domingue revolution); Victor Hughes and, 74-75
Reflections on the Revolution in France (Burke), 121
Religion: and abolition, 163-64; aristocracy and, 121; influence on imperial government, 117; as a means of managing slavery, 63-65; as a political tool, 120; and slave rebellion, 82-85; slavery as supression of, 143, 168; of slaves, 63-64; and temperal success, 116. *See also* Christianity
Renny, Robert, *History of Jamaica*, 152

A Representation (Sharp), 136
Revolution, 151; cultural, 100-101; ideology of, 102-3; slavery as propaganda for, 163. *See also* French revolution; St. Domingue revolution
Robertson, William, *History of the Discovery and Settlement of America*, 77-78
Roman Empire, 153
Roughley, Thomas, *Jamaican Planters Guide*, 56-59
Royal African Company, 40
Royalist party, 28
Ruling class, divisions in, 80-81. *See also* Aristocracy; Imperial government

St. Christopher, island of, 26, 152
St. Domingue revolution: and the breakdown of slaves' fear, 159-60; British intervention in, 179; as an example of the dangers of slavery, 144, 153-54, 155-56, 166; as indictment of humanitarianism, 61; ruling-class divisions and, 80
St. Kitts acts of, 1711, 54
Saints, the. *See* Clapham group
Scripture, 139-40
Searle, Daniel, 28-29
Self-interest, 124
Sharp, Granville, 135-36; *An Essay on Slavery*, 139-40; *The Law of Liberty*, 140; *The Law of Passive Obedience*, 140; in lawsuit over aiding an abused slave, 136-38; *A Representation*, 136
Sharp, Samuel, 85-86

Sierra Leone, 104
Slave codes, 52-54
Slavery: abolition and the perpetuation of, 143; and American
plantation agriculture, 31;
ancient vs. modern, 145-46;
and Caribbean prosperity, 42;
and colonial dependence, 40,
97; compared to prison, 125;
conversion from indentured
labor force to, 36, 39-40;
cooperation of slave community, 54-55, 57-58, 78, 89-90;
culture of, 56; as danger to
liberty, 138-39; and the degradation of blacks, 142; and
demographics in Caribbean
society, 7, 87-88, 152-53,
170-71; development of industrial capitalism and, 4-5; as
distortion of principles of
justice and morality, 168; and
divine retribution, 163-64;
English law and, 137-38;
European demand and, 146; as
exception to Britain's benevolent imperial record, 162-63;
and the growth of resistance in
the colonies, 41; head Negro
driver and, 58-59; impact on
British culture, 167; as an
inefficient system of labor,
165-66, 169-71; justified by
tradition, 145-46; management
of (see Management of slavery);
master-slave relationship (see
Master-slave relationship);
moral judgements concerning,
13; and narrowing opportunities for small farmers, 38; as
propaganda for revoultion, 163;
racial prejudice and, 149-50;

rebellion against (see Rebellion,
slave); and social instability (see
Social instability); social stratification of, 77-78, 88; in St.
Domingue, 156; sugar cultivation and, 33-34, 51-52, 171; and
the supression of religion, 143,
168; as symbol of patriarchal
society, 10; in Trinidad, 179-80;
in the West Indies vs. elsewhere in the empire, 2, 7, 69,
98. See also Anti-slavery
Slavery (Stephen), 167-69
Social inequality, 117-22
Social instability, 98; concern of
humanitarians, 51, 125-26,
144-46, 148-55; James Stephen
on, 157-58, 160-61; psychological management of slavery
and, 70
Social stratification, of slave
society, 77-78, 88
Social transformations, of British
society, 8-9
Southey, Thomas, Chronological
History of the West Indies, 79
Spain, 19-20
Stephen, James, 116, 154-55,
171-73; Crisis of the Sugar
Colonies, 155-60; The Dangers
of the Country, 160-64; Eng-
land Enslaved, 164-66; Slavery,
167-69
Steward, James, 35
Style, John, 39-40
Subject races, 100, 102, 181.
See also Slavery
Success, 116
Sugar cultivation: imperial
support for, 166; need for
aristocracy and concentration
of holdings, 34-35; need for

slave labor, 33, 51-52, 171; and population decline in the Caribbean, 170-71
Supple, Barry: *Commercial Crisis*, 23
Surinam, 71-72

Textiles, British vs. Dutch trade in, 21-23
Thomas, Dalby, 42; *The Rise and Growth of the West India Colonies*, 20-21
Thompson, Thomas, *The African Trade*, 139
Thornton, John, 110
Thoughts and Sentiments on the Evils of Slavery (Cugoano), 84
Trade: British vs. Dutch, 21-24; control by chartered companies, 30-31; free, 32; as a measure of wealth, 19-20; triangular, 41-42
Treaty of 1739, 74
Triangular trade, 41-42

Trinidad, 170, 179-80

United States, 71, 101-2, 164, 170

Vassa, Gustavus, 83
Voltaire, 8
A Voyage to Guinea, Brazil and the West Indies (Atkins), 72

Warner, Thomas, 26
Wealth, 19-21, 121-22
The West India Colonies (M'Queen), 69
White supremacy, 53
Wilberforce, William, 106, 134; *An Appeal*, 141-45; and the moral dangers of upper-class life, 115; and the needs of the poor, 123; *Practical View*, 118-19. *See also* Clapham group
Williams, Eric, *Capitalism and Slavery*, 4-6

ABOUT THE AUTHOR

RONALD KENT RICHARDSON has taught at the State University of New York at Binghamton, the University of Rhode Island, and Fordham University. Dr. Richardson has lectured extensively in British history and European colonial studies and is currently at work on a study of the culture of the British imperial elite, 1890-1960.